DISARMAMENT

DISARMAMENT

BY

PROFESSOR P. J. NOEL BAKER

Cassell Professor of International Relations in
the University of London ; late Whewell Scholar
in International Law ; late Fellow of King's
College, Cambridge ; late Vice-Principal, Ruskin
College, Oxford

" Who in Europe does not know that one more war in the West
and the civilization of the ages will fall with as great a shock as that
of Rome ?"—Rt. Hon. Stanley Baldwin, M.P., Jan. 8, 1926.

THE HOGARTH PRESS
52, TAVISTOCK SQUARE, W.C. 3
1926

PRINTED AND MADE IN GREAT BRITAIN

First published 1926

BILLING AND SONS, LTD., GUILDFORD AND ESHER

TO

THE MEMORY OF

MY FATHER

FOREWORD

THIS book has been written principally because there is so very little else in published print on the topics with which it deals. It is a straightforward attempt to estimate the importance of disarmament in national and international policy at the present day, and to face the difficulties, both technical and political, which will certainly arise in the practical discussions of the subject now shortly to begin in the Preparatory Disarmament Committee of the League of Nations.

From the first page to the last no difficulty has been consciously avoided. Indeed, any shirking of difficulties would have defeated the main purpose for which the work was undertaken. That purpose was to explore, as thoroughly as might be in a book intended not so much for the expert as for the general reader, the obscure problems involved in the preparation of an international agreement for the mutual and general reduction and limitation of national armaments; to show the complexity of these problems to those who think them simple; and to suggest solutions to those who think them insoluble. Incidentally, many concrete proposals for a scheme of practical disarmament have been made. The author may express his hope that they will not all be value-less. But if they should *all* prove to be impracticable, he would still feel that his work had not been wasted, if they served to stimulate discussion of questions which are now becoming, and which must long remain, matters of first-rate importance in current politics.

It may be that some of the discussion will seem unreal to those who have not given much attention to the subject. It is, in fact, founded on the author's personal experience of debates among soldiers, sailors, and other experts who have had to consider at Paris, Geneva, and elsewhere, the practical realization of a disarmament policy. One example of its "reality" may, perhaps, be given, by way of anticipatory self-defence. Much of the argument about the ratio in Chapter XIII must appear at first sight artificial, but a study of the proceedings of the Washington Conference, and particularly of the Report of its Aircraft Committee, which is quoted on pp. 268-9, will show that the points dealt with are points of substantial importance, which Government experts engaged in practical negotiations are obliged to take into account.

It is hoped that the detailed Table of Contents will serve as an adequate index.

The author must express his gratitude for the help and encouragement which has been given to him by his wife.

P. J. N. B.

March 31, 1926.

CONTENTS

CHAPTER VIII

SUCCESSFUL DISARMAMENT TREATIES (LAND AND AIR FORCES)

CHAPTER IX

LAND DISARMAMENT: SUGGESTED PRINCIPLES FOR A GENERAL SCHEME

CHAPTER X

NAVAL ARMAMENTS: EXISTING TREATIES

CHAPTER XI

PRINCIPLES OF GENERAL AGREEMENT UPON NAVAL DISARMAMENT

CHAPTER XII

AERIAL DISARMAMENT

CHAPTER XIII

PROBLEM OF THE RATIO

DISARMAMENT

CHAPTER I

A PRACTICAL POLICY OF DISARMAMENT

On September 25, 1925, the Sixth Assembly of the League of Nations adopted the following resolution:

"The Assembly . . ., in conformity with the spirit of Article 8 of the Covenant, requests the Council to make a preparatory study with a view to a Conference on the Reduction and Limitation of Armaments, in order that as soon as satisfactory conditions have been assured from the point of view of general security . . ., the said Conference may be convened and a general reduction and limitation of armaments may be realized."

Just three weeks later, the Conference of Locarno, summoned to consider how " satisfactory conditions from the point of view of general security " could be assured, brought its historic labours to an end. In its Final Protocol, over the signatures of Luther, Stresemann, Émile Vandervelde, Aristide Briand, Austen Chamberlain, Benito Mussolini, Al. Skrzynski, Edouard Benes, the Governments of the Great Powers of Europe made the following declaration:

"The representatives of the Governments represented here declare their firm conviction that the entry into force of these treaties and conventions will contribute greatly to bring about a moral relaxation of the tension between nations, that it will help powerfully towards the solution of many political or economic problems in accordance with the interests and sentiments of peoples, and that, in strengthening peace and security in Europe, it will hasten on effectively the disarmament provided for in Article 8 of the Covenant of the League of Nations.

> "*They undertake to give their sincere co-operation to the
> work relating to disarmament already undertaken by the
> League of Nations and to seek the realization thereof in a
> general agreement.*"

A few days after his return from Locarno, Mr. Chamberlain,
speaking in London as Secretary of State for Foreign Affairs,
used these words.

> "The agreements (of Locarno) do not make war im-
> possible—no human undertaking or human force can do
> that—but they render war infinitely less probable than it
> would otherwise have been. I feel, therefore, that Locarno
> has made a real contribution to the peace of the world.
> *And the British Government*, like the other Governments
> there represented, *mean to give their full force to these agree-
> ments, and to draw the natural consequences from them. In
> removing suspicion and fear, and giving a sense of security,
> we make disarmament possible, and disarmament ought to
> follow.*"

It is often said in Geneva that when Great Britain and France
are agreed, the League of Nations is agreed. That exaggerates,
no doubt, the influence of the two leaders of the League. But
when Great Britain and France, Italy and Germany, are all
pledged to a policy which the smaller members of the League
have for years been vigorously demanding, it is reasonably safe
to say that results will follow. The policy of disarmament
through the League, on the basis of Article 8 of the Covenant,
is at last a question of practical politics; and it is a question
on which the British Government is to take the lead.

But what does the British Government mean when it speaks
of "Disarmament"? It does not, we may be sure, use the
word in its literal sense; it does not mean the disbanding of
the whole nor even of the greater part of the armed forces of
the world. It means, rather, the reduction, the modest but,
we may hope, not negligible reduction, of those forces, and
their limitation by a general international treaty to new scales
voluntarily accepted by the various nations who take part. It
means, in other words, a definite start in the slow and arduous

journey back along the road which Europe and the world have travelled—ceaselessly and ever faster—since 1860. It means a beginning of the demilitarization of human society, a reversal of the insidious and devastating perversion of life and riches to military ends which the last two generations of European statesmen thrust upon the peoples of the world. The vast majority of men, so fast does human mentality adapt itself to what it finds around it, regard the burden of their present armaments as part of the divine ordering of things, a legacy from the remote and distant past, a normal condition of the civilized state. They do not realize that twentieth-century armaments have by far surpassed anything of the kind in history; that Europe to-day is militarized as no other civilized society has ever been. Lord Grey has told the story of the Japanese in England, who, finding himself and his nation to be objects of admiration, reflected thus upon the course of events: " Yes," he said, " we used to be a nation of artists; our art was really very good; you called us barbarians then. Now our art is not so good as it was, but we have learnt how to kill, and you call us civilized."[1] That story still strikes the average European with a shock of surprise; but no one who looks impartially at the history of the last sixty years can see why it should do so.

On the eve of the world war in 1914 the war strength of the armies of the six Great Powers of Europe numbered, in first and second line troops alone, more than eighteen million men; their full mobilized strength in all services was thirty-seven million, eight hundred thousand.[2] There is no need for more elaborate figures to prove the point; in such a society military power was not only the foundation of national and international policy, it became insensibly but, let the reader frankly ask himself if it was not so, quite certainly, the criterion of spiritual and moral values too. It is this great process of the militarization of national and international life that we are now, through the machinery of the League of Nations, not only to arrest, but gradually and cautiously to undo. What can we hope to

[1] *Twenty-five Years*, by Viscount Grey of Fallodon, vol. i., p. 57.
[2] Cf. official statistics collected and discussed in *Encyclopædia Britannica* under heading " Army."

accomplish ? What rate of progress can we look for ? What do we mean by caution ?

Much will be said in later chapters about the early stages of disarmament, and the kind and measure of reduction in military preparation which can be at first expected. The purpose now is to make a guess at what the present generation may achieve, not, of course, at once, but by successive and unremitting efforts; to make a guess at what the men who fought the war to end war can hope to see before they die. It may sometimes help in searching out the path to try beforehand to visualize the goal.

What can be taken as the starting point for such a guess ? Surely we can at least hope that the process of undoing will be quicker than the process of growth, that we can unbuild armaments faster than our fathers built them. Let us see then first how old a thing is the militarism with which we have to deal.

Again it comes with a shock of surprise to the average European to find just how new it really is. Nations are accustomed to cast back long centuries for the beginnings of their military traditions and for their national glory in the prowess of their arms. They forget that their present fleets and armies date from yesterday.

It is only from about 1860 onwards that the Governments began to build up their modern forces, and to give their fleets and armies their present scale and form. Until then the strength which they maintained in time of peace was little more than could be fairly held to be required for the maintenance of peace and order. But from about that time, of course with sudden temporary increases when wars broke out, but by a continuous process, these forces consistently increased until they reached the figures at which they stood when war broke out in 1914, when it could be said without exaggeration that Europe was no better than an armed camp.

And what is most remarkable about the growth in military preparation which these figures show is the rapid increase in its rate as the catastrophe of 1914 came near. At the end of the century the speed increased; in ten years from 1898 to 1908 all the Great Powers among them increased their military and naval budgets by about £100 million—£10 million a year. For the next six years, from 1908 to 1914, the six Great Powers of Europe alone increased their budgets by more than £100 million a year. It is from 1860, therefore, that modern militarism must be said to date, and its greatest strides were in the last two decades before the war broke out.

What two generations have created, one generation should surely be able to undo. It cannot be beyond our power to go back to the standards and the conceptions of sixty years ago. Indeed, it should be a relatively simple process, for it only needs the joint will and action of a few great Governments to lead the way. If the Great Powers of Europe can but be persuaded, the work is done. A simple comparison will show how Europe stands in this respect. In 1919 disarmament was imposed on Germany by the Treaty of Versailles; her military strength was cut down in all respects to the lowest point which the most determined of her enemies thought it worth his while to demand; her military organization was so destroyed that all her friends, the pacifists not last among them, denounced it as a shame and scandal that she should be left " helpless " and without defence, unable even, they often said, to keep the peace within her borders. Yet there is only one of the South American republics which has armaments proportionately as great as those which the European enemies of Germany in 1919 allowed her to retain.[1] On any basis of comparison that may be desired, population, length of frontier, area, economic wealth—by every test the republics of Brazil, Chile, Argentine and all the rest have less armament in proportion to their size and strength than that which Germany is granted under this " outrageous " system of the Treaty of Versailles.

The idea that the German scale of armament should be accepted by the rest of Europe as the basis of the general scheme of reduction which they are going to adopt would probably be scouted by the other great Governments at the present time. But may we not hope that when we have passed the early stages

[1] In this comparison the German military police are counted as part of Germany's armed forces. This is justifiable because they are no doubt of greater military value than the regular troops of any South American country.

of this backward march to the standards of sanity, the German scale will then become not a European minimum but a European maximum; that by successive agreements, as international confidence is increased and the structure of the League grows stronger, we may be able to go perhaps even well below the scale against which Germany to-day protests. And if confidence increases as it is doing now, if the League continues its present growth in strength, shall we not be entitled to demand, and to demand with insistence, that we reach that scale, not in a dim and distant future, but now while our generation is still there to see it, and before the living memories of the war have died away ?

CHAPTER II
THE REASONS FOR DISARMAMENT

IT is commonly agreed that the purpose of disarmament is twofold: first, to reduce the economic burden laid upon the peoples of the world by excessive preparation for war; second, to prevent that competition in preparation from which war results. It may make for clearness in the subsequent discussion if, as an introduction to it, and at the risk of repeating what is well known and even what has perhaps become mere platitude, a brief survey is attempted of the reasons why it is desirable that this twofold purpose should be fulfilled.

THE ECONOMIC BURDEN OF ARMAMENTS

The Financial Conference which, on the summons of the Council of the League, met in Brussels in October, 1920, was an expert body of great competence; in its resolutions it made a statement which may well serve as the starting point for any fresh discussion of the economic cost which warlike preparations to-day involve. In the course of this statement it reviewed the amount of wealth which the different Governments were devoting to their military and naval budgets; it struck an average between those which—like Great Britain, Japan, France, Italy, and others—were spending a great proportion of their total budgets in this way,[1] and others which were spending relatively less; it declared that on the average " some 20 per cent of the national expenditure is still being devoted to the maintenance of armaments and to preparation for war "; and it ended by calling upon the Council of the

[1] According to calculations made by Sir Josiah Stamp (*Current Problems in Finance and Government*, pp. 96-7), Great Britain, France, and U.S.A. were, before 1914, spending between 34 and 38 per cent of their national budgets for military purposes; Italy, Japan, and Sweden, between 25 and 30 per cent; Belgium and Spain, between 15 and 20 per cent, etc.; and he holds that the proportion has increased in many post-war budgets.

7

League to confer at once with the Governments " with a view to securing a general reduction of the *crushing burden, which on their existing scale armaments still impose upon the impoverished peoples of the world, sapping their resources and imperilling their recovery from the ravages of the war.*"

Armament expenditure has been reduced a little since the Brussels Conference met, but no one who compares the situation with what it was when the Conference made this declaration will deny that it still constitutes " a crushing burden on the impoverished peoples of the world."[1]

How can we estimate what the weight of this burden is, what it means in terms of the general welfare of the nations ? We have happily the guidance of two distinguished economists, Professor Pigou and Sir J. Stamp, who since 1920 have published brief studies on the real economic cost of armaments.[2]

They both devote most of their attention, as the Brussels Conference did, to the cost of peace-time preparation, not to the cost of actual war itself. It may be convenient, therefore, to discuss first the cost of armaments in peace.

1. Both Professor Pigou and Sir Josiah Stamp begin, of course, by pointing out that the Brussels calculations did not mean that 20 per cent of the total economic income of the nations was being spent on military preparation; " national

[1] The following figures show the cost of military forces of various nations in 1913-14 and in 1924-25; they show that the burden, even allowing for the rise in prices, has been very little lightened, if indeed at all.

(£ Sterling.)

	1913–1914.	1924–1925.	1924–1925. (*Reduced to Pre-War Price Level.*)
Great Britain	72,436,000	123,182,000 (estimates)	79,500,000
France ..	68,941,000	57,775,000 (approximately)	47,200,000
U.S.A. ..	61,812,000	121,100,000 (revised estimates)	78,100,000
Japan ..	19,358,000	44,900,000 (estimates)	21,700,000

These are figures given and calculations made in the League of Nations Armaments Year Book, 1925-1926.

[2] A. C. Pigou, *The Political Economy of War*, chap. ii. ; Sir J. Stamp, *Current Problems in Finance and Government*, chap. iv.

expenditure " is used to mean the *expenditure of the Governments* as provided in their annual budgets. The real economic cost to a nation of its armaments lies in " the withdrawal from ordinary productive industry of a large number of men above the average level of physique, of much intelligence, of organizing and inventive power, and of many ingenious machines."[1]   This cost is represented in terms of money, according to Professor Pigou, roughly by the total budgets of the Government departments charged with the national defence; Sir J. Stamp holds that to the budget figures there must be added another 25 per cent, to allow for other elements of waste involved in the devotion of wealth and industry to military ends.   This cost bears to the total real resources of a nation approximately the same proportion as the total budgets of the defence departments (or these budgets plus 25 per cent) bear to the nation's aggregate money income, or as economists usually call it, its " national dividend." Working on the basis of 1913 figures, Professor Pigou estimates that the cost of the army and navy to the British people was in that year somewhere between 3 and 4 per cent of their " national dividend,"[2] that is to say, " the equivalent of about a fortnight's work of the brain workers, hand workers, and mechanical equipment of the country every year."

Professor Pigou goes on to say that this figure would be a much higher one for continental countries where conscripted soldiers are paid a very much lower wage than they would receive in industry, and where therefore the defence budgets do not represent the whole cost of the withdrawal of these soldiers from productive work. And Sir J. Stamp, taking post-war figures and allowing for this and for other factors which he thinks must be taken into account, estimates that the cost of armaments to-day, taking an average of the nations with big fleets and armies, is not 3 to 4 per cent, but more nearly 8 per cent, of the national dividend, or the equivalent of at least a month's work every year of all the producers and plant of those nations.

Whether the proper figure be 4 or 8 per cent, it may seem

[1] Pigou, *loc. cit.*, p. 4.
[2] The national dividend of the British Isles was in 1913 estimated at roughly £2,000 million to £2,400 million.

relatively small to anyone who does not look at it more closely. But Professor Pigou goes on to explain that in every country the national dividend gives very little margin over and above the bare subsistence level of the nation. He quotes Dr. Bowley as saying that " the wealth of the country (Great Britain) was insufficient before the war for a high general standard: there is nothing as yet to show that it will be greater in the future."[1] After the absolutely indispensable needs of individual existence have been provided—apart altogether from the need for building up new capital—there is very little " surplus income " for the comforts and amenities of life. Of this meagre "surplus income " military budgets absorb, of course, a far greater proportion than they do of the total dividend. Professor Pigou indicates that in Great Britain they must reduce the surplus income by at least 15 per cent; in continental countries, where the real cost of armaments is greater and the average income per head much less, the percentage must, he says, be " certainly much bigger "; and in the light of Sir J. Stamp's calculations a guess of anywhere from 30 to 50 per cent would probably be safe.

But even when we have arrived at such a figure, it does not give the average man any exact idea of the sacrifice in material well-being which military budgets now involve. Again Sir J. Stamp comes to our assistance, and on such a concrete problem of practical economic science there is no one better qualified to speak.

Allowing for both the direct and indirect effects of armament-taxation, he says that "one could . . . state, without much fear of serious error, that the standard of life throughout great industrial powers would be lifted by over 10 per cent by the cancellation of the expenditure on armaments. Such an increase would have a much greater influence upon the comforts of life and on the economic well-being of the people, than the mere figure itself might convey. At the stage at which we stand, *it is for the mass of the peoples of these nations the difference between grinding penury and a reasonable standard of comfort*."[2]

2. But this 8 per cent of the national dividend, this difference between reasonable comfort and grinding penury, is only the *direct* economic loss in time of peace represented roughly by

[1] *The Division of the Product of Industry*, p. 58.   [2] *Loc. cit.*, p. 97.

the normal money cost of the departments of national defence. To that there must be added various other factors, which do not figure in the budget, of which there can be no measurement in terms of cash, but which *indirectly* increase the economic burden which armaments impose.

First, for example, there is the organization on uneconomic lines of the transport systems of the world. The navigation laws in England, which had the military purpose of training in peace-time seamen who could be used in war; the diversion of railways from their proper economic routes in order that they may be made to serve strategic ends; such economic follies as the broad-gauge lines in Russia or the forbidding of the Channel Tunnel between France and England—these are policies due to the fear of war, which " create a strong presumption " that the countries which adopt them " will be *somewhat* less well off than they would have been if the claims of defence had been silent."[1]

3. In the same order of indirect economic cost must be counted the loss which results from policies for promoting the uneconomic production of food, or for diverting the normal channel of industrial development. Iron and steel industries, the engineering industry, some chemical industries, iron-mining and coal-mining, are all of exceptional importance in the conduct of modern war; so are big shipyards and aircraft factories. A country which is without industries, or which, like many European states, possesses industries but cannot produce its own supplies of food, may find itself in a position of difficulty or danger when it is engaged in war. For reasons such as these many Governments give artificial encouragement to various industries which otherwise would not flourish on their soil. They regard the cost of such encouragement as an insurance against a greater loss, but, says Professor Pigou, " if the policy is carried far enough to be effective, the costs are likely to be high and the real sacrifice involved large."[2] There can be little doubt that in fact the loss so caused, particularly in post-war Europe taken as a whole, is very large.

4. A similar kind of economic loss is caused, again especially in Europe, by the elaborate frontier barriers of every kind which states create against their neighbours. This loss is not

[1] Pigou, *ibid.*, p. 10.   [2] *Ibid.*, p. 13.

merely that which results directly from restrictive customs tariffs; it results from the whole complex system of customs, restrictions on the import and transit of goods, restrictions on individual travel, restrictions on international trains, disabilities of foreigners established abroad, and so on, a great part—though, of course, not all—of which is due to military reasons of various kinds. Again it is impossible to estimate in terms of cash the economic loss which the frontier system of modern Europe thus involves; but Sir Josiah Stamp assures us that its freedom from this system is one of the important causes of the superior economic development of the United States, and of the high standard of living which has been there set up.[1]

5. Sir Josiah Stamp also calls attention to another kind of loss which results from the inflation of military budgets. It is that of the peculiarly deleterious effect of the heavy national taxation which modern military expenditure has caused. The continuance year after year of such heavy taxation for wholly unproductive ends has a repressive influence on the general economic activity of a nation, which is not only persistent but actually *cumulative* in its effect, so that in fact it causes a greater actual loss than the money total of the taxation represents. Not only so, but a high level of taxation for unproductive military ends inevitably reduces national expenditure on productive social reform of every kind. It thus diverts the national wealth from uses in which the returns in welfare, and often over a period of time the returns in actual economic prosperity, are particularly great.[2]

6. Such are some of the elements in the direct and indirect economic cost of armaments in time of peace. To them must be added—at the present time it is, of course, particularly important—the vast additional cost of armaments in time of war.

Apart from moral sacrifice and spiritual degradation, the whole life of the present generation of European nations has been changed and warped by the burden which the world war

[1] " One of the most important historical reasons for the rapid economic development of the American continent is that it has been able to develop its resources as a unified whole instead of being split up into a large number of separate military areas " (Stamp, *loc. cit.*, p. 87).

[2] *Loc. cit.*, p. 86.

has imposed upon them. Any measurement of its cost in terms of gold must be in great part guess-work. An American economist, Professor Bogart, has essayed an estimate, including in his calculations not only the material capital that was expended and destroyed, and the cost of the war effort of those who took part in it in various ways, but also an average allowance for the productive work which the killed, both civilians and soldiers, would have done in the remainder of their lives, had no war occurred. The result is a net total cost for all the belligerents and neutrals put together of £70,000 million—the equivalent of twenty full years' work of all the brain workers, hand workers, and mechanical equipment of the British Isles.[1]

7. That figure, for what it is worth, represents the direct economic cost of the last world war. To that there must be added various elements of indirect loss, not allowed for in any way by Professor Bogart, some of which have been the cause of important additional burdens on the peoples of the world.

There is, for example, the fact, pointed out by Sir Josiah Stamp,[2] that the war caused an enormously rapid wastage of some of the mineral resources of the world—steel, coal, oil—which are vital to the prosperity of its industrial civilization, and of which the total known supplies are relatively very small. A single figure will serve to illustrate the point. Between 1915 and 1918 the consumption of steel in Great Britain for shells alone rose from an average of about 2,000 tons a month to more than 180,000 tons a month—and of this total, of course, the whole was blown away and immediately destroyed.[3] These figures concern only one of the many countries who fought the war, but they demonstrate the vast waste of vital resources due to the fighting methods of to-day—what Sir Josiah Stamp calls " the rake's progress to physical bankruptcy by the waste of the irreplaceable factors of modern economic life."

8. But much more important as factors of indirect economic loss are the various catastrophes and dislocations of the

---

[1] Economists calculate the national dividend at present prices (1925) at roughly £3,500 million. Cf. *Direct and Indirect Costs of the Great World War*, by E. L. Bogart, Professor of Economics at the University of Illinois. [2] *Loc. cit.*, pp. 83-4.

[3] Statistics given by Enoch, *Problem of Armaments*, p. 113.

economic system which the war produced.   Each enormous
exodus of refugees—Belgian refugees, Russian refugees, Greek,
Bulgarian, Turkish refugees; they numbered millions altogether
—each exodus meant a violent upheaval in the European system,
a diminution of production, economic waste in keeping the
refugees alive and finding them new homes and new employment.   The civil wars in Russia, following the Great War and
followed in turn by the Russian famine,[1] swept away the
Russian export of grain, wiped out the Russian market for
manufactured goods, and so lowered the whole standard of
living throughout the Continent of Europe.   The demoraliza-
tion of the international exchanges, due to war finance, the
problems of reparations and Allied indebtedness, the burden of
war pensions, the reduced capacity of disabled men to work—
these were all contributing factors in the disorganization of the
economic mechanism of the world which left England for six
years with a million unemployed and which for all that time
has substantially reduced the material comfort and well-
being of 95 per cent of the population of the Continent of
Europe.

It is relevant to note that, great as was the scale of the last
war, the next, if there is a " next," will, in the opinion of almost
every expert, be far more destructive still, both of life and of
material capital and wealth.   In calculating the economic
burden imposed by armaments in use, this fact must not be
overlooked.

9. There is one more element which is common to both peace
and war, which is in part allowed for in what is said above, but
which, none the less, requires another word.   It is the loss due
to the perversion of scientific and inventive genius from productive to unproductive ends.   The modern industrial system
is founded on the application of science to the production of
wealth; its progress in prosperity depends, and must depend,
on improved methods of such application.   It is so organized
that a single new invention may mean extra comfort to half
the population of the world.   But inventive genius is not a
commodity to be ordered on the public market.   It is a fortuitous

---

[1] Forty million people were affected by the famine; it is estimated
that four million of them died of hunger.

and infinitely precious gift. But if those who have it spend their lives in perfecting the wireless steering of marine torpedoes, or a poison-gas against which no gas-mask can be made, not only do they make no contribution to the economic welfare of mankind, they actually help to destroy the wealth upon which that welfare rests. We cannot calculate what loss we suffer in this way; we know it must be great, we believe it *may* be very great indeed.

10. Was the Brussels Conference not right, then, to denounce the cost of armaments as a crushing burden which saps the resources of the peoples of the world and imperils their recovery from the ravages of war ? Is it not a barrier which stands everywhere across the path of social progress ? For why do we prize economic welfare ? Why do we seek by every means to raise the standard of life among our citizens ? Is it not because we know that for the vast mass of the democracies a higher standard of material comfort is but the gateway to a new vista of moral and spiritual well-being ?

If we judge things, then, in terms of life and welfare, we may be very sure that in Great Britain, and even more in other highly developed countries, the reduction and limitation of armaments is the essential preliminary to substantial social progress and reform. We may be no less sure that in less-developed countries the economic burden of modern armament presses still more hardly on the struggling forces of civilization. No one can doubt, for instance, that the relative freedom of the South American republics from large armies and navies is a most important factor in their general social, economic and political advance—an advance which constitutes a striking feature of international life to-day. Still less can anyone who knows them doubt that for the Balkan States disarmament might mean the whole difference not only between penury for their peoples and reasonable comfort, but between education and illiteracy, between sound administration and corruption, between the steady growth of responsible self-government and the debauchery of democratic institutions to violent ends—between, in short, their whole social and moral progress and their retrogression to the barbaric standards of the Turkish empire of the past.

That, then, and no less is the price of militarism, the economic cost of armament, in the Europe that to-day still lies around us prostrate from the ravages of war.

THE PREVENTION OF COMPETITION IN ARMAMENT

The second purpose of disarmament is to prevent competition in preparation for war, and it is generally agreed that this is even more important and more urgent than the first. It is important not only because competition, if it is unchecked, adds greatly and rapidly to the economic burden which has been above discussed, but also because in many different ways it is itself a cause of war. It is urgent because, once started, it is hard to stop, and because there is ground for fearing that to-day several dangerous competitions have already been begun.

It is worth while to look more closely at the arguments for checking competition thus briefly summarized, and at the ways in which competition itself becomes a cause of war.

1. It used often to be said that armaments are not a cause of policy, but a result; that nations arm because for other reasons they are in danger of attack; that when they cease to be in danger they will cease to arm; that armaments may, therefore, safely be neglected, and attention concentrated on removing the economic or political causes which lead nations into conflict or dispute. This is really nothing but a modern version of an ancient but exploded maxim, *Si vis pacem, para bellum*, and if experience could teach us, it ought to be as much discredited as that.

It is true that nations in building up their armies and their fleets believe that in that way they can make their frontiers safe against attack. It is true that many politicians and their military advisers believe that with unrestricted liberty to arm they could make their countries more secure than they could be under any scheme of general and mutual disarmament. That conception reappeared in paper after paper sent to Geneva by the Governments of the world when the League of Nations first began its serious discussions of the subject. Thus, for example, a Spanish admiral, speaking for the Government of Madrid: " We may take it for granted that the armaments (capital ships, etc.) allowed at Washington are the minimum compatible with the national safety of the signatory powers ";[1] as though the signatory powers would have run a dangerous risk if they had agreed each to give up another battleship or two.

The present argument, of course, is not that armaments *never* serve the purpose with which the nations build them up; it is simply that when nations begin to arm in rivalry against each other, that rivalry leads to ever greater preparation, first on one side, then upon the other; that it leads thus to the formation of alliances and groups, each group suspecting always that the other is about to strike, fearing always that the other is out-stripping it in power, and striving always by some new effort to redress the balance; and that thus by a process Europe ought to know too well their rivalry leads them to the catastrophe of war itself, and thus destroys by their very preparation for defence against attack the security which each of them set out to seek.

This argument needs no elaborate historical defence, for we have the evidence and the verdict of the best qualified historian we could desire. Lord Grey, discussing the events that led to war in 1914, has written thus:[2]

" The moral is obvious; it is that great armaments lead inevitably to war. If there are armaments on one side, there must be armaments on other sides. While one nation arms, other nations cannot tempt it to aggression by remaining defenceless. Armaments must have equipment; armies cannot be of use without strategic railways. Each measure taken by one nation is noted, and leads to counter-measures by others.

" The increase of armaments that is intended in each nation to produce consciousness of strength, and a sense of security, does not produce these effects. On the contrary, it produces a consciousness of the strength of other nations and a sense of fear. Fear begets suspicion and distrust and evil imaginings of all sorts, till each Government feels it would be criminal and a betrayal of its own country not to take every precaution, while every Government regards every precaution of every other

[1] L. N. Document C. 477, 1922, ix., pp. 4-5.
[2] Lord Grey of Fallodon, *Twenty-five Years*, vol. i., pp. 91-2.

Government as evidence of hostile intent. . . ." (Here follows
an account of the diplomatic negotiations between Lord Grey
and the Germans for the prevention of war in 1914.)

" But, although all this be true, it is not in my opinion the
real and final account of the origin of the Great War. *The
enormous growth of armaments in Europe. the sense of insecurity and fear caused by them—it was these that made war
inevitable.*   This, it seems to me, is the truest reading of history,
and the lesson that the present should be learning from the past
in the interests of future peace, the warning to be handed on to
those who come after us."

There are few Englishmen who will dispute Lord Grey's
contention, or who will doubt hereafter that competition in
military preparation, by creating its own international crises,
directly leads to war, and thus destroys the security at which it
aims.   And this is not a danger of the past alone.   If Germany
ever arms again—as, if there is no general disarmament, she
surely will—another Franco-German armament crisis of this
sort is certain to occur.

2. The passage quoted from Lord Grey gives perhaps a conclusive, but not a complete, account of the ways in which
armament competition becomes a cause of war.

Competition leads to great and ever greater fleets and armies.
But great fleets and armies are themselves in various ways a
danger to the peace.   They create a standing temptation to
the Governments and the staffs which build them up to put
them into use whenever a favourable opportunity may occur.
That is a temptation natural enough to soldiers who have spent
their lives in planning and preparing for a war; but it is a temptation which, as history shows, appeals only less strongly to those
whom the military staffs advise.   And it is a temptation which
comes no longer in the crude form of the desire of professional
soldiers for active service, and for all that active service may
mean in promotions and rewards, but in the form of a difficult
and an insidious choice: since they have no security against
attack, since, as they daily calculate, they may sometime have
to fight, should it not be at a moment when they are strong,
when they can count perhaps on rapid and decisive victory ?
How can they know that in a few years' time their rivals may

not have outstripped them in the race? They cannot know, and so they strike.

3. And the temptation of great armaments acts also in another way. There are many naval and military operations which can be carried out by a great fleet or army, but which might be *made* quite impossible if only smaller forces were at command. This result might follow from reduction, even if the enemy against whom operations were to be directed had been proportionately disarmed as well. For the number of divisions needed for a given military task does not depend only on the strength of the army opposition which they have to meet; it depends also on other invariable factors, such as the nature of the country in which the operation is required, the distances to be controlled, and so on. History gives many an example of an army dispersed too thinly over conquered country which has been beaten by an unorganized but national civilian defence. There are many modern cases in which general reduction might render impossible sudden overwhelming aggressions to which otherwise statesmen might be tempted by great military power. To take an example which we may hope is becoming every year less credible, the lightning conquest of Germany by France might be quite possible if she could mobilize the forces which she has to-day, but quite impossible if those forces were considerably reduced.

In this way again, therefore, a reduction of the present great competitive armaments of the world might remove temptations to military enterprise which still to-day exist.

4. Next, great armaments necessarily mean great military castes, and when competition is keen and national fears have been aroused, the military staffs acquire, and necessarily acquire, a great power to influence not only the military policy, but the whole international and even the internal policy of the state. It is inevitable that this should be so. At moments of crisis this influence of the military staff, pressing for a decisive blow at a favourable moment, may become irresistible in circumstances when the statesmen, left to themselves, might avert resort to war. And even in normal times their influence is strong. In the exercise of their proper duty of advice, they often propose, and indeed insist on, policies which, while they

may be sound if war is certain, are dangerous to the maintenance of peace. Anyone who knows the continental countries where the sense of insecurity is great, and where in consequence the power of the military machine is great, will be able to supply examples. The building up of so-called "defensive" group alliances, corrupt international bargains in the interest of an ally, the creation of great black armies of colonial troops, the repression of racial and linguistic minorities, espionage in the services and ministries of friendly states, the organization of the frontier barriers to which reference has above been made—these often, if not always, seem to those who order them precautions essential to the national security entrusted to their charge. But they are none the less the things which sow distrust, suspicion, and unrest, which create the atmosphere of conflict, and which often furnish the reason or excuse for war itself.

5. But the supreme danger of rival competition in " preparedness " lies in the sense of insecurity which it creates—a sense of insecurity which eventually becomes a veritable passion of fear, in the minds not only of Governments, but also of their peoples. Whoever has travelled in the storm-centres of Europe knows how acute and all-pervading this fear can become. It is this that often enables them to persuade their democracies to accept the policies, described in the last paragraph, which make for war, and which, if they were free from menace, these democracies would unhesitatingly reject.

6. And this sense of fear acts both directly and indirectly, both by concentrating attention on preparation for war and by creating distrust of the motives and intentions of foreign Governments. The point has never been more clearly stated than by the British Government itself in an *aide-mémoire* on the Anglo-French controversy at the Washington Conference about the use of submarines. The note runs as follows: " His Majesty's Government consider the first condition of a true entente is the avoidance of naval competition between the two countries. . . . British opinion would inevitably insist on a heavy programme of anti-submarine craft if the French submarine programme were to be carried out, and the two countries would thus be launched on a course of competitive naval

construction. The British Government cannot disguise the fact that any such development would react very seriously on British sentiment towards France and on French sentiment towards Great Britain. . . . *Naval competition in any form between Great Britain and France would corrode goodwill.*"[1] These are arguments and conclusions which carry the highest authority, and which deserve to be remembered.

7. Last, the force of all these arguments is much increased by the present rapid changes in the art of war. These changes operate in two different ways. First, the fact that armament is never static renders competitive preparation an almost inevitable result; if a Government knows that other states are always making new and secret improvements in their military equipment, it is almost irresistibly compelled to take precautions by making greater and ever greater efforts of its own. Second, the recent progress in the science of destruction, the improvements in every sort of weapon and above all in aircraft and the use of gas, have enormously increased the potential swiftness and deadliness of an attack. In so doing, they have increased the general sense of insecurity, the keenness of the race in preparation, the incentive to the " decisive blow " by sudden and unscrupulous attack; and in due course they would no doubt complete the subordination of general policy to military ends.

Is it unfair to conclude that it is truer to-day—and that it has perhaps been truer for fifty years—to say that policy follows armaments, rather than that armaments follow policy; and that therefore the ending of armament competition is the first and overwhelmingly important objective of a disarmament agreement ? It is not so much the scale of armament adopted that, in the early stages, matters; it is the stopping of the rivalry in preparation, and the prevention of the results to which it leads.

Moreover, as was said above, the discussion of this aspect of the armament problem is far from academic, for, in spite of the exhaustion of the war, several dangerous competitions have,

---

[1] *Aide-mémoire* issued on January 4, 1922.

in recent years, begun. No one has forgotten the race in
battleship construction between the United States of America
and Japan which preceded the Washington Conference in 1921,
nor the very threatening political situation which that race
produced. Between 1917 and 1921 the Japanese expenditure
on their navy rose from roughly £19 million per annum to
£54½ million, and if their programme had been fulfilled it would
have cost them in 1927 the sum of £85 million. The cost of
the United States Navy rose from £27½ million in 1914 to the
stupendous figure of £94 million in 1921, and if the Washington
agreement had not stopped the race, it would certainly have
risen still more.[1]

But the Washington agreement only stopped the race in
certain categories of ships—those which the naval staffs then
thought the most important. Since 1921 it has begun again in
other categories, and threatens to assume proportions hardly
less dangerous than the race in battleships itself. The U.S.A.,
Japan, and the British Empire are building against each other
just as Great Britain and Germany built against each other
before the war. *In the year* 1925 *alone roughly* 300,000 *tons of
new warships were launched.* These included, indeed, two big
new British battleships, allowed under the Washington Convention, and accounting in displacement for 70,000 tons. But
the rest was made up of Japanese aircraft carriers, of American,
Japanese, British, French, and Italian submarines and cruisers.
Since the Washington Conference took place, 154 submarines
have been built or voted by the Parliaments of these five powers,
and 53 big cruisers and 144 destroyers have similarly been built
or voted: a total of 351[2] ships, most of them the largest and
most powerful in the world of their respective classes (the
cruisers alone will cost perhaps £150 million), built or voted
by the powers who agreed in 1921 " to reduce the burdens of
competition in armament."[3]

The situation is hardly less alarming in respect of aircraft.
The French Government, disturbed by the large-scale and

[1] Cf. for these and other valuable statistics, reproduced in a convenient
form, Buell, *The Washington Conference*, chap. v.
[2] Vide White Papers, Cmd. 2349, 1925, and Cmd. 2476, 1925.
[3] Preamble to the Washington Naval Convention.

successful development of German civil aviation, has decided
to have the strongest military air force in the world. Great
Britain, unable to admit the standing menace to her industrial
centres which French supremacy in the air may mean, has
decided that she must have at least a one-power standard in
both fighting and bombing aircraft. In consequence—and it is
a direct reply to France, a direct competition with our closest
ally and friend, with whom in 1918 we were fighting side by side
in a struggle for our lives[1]—we have made plans since 1922
to increase our military air force to *eighteen times* what it then
was, and to add to it a supplementary force of volunteers.

May it not, then, be fairly claimed that, in spite of the exhaustion of the war, the discussion of armament competition is,
unhappily, far from academic at the present time.

OTHER REASONS FOR DISARMAMENT: THE POLICY OF THE LEAGUE OF NATIONS

To these now classical arguments for the reduction and
limitation of the armies and navies of the world, there are
to-day others which must be taken into account.

The first is the consideration whether armament competition
is compatible with the general international policy to which the
vast majority of states have pledged their word. That policy—
and every month that passes shows that both Governments and
peoples are more and more in earnest in its pursuit—is the policy
of the Covenant of the League. But the authors of the Covenant
never dreamt that the institutions of the League could work,
that they could fulfil their supreme purpose of averting another
cataclysm like that of 1914, if international society was dis-
tracted by competition in armament preparation. For that
reason they inserted Article 8 into the Covenant, believing
it to be a vital part of the whole system they set up. They
believed, with Lord Grey, that reduction and limitation of
armament would remove a fruitful cause of international
suspicion and distrust; and they expected from it too a profound
psychological effect upon the vast masses of the democratic

[1] Cf. sundry speeches in the House of Commons by Sir S. Hoare,
Secretary of State for Air, *Hansard*, March, 1925, and at other times.

peoples who form the League. The reduction of military service, economies—perhaps great economies—in taxation, a new sense of security in their relations with other peoples—these changes brought suddenly to the world would, it was believed, place behind the new institutions of the League a vast body of public support. Without such support the authors of the Covenant never hoped that the Covenant could do its work.

The incompatibility of continued disarmament competition with the policy of the League is increased, and much increased, by the unilateral disarmament which has been imposed on Germany and her late allies by the Versailles and other Treaties of Peace. There is good evidence for believing that in 1919 that disarmament was welcomed by a great majority, at least, of the four peoples on whom it was imposed, because they believed it to be a first step to general disarmament. But no one who has followed German politics can doubt that unless general disarmament *does* follow, the German people, sooner or later, will make a desperate attempt to regain their freedom to defend themselves; no one can doubt that France will combat that attempt, and that the League will thus be rent in sunder by a great internecine war. The prospect is the more alarming for Great Britain, and her interest in general disarmament the greater, since to both peoples—one of them the greatest military power in the world, the other relatively without defence—she has given by the Locarno pact an equal and a binding pledge of military help. A failure to secure a general disarmament agreement would mean, therefore, to Great Britain an intolerable risk, and to the League of Nations a menace to its whole policy, perhaps even to the continued existence of its institutions.

TREATY OBLIGATION TO DISARM

This chapter may be ended, as perhaps it should have been begun, by a reference to the Treaty obligations of the Governments to disarm.

Article 8 of the Covenant not only contains a declaration that the reduction of armaments is necessary for the maintenance of peace; it contains also specific stipulations as to the method by which such reduction shall be carried out. These stipulations involve a binding obligation to disarm. It is what Professor Westlake[1] used to call an " imperfect " obligation, in the sense that it requires a further supplementary agreement to bring it into force; but it is none the less for that a legal undertaking of a particularly important kind.

In addition to Article 8, there is also the Preamble to Part V of the Treaty of Versailles, and to the corresponding parts of the Peace Treaties with Austria, Hungary, and Bulgaria. This Preamble reads as follows: " *In order to render possible the initiation of a general limitation of the armaments of all nations,* Germany (Austria, etc.) undertakes strictly to observe the military, naval, and air clauses which follow." When the draft of the Peace Treaty of Versailles was first presented to the German Delegation in May, 1919, they made the following observation upon Part V: " Germany is prepared to agree to the basic idea of the army, navy, and air regulations . . . provided this is a beginning of a general reduction of armaments." To which the Allied Powers in their famous answer replied as follows: " The Allied and Associated Powers wish to make it clear that their requirements in regard to German armaments were not made solely with the object of rendering it impossible to resume her policy of military aggression. They are also the first steps towards that general reduction and limitation of armaments which they seek to bring about as one of the most fruitful preventives of war, and which it will be one of the first duties of the League of Nations to promote." The ex-enemy people hold that this Preamble to Part V, and this exchange of Notes upon it, together constitute a solemn pledge towards themselves—a pledge in virtue of which their own disarmament has been effected—that a general scheme for the reduction and limitation of the armaments of all nations will be carried through.

There is no answer to this argument, nor any question, therefore, that to the Governments of Europe disarmament is a matter not only of policy and interest, but of legal and honourable obligation too.

[1] Cf. *International Law*, part i., chap. vii.

CHAPTER III
METHOD OF PREPARATION OF THE DISARMAMENT TREATY

THE purpose of the present chapter is to examine the method of procedure laid down in Article 8 of the Covenant for the preparation of a disarmament agreement among the Members of the League.

THE PROCEDURE PRESCRIBED BY ARTICLE 8

Article 8 provides as follows: The necessary preparatory work for a treaty is entrusted to the Council of the League; the Council, acting on the basis of the declaration referred to in the last chapter concerning the necessity of reduction, and "taking account of the geographical situation and circumstances of each state, shall formulate plans for such reduction" (Paragraph 2 of Article 8).

When these plans have been prepared by the Council, they are to be submitted "for the *consideration* and *action* of the several Governments" (Paragraph 2). In other words, the Members of the League are not bound by the plans which the Council may at first submit.

But after "consideration," "action" is to follow. Paragraph 4 begins: "After these plans" (that is to say, the Council's plans, with or without amendment to meet the views of the Governments) "shall have been *adopted* by the several Governments. . . ." *Some* plan or other the Members of the League are under an obligation to accept.

And when they have adopted a plan, "the limits of armaments therein fixed shall not be exceeded without the concurrence of the Council" (Paragraph 4).

But these limits as originally fixed are not to be eternal, for the plans "shall be subject to reconsideration and revision every ten years" (Paragraph 3).

26

What have these provisions meant when they have been translated into the practical details of the procedure of the Council and Assembly of the League?

1. In order to enable it to fulfil its duty to " formulate plans," the Council, acting on a recommendation made to it by the First Assembly, appointed in 1921 a special Preparatory Committee to study the whole question of executing Article 8 and to draft " reports and proposals for the reduction of armaments."[1]   This committee, known as the Temporary Mixed Commission, was composed not of Government representatives, but of independent persons, acting some of them in close contact with their Governments, but chosen primarily for their personal authority or expert knowledge.

In constituting such a non-governmental committee to carry through the early stages of the work, the Council acted in accordance with a well-established principle of democratic government,[2] and followed a plan which had served it well a year before in the preparation of a statute for the Permanent Court of International Justice. Again in connection with disarmament the plan was successful, for it enabled the Council, without engaging its own direct responsibility, to lay before the Governments of the League proposals which were, we are entitled to hope, destined ultimately to lead to practical results, but which no Government would at the beginning have even ventured seriously to discuss. The Temporary Mixed Commission, under the leadership of Viscount Cecil, prepared the Draft Treaty of Mutual Assistance, upon the principles of which were founded in turn the Geneva Protocol and the Locarno Pacts. It thus rendered great services to the world by its pioneer work on the security problem, but these services were ill requited by its dissolution by the Fifth Assembly, before it had been able to complete its task by making plans for the solution of the technical problem of disarmament itself. It was replaced in 1924 by the so-called Co-ordination Committee, which undertook the drafting of these plans. This body was largely governmental in composition; if the Geneva Protocol had been carried into effect, a disarmament conference would

[1] Resolution 3 of First Assembly: cf. Council Document 124, 1920.
[2] Cf., *e.g.*, Royal Commissions in Great Britain.

have been summoned within a short delay, and it was believed that responsible governmental preparation was for that reason required.   But the Protocol was not accepted; the summoning of the disarmament conference is not yet; the Co-ordination Committeee did nothing of any value.   For the work of preparing the disarmament plans that are required, the Sixth Assembly in September, 1925, invited the Council to make an entirely new start, and to begin virtually at the point where the Temporary Mixed Commission had left off; and for this purpose the Council set up first a special Council Committee, which met once in December, 1925, and which was then replaced by a new Preparatory Committee composed of Government representatives, with other sub-committees of independent experts to assist it.   Thus the Council adhered to the main principle of its previous practice, that of having prepared for it by an *ad hoc* and expert body a draft of the " plans " for the reduction of armaments which it is its task to formulate.

2. The report of this Preparatory Committee must, of course, when it is ready, be made to the Council of the League, and the next step in the procedure is for the Council to submit this report and the plans which it contains to the Governments of the Members of the League for their "consideration."   This it is free to do, either in the draft form in which the plans are first proposed by the Preparatory Committee, or after it has amended them and adopted them as its own.   In other matters it has in the past followed both these procedures; it did the former, for example, when the Temporary Mixed Commission laid before it their draft Treaty of Mutual Assistance; it did the latter with the draft Statute of the Permanent Court of International Justice, freely amending the proposals of its Jurists' Committee before it sent them on to the Members of the League. But it is probable that in a matter such as disarmament, in which the Great Powers must play a predominating part, the Council will want itself to agree upon the plans before they are sent on to other Governments.

3. But whichever of these courses it may adopt, the plans at this stage will be no more than a draft, though perhaps a draft to which the members of the Council—at least, in a provisional way—are individually and collectively committed.

But since they will be only a draft, the Council in sending them to the other Members of the League will invite the Governments of these Members to make upon them whatever comments they may wish to make.[1] Each of these Governments will be absolutely free to offer criticisms of any kind, either upon the plans as a whole or upon their particular application to itself, or even, if it wishes, either alone or with a group of other Governments, to make counter-propositions. It is in this way that the Members of the League will have their first opportunity for that " consideration " of the plans which the Covenant assures to them.

4. Having received the comments of the Governments so consulted, the Council will consider the plans again, and will confirm them or amend them as it then sees fit. When it has agreed on them, it once more has discretion as to the action it will take; it may either decide definitely to adopt them as its own, in which case its members would be thereafter committed to them; or it may prefer, without engaging its own responsibility, merely to submit them to a general conference of all the states concerned. In any case, the stage of preliminary " consideration " will probably be over, and the stage of " action " will begin.

5. The procedure to be adopted for this stage of " action " will almost certainly consist in the summoning by the Council of a general conference of all civilized states, whether Members of the League or not. At this conference every state would be represented by its responsible ministers—Great Britain no doubt would send the Foreign Secretary, the First Lord of the Admiralty, the Secretary for War, and the Secretary for Air—each accompanied by whatever expert staff he might require. It will almost certainly be the intention of the Council that the Conference should itself prepare a definite and binding agreement to disarm, which should be both drawn up and signed at its own meetings. This would be in accordance with the procedure usually followed by the League in other technical matters with which it has been called upon to deal. But it is also possible that in so difficult and important a matter as

[1] No doubt they would also be sent to Governments of Non-Members of the League, as such documents always are.

disarmament the Members of the League might wish to interpose yet another preparatory stage, and that they might decide
at the disarmament conference merely to draw up the scheme
of a concrete and definite agreement, leaving the final " adoption " of this agreement to be done by the Assembly of the
League. This also would be in accordance with some precedents
and with the general principles of the working of the League,
and it might well be that when the time came there would be
great practical advantages in so proceeding.

THE NATURE OF THE COUNCIL'S PLANS

Such being in outline the practical procedure for the preparation of a disarmament agreement which Article 8 of the
Covenant prescribes, the next question that arises is that of
the nature of the " plans " which the Council is to lay before
the Members of the League. What is meant by the word
" plans " ?

The terms of Article 8 itself provide no answer, but various
resolutions adopted by the Assembly plainly do. The Assembly
has several times suggested that the Council's Preparatory
Committee should be instructed to make proposals which, " in
order to secure precision, should be *in the form of a draft treaty*
or other equally definite plan."[1]

A little reflection shows it clearly to be desirable that the
plans should be " in the form of a draft treaty." The later
chapters of this book will indicate some of the formidable
technical and political difficulties which must be overcome
before any disarmament agreement whatever can be made.
There can be no doubt that the real nature of these difficulties,
and the methods by which they can be dealt with, will fully
appear only when an attempt is made to solve them in an
international convention. It is a common experience that
much of the real substance of a problem first emerges when
drafting is begun.

Whatever else the Preparatory Committee may or may not do,
therefore, it must draw up its proposals in the form of a draft

---

[1] *E.g.*, Resolution 2 of Third Committee, Second Assembly, 1921,
A. 158 (I.), 1921, p. 1.

convention. This will have, moreover, not only the advantage of bringing out the points that must be dealt with, but also the further highly practical advantages of providing a precise basis for the criticisms and counter-propositions of the various Governments, and of much facilitating the arduous task of the Council and of the Disarmament Conference itself, when matters reach that stage.

If, then, the plans are to be in the form of a draft treaty, what should this draft treaty contain?

It may be that it will have to consist of two parts: one dealing, in the words of Article 8, with "national safety and the enforcement by common action of international obligations"; the other with disarmament proper. This was the theory upon which the draft Treaty of Mutual Assistance and the Geneva Protocol were based; for that reason, the Temporary Mixed Commission proposed its general "security" plan, upon which both these documents were founded. But it may be that the security problem will be settled apart and in advance by preliminary and separate agreements such as the Locarno Pacts;[1] in that case the draft treaty which the Council will propose will only consist of one main part, that relating to the reduction and limitation of the national armaments of the signatory states.

In any case it is the reduction and limitation of armaments that are here to be discussed, and it is plain that when the final agreement on this part of the matter has been made, its main substance will consist in the laying down in treaty form of definite scales of national armament which each signatory power will undertake not to exceed. Must, then, the Council "plans" contain draft schedules setting forth in concrete figures precise proposals for these scales? Or should they only, in the words of the Second Assembly, draw up "a model skeleton treaty which could be adapted to the requirements of the situation when the actual agreements came to be made?"[2] Should they, that is to say, carry the precision of their plans to the point of inserting in them actual detailed propositions concerning the size and strength of the armies, navies and air forces which the various countries of the world shall respectively

---

[1] On the general question of security, cf. chap. v., *infra*. [2] *Ibid.*

maintain, or should they merely determine the principles and
the form of the treaty to be made, either using for the
purpose of their " model skeleton " imaginary figures or leaving,
in place of figures, blanks which the disarmament Conference
itself should subsequently fill in ?

It is a large question, and one which will be of practical
importance when the Preparatory Committee comes to grips
with its work. The subsequent chapters of this book may
provide material for an answer; in the meantime it may be said
that there is no obvious *a priori* conclusion. The question
requires double consideration, in connection first with the
function of the Preparatory Committee, and second with that
of the Council itself. Clearly the Preparatory Committee
could perform a useful work by making such a " model skeleton
treaty " as the Second Assembly proposed, without embarking
on the difficult and perhaps dangerous political task of proposing
actual scales of armament for different states. It would probably in any case do well to *start* by doing this, finding solutions
in principle for the technical problems that will arise, and reserv-
ing for a secondary stage their concrete application. It is
obvious from the records of the Temporary Mixed Commission
that its leading members intended to proceed in this way had
their work not been cut prematurely short. Indeed, these
records give some ground for the view that they considered that
if they could succeed in drawing up a " model skeleton treaty "
their whole function would thus have been fulfilled, and there
is an obvious force in the contention that an independent,
non-governmental committee might have difficulty in making
propositions on so thorny and so important a matter as scales
of national armament. But against that contention it can
equally be argued that the very independence of such a body
might enable it, perhaps after private and non-committal
negotiations with the Governments, to put forward proposals
which an official body might find it impossible to make.

But, of course, if the Preparatory Committee decided only
to make a model skeleton, the problem would then arise for the
Council itself. Should it in this case be content to pass on the
skeleton, leaving the Conference when it met to fill in the blanks?

No doubt this is a possible course for the Council to adopt;

but in fact it is improbable that it will adopt it. The records of the Fifth Assembly show that when the Geneva Protocol was made, and the Council was invited to communicate to the Governments by March 15, 1925, "a general programme for the reduction and limitation of armaments,"[1] it was universally agreed that this programme should include not only technical principles but also the practical application of these principles in definite scales of national armament. Moreover the terms of Paragraph 4 of Article 8, though they are not conclusive, certainly support the view that it is the duty of the Council to make such a programme. There is also the consideration that if it were to confine itself to a model skeleton, the Council would inevitably lose in the whole question of disarmament the initiative which the Covenant has given it, and which its Members will in all likelihood be most anxious to retain.

But it must be recognized that if the Council does include actual scales of armament in its plans, it will almost certainly be obliged to enter on difficult and perhaps prolonged negotiations. When the technical skeleton of its treaty has been provided, it (or, of course, its Preparatory Committee, if that Committee undertakes itself this part of the work) will have to consult with the different Governments as to the manner in which the blanks in the skeleton shall be filled in. It would be risky and perhaps quite useless for them to draw up, even as a preliminary proposition, elaborate scales of figures every one of which the Governments concerned might subsequently resist. And since—the security of each state being dependent chiefly on its neighbours' preparations—the original figures to be inserted in the plans for any one Government must depend upon the figures inserted for a number of other Governments, the Council (or the Preparatory Committee) would probably require to hold a number of informal regional conferences with Government representatives to discuss in general terms the scales it should insert. Neither the Council nor the Governments would be bound by the results of such consultations, but unless they had taken place the chances of ultimate success might well be much reduced.

[1] Article 17, para. 2, of Geneva Protocol; cf. *The Geneva Protocol*, by P. J. Noel Baker, chap. x.

Even with this prospect of protracted negotiations before it, however, it is virtually certain that, for the reasons given above, the Council will decide to include in the plans which it puts forward not merely a model skeleton, but also concrete figures on which the Disarmament Conference can base its work. Its " plans " then will be in the form of a Draft Treaty, which will include a definite proposal for the necessary schedules with their scales of armament provisionally filled in. What else must it include ?

Obviously any disarmament agreement must follow the lines indicated in Articles 17 and 21 of the Geneva Protocol, and must lay down the methods by which, and the time-limits within which, reduction of armament to the scales adopted shall be carried out. It must also—in view of the nature of the problem—lay down the conditions in which the whole agreement may be declared to have been unfulfilled, and it must make arrangements for what shall then be done. And since these thorny questions constitute an essential part of the problem of disarmament, and a considerable element in its technical difficulty, they must be dealt with, not only in the ultimate disarmament agreement which the Conference will adopt, but also in the plans which the Council will prepare. No proposals for disarmament would be complete which did not suggest how they should be practically carried out and define the circumstances in which they must be deemed to have failed of execution.

THE ACTION OF THE LEAGUE

Such is in outline the procedure and the preparation which, in pursuance of Article 8 and the decisions of the Assembly, are required. One concluding reflection on the subject may be allowed.

If any practicable plans are to be laid before the Conference when it meets, there must be first an elaborate theoretical study of the problem, and then a whole series of negotiations which will probably be protracted, and which will certainly be difficult both from the technical and the political points of view. When the plans are made and the Conference has met, the securing of agreement may even then be very hard. After the conference has made its treaty and dispersed, there will remain the task of obtaining ratification by the Parliaments of the very numerous Governments concerned. After the Parliaments have ratified, and the treaty has entered into force, it will still be necessary to supervise the long and complicated process of its execution, and to settle the many international disputes that will arise.

All these many processes can only be carried through, all the many obstacles can only be overcome, by action taken through the institutions of the League of Nations on the basis of the positive obligations which, by Article 8, the Members of the League have all assumed. The authors of Article 8 and the Assembly have not invented needless and tiresome elaborations; disarmament is, in fact, as they conceived it, an immensely intricate and difficult affair. A comparison may, perhaps, be made with another problem with which the League has dealt, a problem smaller in scale and different in nature, yet similar in its combination of technical and political difficulties to be overcome—the problem of Austrian financial and economic reconstruction. The League was only called upon to take the matter up after the Allied Powers in conference after conference had failed. Its Council carried through technical investigations for which no diplomatic conference could have had the means; in this way it reached agreement where the Allies had been unable to agree. But this agreement, and the treaties which it made, were not the end, but only the beginning of its task. Three years were needed before the Austrian Republic could stand alone. And during those three years new problems of every kind arose, disputes between the Austrian Government and the agents of the League were brought to almost every session of the Council, grave political crises threatened to overthrow all that the League had done. The Council and its technical committees carried through, in short, a work which, by its very nature, could not possibly have been accomplished by the ordinary machinery and methods of diplomacy.

What was true of Austrian reconstruction is no less true of disarmament. Only by the constant pressure exerted by permanent international institutions, by the continued and systematic work, technical and political, which such institutions alone make possible, can success be achieved in a matter so difficult as this. Through the machinery of diplomacy we could never hope to get results. That machinery could never do the preparation that is needed; no diplomatic conference summoned *ad hoc* could make a treaty; no Foreign Office staff could supervise its execution. The experience of Washington in 1921 only strengthens this conclusion,[1] and the whole course of the League discussions does the same. It is a cause for satisfaction, therefore, that the matter is to be dealt with as the Covenant prescribes, that Washington excursions are no more in favour, and that the League is to be enabled to fulfil the first and greatest of its allotted tasks.

---

[1] Cf. chap. x., *infra.*

CHAPTER IV

SPECIAL DIFFICULTIES DUE TO MODERN CONDITIONS

THE object of a disarmament policy is to make an international agreement which shall strike a balance between the armaments maintained by different nations at a level lower than that which they at present maintain, without either involving injustice as between one nation and another, or exposing any of them to dangers to their national security to which they are not exposed when they are free to maintain whatever armaments they please. This object is made more difficult to achieve by various factors arising out of and peculiar to the conditions of modern war.

WAR VETERANS

The first factor of this kind which must be mentioned is one of importance at the present time, but of an importance which diminishes with every passing year. It lies in the existence in most of the countries involved in the Great War of large numbers of veterans who have had prolonged experience of active operations. There is no doubt, for example, that the potential military strength of Germany is far greater than that of the small army which she is allowed under the Treaty of Versailles. It is greater because there are in Germany ready to answer a summons to the colours several million men who underwent the training of the world war, and who with some further training would be first-class soldiers. The same would be true of the potential strength of other belligerent countries were they now to accept a fixed limitation of the armed forces they maintain.

This factor is important because it increases the difference between the armed forces allowed to any given nation under a disarmament agreement and the forces which that nation could mobilize in the early stages of a war; and the greater the difference which there is in this respect the greater will be the difficulty of securing agreement upon the technical terms of any disarmament treaty.　It is important also because the initial period of a disarmament scheme, the years during which its clauses are being carried out and the next few years which immediately succeed, will evidently be the most critical time for its success.　If the scheme works satisfactorily during this period, the nations thereafter will have so much greater confidence in it that its ultimate success will, in all probability, be assured.

But if it is important in the initial stages this factor will later on be wholly negligible.　The veterans of the Great War, if they were mobilized to-day, would no doubt already make far less efficient soldiers than they were in 1918.　Experts say that by 1933 they will be little better—if, indeed, they are better at all—than raw recruits.　That being so, it is probable that the existence of the war veterans will be neglected when the scales of armament for different nations are laid down.　It may be added that the desire of Europe for repose, and its repugnance to the renewal of war, are now so great that such neglect would probably be safe.

CONSCRIPTION

The conscription system is another element in modern military preparation which complicates the problem of disarmament.　Any agreement made now must deal, not with the relatively small professional armies of the past, but with nations in arms.

The conscription system is relatively new, but, nevertheless, it cannot be expected that the continental nations of Europe will agree to give it up.　They may agree to limit the period of compulsory service for which they conscript their subjects; they may equally agree to limit the percentage of the annual " class " whom they oblige to serve.　But they will not agree to give up the right to compel their citizens by law to do military service for the state.

This may be regretted, but it must be accepted.　It is no doubt true that conscription has been the greatest single cause of modern militarism.　But it has become part of the national life of many nations, and is regarded by them not merely as a means of military protection, but as an indispensable method of education and discipline for the manhood of their peoples. It is claimed, for example, by the Italian Government, and by Italians even of the most liberal outlook, that Italy, after her risorgimento, was only welded into a single nation by the common service of all her subjects in the national forces. The Balkan nations no less regard compulsory military service as part of the foundation upon which their national systems rest. Probably none of those countries whose armies it is now most desirable to reduce and limit would agree to abandon conscription. Rather than do so, indeed, their Governments in all likelihood would take the responsibility of rejecting a disarmament scheme altogether. It may also safely be said that all the ex-enemy countries who have been forced to give it up would return to conscription to-morrow if they got the chance.

Conscription makes disarmament plans more difficult to draw up because it permits the creation of very large reserves which can be added to the standing forces when mobilization takes place.

PROGRESS OF INVENTION

Even more difficult than the complication arising from conscription is that which results from the rapid progress of invention and its application to the means of war. This again is modern. For hundreds, indeed for thousands of years, the arms used in warfare hardly changed. Even the introduction of gunpowder made little difference for several centuries, either in the nature of war or in the destructiveness of military operations. The rifles used by infantry remained no more than an improved bow and arrows; the cannon were only a more effective form of the mediæval battering-ram. Even throughout the Napoleonic period, in spite of its prolonged and large-scale operations, armament remained static; not a single new weapon was introduced from the beginning to the end, and even after the Napoleonic wars were over there was little development or change until late in the nineteenth century. It was, indeed, only in the last quarter of that century that steam and electricity and chemistry began greatly to affect the nature of the weapons used. Then in a comparatively brief period

high-explosive shell reached an efficiency hitherto undreamt of;
the rifle was modernized, and to it was added the machine-gun;
to the hand-grenade was added the flame-thrower; poison gas,
aeroplanes, submarines, torpedoes, and tanks came in as entirely
new weapons necessitating the development of new services in
fleets and armies.

This fact of the rapid change in weapons is of great importance
to the present purpose. Incidentally it is, of course, the
fundamental reason why the old international law of war is
no longer really adequate to control the operations which
it was intended to control. But also—and this is the present
point—it must affect, and affect profoundly, the attitude of
Governments towards disarmament. For no doubt the staffs
will now want, under a disarmament treaty, full liberty to
experiment in new forms of warfare. They will be reluctant
to bind themselves not to develop this weapon or that, fearing
always that some disloyal state might by some secret new
invention place them at a disadvantage. Indeed, the mere
knowledge of impending changes and development in the means
of war must make any fixed limitations on armament, at least
when they are first adopted, seem artificial in their nature.
And the difficulty is continually increasing for the reason that
the changes in weapons have gone on with increasing rapidity
ever since the Great War came to an end. The aeroplane,
packed with high-explosive and steered and controlled by
wireless, the torpedo of irresistible destructive power and likewise guided to its allotted prey by wireless, are but two of the
new weapons that have been developed since 1919. Such rapid
change almost gives ground for speculation as to whether, if
the present development goes on, all limitations of the kind so
far proposed will not soon be irrelevant to the purpose they are
intended to achieve.

THE PEACE-TIME USE OF WEAPONS

Another difficulty results from the rapid development of
weapons which has followed the application of modern science
to war. It is this: that no disarmament agreement can now
include and limit all the vital factors on which military strength

depends. Before modern science had changed the methods of warfare, the weapons that were useful in war served, broadly speaking, no other purpose. But nowadays the weapons upon which success in war will probably depend have peacetime uses of great importance. Aircraft furnish an obvious example. Commercial aircraft are in their infancy, but they have already become an important factor in the economic system; and, with every month that passes, their efficiency, and, in consequence, their utility and their numbers, increase. No one who contemplates the great air lines of the world—London to Paris, Paris to Stockholm, Berlin to Moscow, Helsingfors to Tiflis and Teheran, Rome to Constantinople—and the vast network of aerial communication that is being built up around them, can doubt that the commercial aeroplane has come to stay. Nor will most people who examine the great projects now under responsible consideration for linking up Great Britain and India, Africa and Australasia, believe that it would be desirable, even if it were possible, which it almost certainly is not, to limit by international agreement the number of commercial aircraft which each state chooses to produce or to maintain. Yet the qualities required in a commercial aeroplane[1] are precisely the qualities required in a military bombing machine; the transformation from commercial to military use is the work of an hour or two. In the view of many experts, bombing aircraft, by means of which whole cities might be wiped out, and the resistance of an enemy quickly paralyzed, will almost certainly be the principal offensive weapon of any future war.[2]

The same argument applies to what will, again according to the experts, be the chief auxiliary weapon used by aircraft—poison-gas. In his admirable work on chemical warfare Major Victor Lefebure has explained the reasons why gas and aircraft were not used in combination during the last world war, and he has also explained that these reasons no longer hold good. His whole book, indeed, is a demonstration, so far unrefuted, and, to the layman, seemingly irrefutable, that gas, distributed by aircraft, will play a predominating rôle in any future war. But the power to produce gas on a large scale and

---

[1] Cf. chap. xii., *infra.*   [2] Cf. chap. xii., *infra.*

at short notice for warlike use depends on the possession of chemical factories; and—this is the present point—such factories are indispensable for many peace-time industries. Speaking of what he calls " the unique war importance of organic chemicals," Major Lefebure says this: " It so happens that many of them are essential to our daily life as dyes, drugs, photographic and other synthetic products. Industries, therefore, have arisen for their manufacture. And this is not all. Organic chemical factories have proved to be not only arsenals in disguise, but endowed with the flexibility of their parent, the science itself. The factories and plants . . . can develop the production of practically any chemical which research can produce. The will of man can thus silently and swiftly convert the dye factory into an arsenal."[1]   And, of course, such chemical factories and plants, because of their peace-time use, cannot, at least without great difficulty, be limited by any international treaty that can be made. Here, then, is a second factor in military strength, of great, perhaps of supreme importance, which may easily escape the control of a disarmament agreement.

Again, some countries have organized for postal or other Government services great fleets of heavy motor-lorries or tractors. They are devoted to a legitimate peace-time use; they cannot be limited by international agreement; yet, in facilitating the concentration of troops, in the transport of artillery and ammunition, or as an auxiliary to air-force operations, they may be a military factor of great importance.

The point need not be laboured. It is quite plain that a great part of the offensive machinery and equipment of a modern fleet or army serves both a warlike and a peace-time purpose, and that, therefore, it cannot in all probability be limited and controlled by an international disarmament agreement. This is a fact peculiar to modern conditions, which obviously and seriously complicates the problem which the experts have to solve.

The Imponderable Factor of Industrial Strength

The same difficulty reappears in another more extended, perhaps vaguer, but certainly no less important form. The

[1] *The Riddle of the Rhine*, chap. x.

factors already considered—the conscriptive system, the achievements of inventive genius in the means of destruction, and the military value of peaceful machines and products— have all combined not only to change the character of fighting, but vastly to increase the scale upon which warfare is now carried on. Any army worth the name is numbered in millions; it requires for its service almost incalculable quantities of supplies and of material of every kind. For that reason, when a nation goes to war the whole economic system of its country is brought into play; and the power of its army in the field depends very largely upon the industrial resources, the manufacturing plant, the supplies of raw material, the roads, the railways, the ships and other transport, which are organized in its support. It follows as an inevitable consequence that a belligerent with a highly developed national industry is in modern warfare far stronger than one that is without it.

The effect of this must be to make it more difficult to get agreement on a scheme for general and mutual reduction and limitation of armaments. For any such scheme must involve an undertaking by every signatory power neither itself to increase nor to assist any other signatory to increase its armaments above the limits mutually agreed upon. Without such an undertaking, no scheme could be of any value. But, if war were subsequently to break out—always the crucial test in disarmament negotiations—such an undertaking would evidently confer a great advantage upon countries with great industrial resources. This advantage would be felt immediately hostilities began, and would increase with every week of war that passed. For both the rapid mobilization of large forces and the conduct of large-scale operations now depend, as has been said, upon the industrial machine by which the armies in the field are supported. If one power has a great industrial system which its Government can immediately take over, which, perhaps, it can secretly prepare for a long time in advance, that will give it at least a considerable, perhaps a decisive, military superiority over another power which has to depend for its supplies of arms, ammunition, uniforms, and so on, on the industries of other countries, perhaps geographically remote. And both the margin of this superiority and its military importance in case of sudden war will be greatly increased by a disarmament agreement which prevents the country without adequate resources of its own from making, in time of peace, the maximum military effort of which it is capable, and which forbids it to accumulate the stocks or organize the forces which might enable it to diminish the disadvantages from which it suffers.

It is, therefore, sometimes said that if a disarmament agreement is to be made, it must include provisions which will protect contracting parties without industrial systems against the great advantage which industrial states possess. It is agreed that such provisions may be of two different kinds: first, that in calculating the scales of armament allowed to different states—what at the Washington Conference was called the "ratio" between the signatory powers—a large allowance of extra military strength should be given to non-industrial nations, to compensate them for the weaknesses they cannot help ; second, that to reduce and limit, as far as may be, the importance of industrial strength, the disarmament agreement should include obligations on the parties not to adapt their manufacturing plant and their transport systems to preparation for war. It is further suggested that the execution of these obligations could be supervised by an international commission of control, and that this control could be made practically effective by the help and co-operation of the Socialist and Labour parties in the different Parliaments, and of their working-class supporters in the industrial factories and plants.

There is no need at the present juncture to discuss these propositions, nor to decide whether, either among the factors of military strength to be limited and reduced, or as an element in calculating the basic ratio between the parties, economic strength need be or can be specifically dealt with.[1] It is sufficient for the moment to note it as a complicating fact, new in military history, peculiar to our epoch of nations in arms and of industrialized and scientific war.

[1] Cf. *infra*, chaps. xiii. and xv.

The Danger of Secret and Decisive Weapons

There is yet another difficulty in making a disarmament agreement peculiar to the modern character of war.

It is generally agreed as a fundamental principle that such an agreement should only deal with factors of military strength over which it is possible to exercise a real control. Unless the parties to the agreement have confidence that its obligations are really being carried out by every state that signed it, distrust and fear will be increased to such a point that more harm than good might possibly result. But over the preparation of some weapons that may be of great importance in modern war it is difficult to know whether control can by any means be made effective. One party might, therefore, be able secretly to violate its undertakings, and by developing such weapons to increase its offensive power far beyond the strength allowed it in the Treaty. How can this difficulty, which may involve the gravest risks, be met and overcome ?

Though in the future it may arise over other weapons too, this is at the present time really no more and no less than the problem of poison gas. Poison gases have become a part of modern war. Every army that is worthy of the name has studied their use, has prepared its complete system of chemical attack and chemical defence. Most of the civilized powers have signed the most solemn undertakings—in Treaties made at Washington[1] and Geneva[2]—not to make use of gas in war; but their military policy is founded on the belief that these undertakings will not be observed. No one, indeed, who knows what war is like believes that a people fighting desperately in a mortal struggle for its life, attacked by land, by sea, and from the air, with all the hellish power of high-explosive, would hesitate at the crisis of its fate to seek salvation in any weapon it could turn to use. The chance that this may happen makes it very difficult to forbid study and preparation for chemical defence; and defence includes, as, indeed, it plainly must, defensive counter-attack. Thus, while the Geneva and Washington Con-

---

[1] Treaty . . . to Prevent the Use in War of Noxious Gases and Chemicals. Text printed in White Paper Cmd. 1627, 1922, p. 19.

[2] Protocol on Chemical and Bacteriological Warfare. Text printed in L. N. document, A. 16, 1925, ix., c.c. I.A. 91 (3).

ventions perhaps on some occasions may have their value, gas now is and, unless States disarm, it will remain a part of war.

And the preparation of poison gas is admittedly very difficult to control. If once the study of its use is undertaken, if once the necessary military apparatus is allowed, the preparation of vast quantities of gas can be carried on in secret in civilian chemical factories and plants, perhaps in such conditions that a great number of the factory hands themselves would be in ignorance of what was being made. Great stocks could be prepared and hidden, and would be extremely difficult to detect. Measures have, indeed, been suggested for the control of gas and the prevention of violations of a disarmament agreement on the subject; they will be discussed in a later chapter.[1] Here it is enough to indicate the great difficulty which is caused by the risk that such violations may occur.

This same difficulty arises, moreover, in another special form. There is to-day, as there has never been before in military history, the danger that someone may discover a new scientific principle or device which will enable him to make a weapon against which there is no known or discoverable defence. If this could be done, such a weapon might perhaps be made even without contravention of a disarmament agreement, yet its possession by one party to that agreement would give it such advantage that the whole meaning and balance of the treaty would be destroyed. For if one party acquired the power to strike a sudden and decisive blow, the armament restrictions of the other parties might become not only valueless but dangerous and unjust. Much has been heard in recent times of such a weapon. The "electric" death-ray, the deadly bacteria, the atomic bomb—writers of fiction have familiarized the public with fantastic hopes of winning easy wars and endless power by such means. Neither electricity nor bacteria nor radio activity have been so easy to harness as these writers tried to make us think; the revolutionary and irresistible weapon is still to find.

But the advent of chemical attack has given an imminent and terrible reality to a hitherto imaginary risk. Let us quote again from Major Lefebure: " In organic chemistry a single

[1] Cf. chap. xiv., *infra*.

worker, following up some rare family of compounds, may stumble upon a substance not far removed chemically from related compounds, yet infinitely more potent for war. Mustard gas, or B : B-dichlordiethylsulphide, is a member of a group of compounds differing only slightly in chemical structure the one from the other. Yet its nearest chemical relative is comparatively harmless. *The persistent lethal compound which will vastly change the nature of warfare will be but a slight chemical modification of some harmless substance.* . . . These inherent possibilities of chemical warfare . . . make chemical warfare the most important war problem in the future reconstruction of the world."[1]

Force is lent to Major Lefebure's contentions by the facts now known about Lewisite, the gas prepared by the United States Chemical Department for the campaign of 1919 but never used. Lewisite is invisible, it is a sinking gas, which would reach down to cellars and dugouts; if inhaled it is fatal at once; if it settles on the skin it produces almost certain death; masks alone are of no use against it; it is persistent; it has *fifty-five* times the " spread " of any poison gas actually used in the war. Indeed, it was estimated by an expert that one dozen Lewisite air bombs of the largest size known in 1918— far larger sizes could now be used—might in favourable circumstances have wiped out the population of Berlin.[2] And Lewisite is not the last word in gases. It is known that later research has given yet " better " results in fatal effect, in penetrative power, in persistence and in " spread."

It is in the realm of chemical attack that there is at present the greatest risk of the discovery of the new, secret, deadly and decisive weapon. But it is not only in that realm that the risk exists. Science no doubt holds many other unknown dangers of the sort, and from one day to the next she may spring a cataclysmic surprise upon a careless world.

In the consideration, therefore, of plans for the reduction and limitation of national armaments, we must bear continually in mind, together with the other difficulties which the nature of modern war imposes, that of the possible invention of some new and irresistible device for making war.

[1] *Riddle of the Rhine*, chap. x.
[2] Even if he exaggerated, the substantial point is unaffected. Cf. Irwin, *The Next War, passim.*

CHAPTER V

THE CONDITIONS OF SUCCESS

THE purpose of this chapter is to indicate in as few words as may be the main conditions that must be fulfilled if the Disarmament Conference to be summoned is to have a reasonable chance of succeeding in its task.

THE PROBLEM OF SECURITY

It was said in Chapter II that the plans for disarmament to be formulated by the Council of the League might have to consist of two parts: one dealing with " national safety and the enforcement by common action of international obligations," the other with the schedules of national armament. This must be so unless the problem of " security " is separately dealt with in advance and by some other means. For the problem of security is now universally agreed to be a part of the problem of disarmament; the two now go, and must go, hand in hand; the solution of the first is therefore the chief and indispensable condition of success in the solution of the other.

Why this should be so is shown, at least in part, by the arguments put forward in Chapter IV above. For it results from the modern difficulties there discussed that the incidence of a disarmament agreement will not to-day be what it would have been in simpler times. The classical proposition that a proportionately equal reduction of standing armaments will leave each reducing party relatively as strong, and therefore quite as safe, as it was before, is no longer obviously true; for an equal reduction in factors of military strength which can be limited by international agreement may much exaggerate an existing inequality of strength in factors which cannot be so limited, and may thus expose some parties to greater dangers than before.

Again, the fact that no disarmament agreement can by itself protect possible nations of good faith against the risk of sudden and treacherous attack by weapons of overwhelming power, the secret preparation of which it may be very difficult to prevent, makes it certain that they will be—whether logically or illogically is beside the point—unwilling to reduce the maximum military effort for their own protection which they are at present free to make, unless they receive other guarantees.

A scheme for general security, therefore, is part of the work which the League must carry through before its Members can execute their obligations under Article 8 of the Covenant. This is laid down clearly enough in Article 8 itself, as a careful examination of its terms will show; and Lord Cecil, when he first brought the reduction of armaments into practical discussion in 1922, did so on this basis. It was, indeed, at the moment when he linked the principles of security and disarmament together, that hope of a solution first appeared. It is not the purpose of this book to debate security, which has been dealt with at great length elsewhere.[1] It is enough to say that in the discussions of the last few years general agreement has been reached about its meaning. Security now means the provision of reasonable safeguards by the joint and common action of the society of states against aggressive attack aimed at any one among them which has not itself been guilty of an international fault or misdeameanour. It is further agreed— as is shown by the whole negotiations for the Draft Treaty of Mutual Assistance, the Geneva Protocol, and the Locarno Pacts—that security in this sense can only be achieved by two essential steps. The first of these is the closing of what the French have called the " gap" in the Covenant; in other words, the giving up of the right still left to Members of the League by Article 15 in certain cases to resort to war against a state which has not itself been guilty of a fault. The abandonment of this right and the consequent complete outlawry of aggressive war as between the parties, was the one vitally important feature of the Locarno Convention between Germany and France. The second step is the elaboration, whether by new general obligations or by supplementary special treaties like the Rhineland Pact, of further arrangements for mutual defence

---

[1] Cf., *e.g.*, *The Geneva Protocol*, by P. J. Noel Baker, chaps. ii., iii., viii.

against aggression. These arrangements must all be founded, as every new negotiation makes more plain, upon the fundamental undertakings already given in Article 16 by all the Members of the League.

It must be added, before the subject of security is left, that, of course, disarmament when carried through will in itself be an important factor in the safety of the participating states. In all the ways and for all the reasons discussed in Chapter II, it will reduce the risk of war. Nor is that all. For if sanctions by joint international action should ever unhappily be required, such action would obviously be simpler against a state whose armaments were small, and this advantage would not be outweighed by the fact that the armaments of the states acting together against it would also be reduced. But this element of safety will not alone suffice. Only when something further has been done to make the system of the Covenant a living reality in the policy of states, and to complete that system by the fuller application of the basic principles on which it has been built, will the disarmament of nations come about.

THE GENERALITY OF A DISARMAMENT TREATY

The second condition of success in a policy of disarmament is contained in the proposition that " no scheme for the reduction of armaments can ever be really successful unless it is general."[1] Unless the great body of civilized states can agree to adopt in common a plan that will equally apply to the armed forces which they all maintain, there is small hope that those among them who desire to do so will be able to reduce the military burden which they bear.

When it is analysed, this generality which is required has a double meaning: first, the disarmament plan must be accepted by all, or almost all, the members of the community of states; second, it must cover, so far as may be, all the factors of their military strength. These two meanings may be discussed in turn.

[1] Resolution 1 of the four Resolutions presented to the Temporary Mixed Commission by Viscount Cecil in July, 1922, and subsequently adopted by the Third Assembly.

First, then, what in fact is meant when it is said that the disarmament plan must be accepted by all, or almost all, the members of the community of states? Can nothing be agreed or done unless Persia and Peru, Abyssinia and Ecuador give their consent? That is obvious nonsense. The mere suggestion shows that it is necessary to examine more exactly what is meant by " generality " in this sense.

The meaning varies, of course, with the nature of the different kinds of armaments to be discussed. A land-locked country need not be consulted about a naval treaty. If two states are so remotely distant from each other that by no possibility could their forces ever meet, they need not mutually agree, for example, to each other's aerial strength. The question may best be looked at, therefore, from this point of view.

Naval armaments come, to the Briton, logically first. What states must be agreed before a naval treaty can be made? It is best to start by considering what it is desirable, if possible, to do. Plainly, if it can be done, a treaty should be made which shall secure consent from all the powers who either have or may have naval forces. To begin with, if it is to be any good at all, it must take in *all* the great naval powers, however geographically remote they may appear. For, in fact, in naval armaments the " continental limitation " has long since ceased to count. The most active naval competition of present times has been between the U.S.A., Great Britain and Japan—between an American, an Asian, and a European power. For America and Japan, indeed, the Pacific Ocean still remains an obstacle to inter-continental warfare. But the British Empire is on all sides of the Pacific, and even between America and Japan a naval war is unhappily a danger that must be borne in mind. It is certain, therefore, that no great naval power will agree to bind itself to limitations by which its potential rivals are not also bound.

Next, if the naval treaty is to secure the reductions for which we are entitled in due course to hope, it should include besides the great naval powers those other powers with navies at present far below them by every test of naval strength, but to whose present level the Great Powers may be brought much nearer than they are. These should include not only the ten (or eleven) other powers[1] which possess among their fighting vessels units which the Washington Convention somewhat arbitrarily defined as capital ships, but also those which have fleets of any kind, and even those which, though they have no fleets to-day, are so placed that they may be able later on to build them up. The grounds for this are plain: those who have no capital ships may later on acquire them; in any case, as will be argued later, it is useless to deal with capital ships unless other sorts of ships are dealt with also; nor is it possible to limit those who have got navies now, and leave others who have not got them to build them up in freedom later on. For reasons such as these the Temporary Mixed Commission, when it drew up for the Council its extended " Washington Convention," included in its draft not only those eleven powers who actually had fighting vessels of the two classes (capital ships and aircraft carriers) with which it was designed to deal, but also thirty-two other states[2] whose interest was less direct.

For the same reasons it is important, if it can be done, that the naval treaty should be a world-wide agreement, covering all states which are or might be able to build up naval forces. Only such a treaty, universally accepted by all such powers, can give the best results.

But if such " generality " as this is not obtained, can nothing then be done ? Obviously something, perhaps a great deal, can be achieved by smaller groups. For example, the great naval powers, if they acted all together, could, by themselves and without a single other state, do much to rid the world of dangers and themselves of grievous burdens. What they did in Washington for two classes of fighting ships, they could do again for others, perhaps for all the rest. If Russia joined their ranks, they could no doubt go further than if she stood aside.[3] But

---

[1] Argentine, Brazil, Chile, Denmark, Greece, Netherlands, Norway, Russia (if not counted as a great naval power), Spain, Sweden, Turkey (cf. L.N. Document C. 477(*a*), 1922, ix.).

[2] The naval advisers of the Temporary Mixed Commission even exaggerated the point to include land-locked states such as Czecho-Slovakia and Switzerland. Vide *ibid.*, Preamble of Draft Convention.

[3] Even if Russia's policy did not much affect their action at the present time, it must certainly affect in a most important way subsequent reductions of armaments in years to come.

Russia is no more a first-rate naval power, as once she was; without her, therefore, the others—Great Britain, the United States, France, Italy, and Japan—can do something, even if their work be less complete and stable than it would be if she too came in.

Again, it is at least in theory possible that another group of countries, the South American republics, might be able to agree upon a separate naval treaty for themselves, even if the powers in other continents did not help. But in practice it is most unlikely that they will. The negotiations of the League Commissions for the extended " Washington Convention " showed no such disposition of the South American states to act alone. Similarly, it might be thought that the smaller European states might make a group agreement, independent of the remainder of the world. But again, it may be doubted whether Spain, to take a fair example, would act without Italy and France, or whether the Baltic or south-eastern countries would renounce their freedom unless Russia did the same; and without these states, it need not be added, no European agreement, however limited, could be made. Such examples, it may be said in passing, show in a striking way the bearing of security upon the problem. But even if the Council's plans for security are strong, the attitude and action of the Russian state may well determine how much naval reduction will be possible, not only for the great naval powers in years to come, but also for the whole of Europe when the treaty is first made. If the policy of one single country can have such effects, no one can doubt that in naval armaments at least, " no scheme can be really successful unless it is general," and that the " generality " required is of the widest kind.

The same is true of armaments on land, but in a more limited sense than on the sea. It is much more likely than in naval armaments the countries of a single continent could act together to limit the land forces which they respectively maintain. There are two reasons for this.

First, in spite of the recent vast improvements in the means of transport, armies remain far less mobile than a modern navy, and far harder to manœuvre at a distance from their national territory. Countries which are geographically distant from each other do not, therefore, come into competition, and continental grouping would have a natural foundation in military fact. Thus, for example, the countries of North and South America could easily combine to reduce and limit their land forces without the simultaneous action of any single outside power, and they could do so without running any appreciable risk.

For the same reasons the European countries could act as a continental group, quite irrespective of what America might do. But it would be harder for Europe to act without her Eastern neighbours. The Balkan Powers might want to wait for Turkey. Once more the Border states could hardly bind themselves to rigid limitations if Russia should remain entirely free; and Russia in her turn, since the vast spaces of her federation link West and East together, could hardly act without China and Japan. Again, the Oriental possessions of the British Empire bring Great Britain also, although she is a European power, into contact and possible competition with Japan. These difficulties, indeed, are not conclusive. Without Russia and Japan a European treaty might be made, and if the system of security were sound, that treaty might bring reductions, even great reductions, in the scales of armament the European countries now maintain.

A continental grouping for American armies and another for European armies must thus both be reckoned as a possible part of the disarmament treaty to be made. Even that limitation on generality would, so far as Europe is concerned, restrict the results that might otherwise be had. And beyond that limitation it is plainly hopeless to expect to go. It has often been suggested in the Assembly at Geneva that it might be possible for the states in certain parts of Europe to agree together on regional arrangements for reduction irrespective of what those in other parts might do. But not even for the geographically most favoured regions have these suggestions passed beyond the stage of words. There are solid reasons why this has been, and why it must be, so. The different parts of Europe are linked together in a single system which they cannot break.[1]

[1] Cf. Right Hon. S. Baldwin in the House of Commons, February 1, 1926: " One of the greatest practical difficulties in approaching the subject of disarmament is that it would be almost impracticable for the

Consider, for example, the Balkan countries. They form as distinct a geographical unit as any group of powers in Europe; yet they would not think of reducing armaments unless Italy, which is outside the Balkans, did so too. But Italy in her turn would not reduce unless France and Spain would do the same. France would not reduce without Great Britain, and so on round the European map. Of course, it would not be fatal to a land-disarmament plan if some one or two unimportant European states stood out; the security arrangements would meet the risks which their defection would involve. But, broadly speaking, the continental group is the smallest that holds hope of real success, and any *serious* gap in the " generality " of such a group would bring disaster.

The second reason why continental group agreements might succeed with armaments on land is that the problem here, unlike the problem of naval forces, is chiefly European in importance. It is true that Russia and Japan have both great armies, and it is also true, as has been said, that without the co-operation of those powers Europe could not get as great reductions as with their help it could. But when all is said and done, in land forces it is the continental powers of Europe that lead the world. It was shown above that South America is already roughly on a level with the ex-enemy countries which have been disarmed. It is the European powers who for fifty years have constantly pressed up the standard of armaments maintained. It is they who first invented and who most rigidly apply the system of conscription. It is they who have invented and produced the new and deadly weapons which year by year have added to the terrors and destructiveness of war. If they will now act together, if they will make the arrangements and the so-called " sacrifices " that may be required, they can alone do very much; without the help of outside powers they can with their land forces make the great beginning which in due time will change the policy of the world.

Thus it may be concluded that, again, in land as in naval armaments, the ideal plan would be a really general scheme,

---

West of Europe to make any progress in disarmament without the East of Europe."

including all the countries which have armies, perhaps divided into group arrangements, but into group arrangements which are only part of one single scheme. If such " generality " as this could not be had, then continental treaties could be made; for America such a treaty would be easy to prepare, useful no doubt, but not in itself important; but for Europe such a treaty, though more difficult to make and less stable and effective than if a greater measure of generality were secured, would none the less be of vast importance for the future of the world.

What has been said about land armaments applies, for the present time at least, quite equally to armaments in the air. Again, intercontinental warfare is not a danger, and a continental grouping might have thus a solid basis in military fact. But again, and for the same reasons, a really general treaty would be much the best.

It has been suggested that it might be simpler to deal with aerial forces not by general or even continental treaty, but by agreement between those relatively few countries which are able to produce aeroplanes for war. It is held that these powers by agreement among themselves for limitation of their own forces and of the machines which they would sell to other countries[1] could exercise the control that is required. This might be possible; but it by no means follows that because the producing powers are few it would be easier to get agreement among them than to get a general treaty. The reverse is almost certainly the case. Moreover, it must be remembered that no such partial agreement could be for long effective, for the sufficient reason that any country which desires to spend the money can easily build up an aircraft industry.

The Second Meaning of Generality

The second sense in which it is true that a disarmament treaty " to be really successful must be general " is that it must cover not only all the states which maintain fighting forces, but also all the different arms which among them they maintain.

There is a prevalent idea that disarmament can be carried

[1] Cf., .*eg*., Art. XVIII of the Washington Naval Treaty (Appendix IV).

through in small instalments: that capital ships, for example, can be dealt with at one conference, other ships at another conference a few years later, armies at yet another, aircraft still later or not at all. The latest form which this idea has taken in Great Britain—a form due to emotions roused by recent and terrible disasters—is that without waiting for general disarmament a conference should be held to agree upon the immediate abolition of the submarine as a means of war.

There is no doubt that in instalments something might be done, but it may be doubted whether the results would deserve to be called "really successful." The response made abroad to the submarine proposals of the British press and public is not uninstructive. To take but one example that is typical of the feeling which they evoked in nearly every foreign country, a high official in the French Ministry of Marine is reported to have said as follows: "If it is a question of suppressing the submarine alone, then France would answer in the negative. France considers that the submarine is an exclusively defensive arm. If the League of Nations calls a conference to deal with the subject of general disarmament by land and sea, however, France would gladly fall in with all measures that would be decided upon."[1] There is, in fact, no real hope that a proposal concerning submarines alone could bring results.

That does not mean that by taking a small part of a single arm it may not sometimes happen that something can be done. The results of the Washington Conference prove the contrary. Washington succeeded in limiting two classes of naval units, and two only: capital ships and aircraft carriers. It was, indeed, only by excluding other classes that it reached results at all, while both on submarines and aircraft it completely failed. But the price of such a limited success comes up for payment later. The conference at Washington was not a failure; it would be absurd to minimize the importance of its work, but it would be no less absurd not to recognize its limitations. Subsequent experience has proved that at Washington only a small part of one single problem had been dealt with, that in spite of its agreements, a new and dangerous competition in other naval units was destined to begin; that

[1] Exchange News telegram, November 22, 1925.

this new competition threatened to destroy the whole balance of the basic ratio of strength—the famous 5:5:3:1·75:1·75—on which the capital-ship Convention was built up.

This is not academic doctrine; it was officially set forth in December, 1924, by Mr. Wilbur, the Secretary of the American Navy, in a departmental paper, in which for these very reasons he demanded another conference to deal with all the types of naval craft not covered by the Washington agreement. While everyone would admit that by good fortune something might perhaps again be done of the same limited kind as was done at Washington four years ago, no one in the light of subsequent events would now deny that such partial agreements are illogical in theory, and that in practice they cannot greatly help. So far at least it is plain that a "really successful" plan for naval armaments cannot be made by capital ship, by cruiser, or by submarine instalments, but that it must be a single treaty covering every ship and weapon used in war at sea.

For reasons similar in principle though not in detail, a larger proposition is just as true. The larger proposition is that if satisfactory results are to accrue, not only the whole of naval armament but also all land armaments as well must be dealt with at the same time and in a single plan.[1] It is true that navies *could* be dealt with first, as is so frequently proposed; technically, indeed, the naval problem is so different from that of land forces that even if both were dealt with at one conference a separate naval treaty could quite certainly be made. But what that separate treaty would contain would depend on whether fleets and armies had been thrown together into one single political arrangement covering both. For, in fact, it is certain that powers which principally rely on naval forces will not agree to great reductions until the continental military powers will do the same. No one who thinks about it will deny that this remark applies to England; neither Government nor public would accept much diminution of our naval strength if our neighbours—France and others—were free to keep whatever army or air-force they desired. And in other parts of Europe— the Baltic and the Ægean, for example—the interlocking of naval

[1] Cf. on this point Buell, *The Washington Conference*, chap. vii.: "The Future Weapons of War."

and military strength is still more important, as disarmament negotiations, if they once began, would quickly show.[1] Once more, therefore, if the best results are to accrue, there must be one comprehensive scheme, prepared from the beginning, both in the technical and the political Commissions, as a single plan, to cover armaments by both land and sea; drawn up and signed, in separate documents perhaps, but in the same agreement, and at one conference.

The same arguments apply, but with still greater force, to armaments in the air. The point is obvious. A state without an aircraft industry, or weak in aerial knowledge and experience, will not agree to reduce its army, if its neighbours, who may be stronger in the air, are free to build up aerial forces to any strength they like. If it is much inferior in the air, its only method of defence against attack may lie in vigorous counter-strokes on land. It has been said above that owing to the peace-time use of aircraft, it is difficult to limit by a treaty all the factors that make up aerial military strength. But what can be done to deal with aircraft—and though not complete, it may not be ineffective[2]—should be done at the same time and in the same agreement as that by which armaments on land and sea are dealt with.

The practical reasons for this course also happen to be strong, for it is certain that unless some new arrangement can be made, there will be a vigorous and very costly competition in aerial preparation, and the further this rivalry is pushed the more disastrous the results will be if another war should unhappily occur. The place of aircraft in military operations is becoming greater with every year that passes, and it may well be that

[1] Cf. statement by Polish delegate to the Moscow Disarmament Conference of December, 1922: " The Russian scheme made no mention of naval disarmament. This point is of interest to Finland, Esthonia, and Latvia . . . whose coasts are threatened by the Russian fleet stationed in the Gulf of Finland. The question was raised by M. Enckell, Finnish ... delegate to the Conference at Moscow. The Soviet Government gave him a very definite reply on the point. It stated that it could not discuss the question of naval disarmament. . . . It was quite clear that, especially to states such as Finland and Esthonia, the refusal to deal with questions of naval disarmament made the other guarantees (*i.e.*, proposals for land disarmament) of no value."—L.N. Document C.T.A. 227 (1923).   [2] Cf. chap. xii., *infra*.

within a not too distant future the aerial arm may dwarf all others in importance. To deal with land and naval armaments and leave aerial armaments aside might, of course, only hasten this result, and from every point of view it would be absurd.

It may, indeed, even be necessary for technical reasons, as will later on appear,[1] to deal with aerial forces not only at the same Disarmament Conference, but actually in the very document which limits armaments on land. And there is yet another technical consideration of a different sort. It is that aircraft now link up land and naval forces more than ever before, and thus make generality, in the second meaning now being discussed, a plain necessity. For aircraft not only operate in close conjunction with land forces, so that even when they are organized as a separate arm or service they also have to be attached in groups to infantry and artillery commanders in the field, but they are now of almost equal importance in naval operations. Even in the last war they played a considerable part in naval reconnaissance, in anti-submarine patrols, and in other ways; since the Armistice they have been much developed as weapons of direct attack against even the most powerful ships of war. The United States Navy have made experiments in dropping bombs, with the most significant results. A bombing hydroplane, dropping a high-explosive bomb of 2,000 pounds in weight—less than half the largest size that could even now be used—succeeded, without even hitting its target, in making a dismantled battleship turn turtle from the mere force of the explosion in the sea. Nor is it only by sinking them in this way that large ships can be attacked. Hydroplanes can now launch torpedoes, and may be able to use them with terrible effect. According to an authority on the subject, aircraft will soon carry artillery of large calibre, the accurate fire of which would be particularly deadly against either merchantmen or fighting ships.[2] Aircraft, operating either from aircraft-carriers or from the shore, have thus become perhaps the most dangerous single weapon of attack against ships of every kind,

[1] Cf. chap. xii., *infra.*
[2] Major Oliver Stewart, *The Strategy and Tactics of Air-Fighting,* Appendix.

and to deal with naval armaments and leave them on one side would be no less foolish than to do the same on land.

It may be concluded, therefore, that to get the best results, a disarmament agreement must combine in a single comprehensive plan restrictions upon every weapon and upon every arm; and exceptions to "generality" of this kind will not simplify the problem, as is often thought, but, on the contrary, may much increase the difficulties to be overcome.

THE SOLUTION OF THE TECHNICAL PROBLEM

Before a plan of general disarmament can be formulated by the Council there is also a preliminary technical problem to be solved. Its solution is, of course, an essential part of the work that should be done by the Preparatory Committee which the Council has set up.

A good deal has been said in the discussions of the Assembly about this preliminary technical problem, and about the importance of undertaking its examination. The kind of thing which the members of the Assembly have had in mind is perhaps illustrated by the following passage from the minutes of the Third Committee in 1925:

M. MUNCH (DENMARK—EX-MINISTER OF DEFENCE):

"While the Covenant did contemplate a plan of reduction for each state, it was apparent that the Council would need a general standard so as to decide whether the proposals of the various states were proper. How would they be able to reconcile the various interests of states with a fixed standard of armaments? Could they reduce armaments without throwing over the principle of compulsory service? Could they carry out such reduction by stages? What was the method of comparison between standing armies, volunteers, militia, etc.? All these questions, apart from economic and industrial preparation, would require profound study."[1]

It must be admitted that there has not been great precision of thought about the subject up to date. Yet such precision is very much to be desired. Just because the matter is obscure,

[1] Minutes of Third Meeting, September 17, 1925.

it has been asserted by some distinguished critics, both military
and civilian, that there is no solution; that there is no method
by which the military strength of different countries can be
measured and compared; that there are no ways in which a
treaty for mutual reduction, even if it could be put on paper,
could then be made to work.

If there were not high authority supporting this view, the
average person would be disposed to qualify it as absurd. It
is the purpose of this book to show that, though it is not absurd,
it is fallacious; that though the problem is extremely difficult,
it can be solved. There is no machine of human making that
cannot be controlled by those who made it; the military
machines of modern times, vast, cumbrous, and puissant though
they be, are no exception.

Let us attempt precision. What is the technical object at
which a Disarmament Conference will aim in the international
treaties it must make? It will be this: to agree upon the
military strength which the contracting parties will thereafter
respectively maintain; that is to say, to agree upon the absolute
military strength of each of them and upon its strength relatively
to that of all the rest; to express this military strength of all the
parties in treaty scales or schedules in which the forces of each of
them will be set out; and so to draw up these scales or schedules
that what is written down will, in fact, when it is applied, secure
the result to which the Conference has agreed.

Analysed into its technical elements, this object involves three
separate problems.

First, it must be determined what factors of military strength
shall be taken into account in drawing up the treaty—*i.e.*, what
factors shall be limited by its terms. Shall the land agreement,
for example, deal only with the peace-time effectives of the
standing armies, as has been proposed, or shall it also cover
the reserves by which they are supported, the weapons, armament and transport with which they are equipped, the stocks
of munitions they maintain, the method of enlistment of their
troops, supplementary cadres, colonial forces, territorial and
other similar formations?

Second, after it is settled what factors shall be dealt with, there must be found some method of measuring the strength of different countries in these various factors when they are combined. This method need not be absolutely precise, but it must be precise enough to enable the negotiators at the Conference to write down in treaty form the strength allowed to any country, to measure approximately what it is that is so written down, and to compare it with the strength allowed to other parties. It must, in other words, enable the Conference to translate into treaty obligations its decisions about the strength of different states, and to ensure, for example, that two states which it decides shall be of equal strength shall not, in fact, be left unequal.

Third, the Conference must decide what amount of each of the factors to be dealt with shall be allowed to each contracting party; that is to say, it must determine the relative military strength which they are all to have, and must thus establish between them what the Washington Naval Conference called the " ratio."

A few words more may be said on these three problems; the last may perhaps be taken first.

The problem of the ratio is essentially a political question.[1] It is for the Governments to determine not on technical but on political grounds what position in relation to their neighbours each of them is willing to accept. It has of course a technical aspect. On what basis should the ratio of strength between different powers be settled ? Should it be the *status quo* in each given factor ? Should it be the maximum demands of each contracting party ? Should it be a fixed percentage of these maximum demands ? Must allowance be made for geographical advantage or industrial strength ? These, it is true, are technical questions; but they are no more than details of the application of the main political agreement to be made.

But if the question of the ratio is assumed to be solved by a political agreement, there remain the first two problems, which are technical and nothing else. They can be, and indeed they must be, studied and resolved quite separately from the third. Their substance may best be shown by a simple illustration. Suppose that by political arrangement the Dis-

[1] For a discussion of the problem of the ratio cf. chap. xiii., *infra*.

armament Conference had agreed that Belgium and Holland should be given equal military strength, and that France should be given four times as much as each; how could that agreement be transferred to paper in a form that would ensure the desired result ? It must be assumed, of course, that equal military strength means equal national preparation, and that in the adoption of the ratio factors like geographical advantage for defence have been neglected or allowed for ,or are cancelled out. The problem is how to transfer a ratio of 4 : 1 : 1 into the detailed schedules of a treaty.

It has been said by an acute military thinker that in the eighteenth century this could have been very simply done. The whole thing was different in the days when professional armies had an existence entirely distinct from that of the nation, when they went to war on the basis of their peace-time armaments, without the rest of the nation taking any part. " Then the only factor that mattered was *effectives*—military strength corresponded exactly to the number of trained men-at-arms." But we are no longer in the eighteenth century; we have to deal with "nations in arms," and the immense material of attack with which they are equipped. Hence the technical problem.

Even to-day there is one way in which it might be comparatively simply solved; that is, by the application of the rigid, comprehensive, scientific system of the Treaty of Versailles. Under that system every detail of the man-power which Germany may maintain, of their enlistment, training, organization, armament and transport, of their general equipment, and of the whole national scheme of fortification and defence, has been laid down. If that were done in the case that has been taken as an illustration, Belgium and Holland would be given an identical number of effectives; among them there would be an identical proportion of officers of each rank; they would be organized in the same numbers of battalions, regiments, divisions, army corps, and so on; they would be given the same supplies of weapons of each class and of ammunition; in every particular their treaty schedules would be just the same. For France every figure in the schedule would be multiplied by four. On this system the preparation of the treaty might be in detail complex, but in its main substance it would be easy to draw up.

But it is said that no Government would voluntarily accept the simple but drastic system of Versailles. If that is true, if some more elastic system is required, some scheme that does not involve the reorganization of national armies, that does not impose a standard pattern of tactical division, that leaves a Government free to choose its weapons, to develop some arms and abandon others, then the technical difficulties indeed are great. How then can the total strength of one country be compared with that of another? How can unequal tactical divisions be compared? How can the power of one weapon be measured with that of another? How can weapons then be limited at all? How can reserves be sufficiently controlled to prevent a great divergence in the war-strength of different powers as compared with the strength they are respectively allowed to maintain in time of peace?

These are thorny questions, as will later on appear. But they are not insoluble, whatever may be true of some of the modern difficulties discussed in Chapter IV. They *can* be solved. But although they can be solved they are not less serious than they seem. It would be absurd to think that a treaty for general disarmament can be simple. In its preparation, in its negotiation, in its actual terms, and in its execution, it will be technically, as well as politically, the most complicated treaty ever made. So far, whatever may be thought of their conclusions, the pessimists whose views were given above are plainly right.

CHAPTER VI
REDUCTION OF ARMAMENTS BY SIMPLE BUDGETARY LIMITATION

IT may be useful to begin the consideration of the technical problem by looking first at certain schemes for its solution which have been put forward in the past, and at the causes of their failure. A brief attempt to do so will be made in this and in the succeeding chapter. Though incomplete, it may at least serve to show that there is no simple plan, as has often been believed, by which the problem of disarmament may be solved.

The most typical of the attempts at such a simple plan is the proposal, frequently discussed before the war in the conferences of the Inter-Parliamentary Union, and since the war in the Assembly of the League, for a disarmament treaty founded solely on a general and mutual reduction of the total military budget of each contracting state. It was urged in support of this proposal that, once the ratio had been established between the parties, budgetary limitations would provide the easiest means of measuring, or writing down in the treaty, and of subsequently controlling, all the various factors upon which their respective military strength depends. There would be no need, it was said, to deal with each factor by itself; military effort of whatever kind, whether it be the recruiting of effectives, the provision of guns and tanks, or the construction of defences, must all in the last resort be paid for by the state; these payments of every kind are all a charge upon the military budget; if this budget be reduced by a fixed amount, it must inevitably mean a corresponding diminution of military strength. A general agreement to reduce and limit budgets would thus achieve the object of disarmament with the minimum of technical difficulty and with the least possible restriction of the Government's freedom.

Unfortunately, the proposal is less simple than it seems. To begin with, it would be impossible to carry it out at all without a complete reorganization and standardization of the budgets of all or almost all the Governments of the world. The sums shown to-day in different national budgets under the various headings of military expenditure at the best only represent in the roughest way, and, in some cases, do not represent at all, the real strength of the respective countries. The systems of accounting vary greatly; some Governments account for gross appropriations, others only include *net* appropriations for expenditure after deduction of various receipts, such as contributions from other Government departments, from colonies or local governments, and so on.[1] Similarly, some Governments account in their army and navy budgets for powder factories, dockyards, etc., while others treat them as independent state undertakings; some include and others exclude such non-effective services as pension charges; some countries pay for their colonial troops in their national budget, in others the whole cost is borne by the colonies themselves.[2] All this being so, it is plain that the mere reduction and limitation of existing budgets would not mean an equal reduction in their respective military strength.

These difficulties of accounting could no doubt be removed by the general adoption of a new standard model of military budget, with uniform tables for showing the various kinds of cost; and if the Governments were in earnest about disarmament, they would no doubt agree to such a change. But even that would not remove the real difficulties of the proposal, which, indeed, the authors of the budget scheme have never really met. There is, for example, the fundamental difficulty that equal sums of money, expended by Governments on military organization and defence, will give completely different results in different countries. The most obvious example is furnished by the comparison of countries which have con-

---

[1] E.g., it transpired at the Disarmament Conference of 1922 that most of the basic supplies of the Russian Army are provided from the proceeds of taxation in kind, and do not figure in the budget cost of the army at all. C. 59, 1923, C.T.A. 205, p. 9.

[2] Cf. *League of Nations Armaments Year Book*, 1924, Preface, p. 9: " The fact must be emphasized that the figures for defence expenditure presented in these monographs do not admit of comparison of the figures for one country with those for others."

scription and which pay their recruits the merest pittance with countries which have to pay their long-term voluntary armies a wage on which a married soldier and his family can live. This difference of system would be an obvious cause of difficulty in any budget plan that could be devised.

But even if this difference were abolished, even if every country had conscription or voluntary service, the difficulty in question would still remain. It results from the difference in the standard of living of different countries; it is that which explains why Greece or Japan, for example, can maintain a soldier for less than France, France for less than Sweden, Sweden for less than Great Britain, Great Britain for less than the U.S.A. For this reason, equal sums of money will never give equal military strength, and therefore no agreed ratio, translated into terms of gold alone, will give a corresponding ratio in the forces of the different states to which it is applied.

It is possible, of course, that in the calculation of the ratio, that is to say, before the allocation of definite appropriations to the various parties had been begun, this difference in the standard of living could be approximately allowed for. All civilized countries now have index numbers, all of them have the economic statistics concerning the consumption of their peoples that would be required. But, even so, if it were attempted in any scientific form, such a series of calculations would be extremely hard to make. They might lead to almost interminable disputes, and even if first an agreement were once made embodied in a treaty, there would remain the difficulty that a rise or fall in soldiers' pay, a rise or fall in the standard of living, or some other circumstance of deliberate or normal change, might upset the whole basis on which the disarmament agreement had been made.

It has been proposed, however, that the whole difficulty might be met, without any such quasi-scientific arrangement, by simply basing the ratio on the actual expenditure and practice of the past.   It is said that if the ratio were founded— it will be seen hereafter that there is a strong case on its merits for this proposal—on the *status quo* of some given year, *e.g.*, 1913, it might then be possible to get all countries to agree only to expend a certain fixed proportion, the same for all contracting parties, of their total military and naval budgets for the selected ratio year. In this way an automatic allowance would be made for differences in their respective systems, in their respective rates of pay, and in the standard of living of their respective peoples. But this scheme rests, of course, on the assumption that the systems of the contracting parties will not change, and it would therefore need a supplementary agreement that any future change in their existing systems, in their rates of pay, in the standard of maintenance of their troops, would be reflected in the budgetary appropriations which they were respectively allowed. But such a supplementary agreement, it is held, should not, with the modern resources of economic and military science, be impossible either to make or to control; and if it once were made, it might be possible, starting first by some such reduction as 20 or 30 per cent of present budgets, ultimately to reach by further subsequent reductions a level of national armament which would ensure the peace and stability of the world.

It is plain that this scheme, if it could be worked, would have great advantages. It would be simple to prepare; it would be comprehensive; it would bring immediate and perhaps great economies in national budgets; and if, under Parliamentary pressure from the parties of the left, it were faithfully observed, it would do much to pacify existing fears and passions and to diminish the power of the military machine. It would thus achieve, at least in a great measure, the objects for which disarmament is desired, and it would do so with the least possible restriction on the liberty of Governments in respect of national defence.

But there remains for consideration whether any such scheme of limitation by budgetary appropriation alone would be accepted by Governments as sound. Would it give to suspicious and hesitating nations the conviction that the sacrifices of strength to which they might agree would not turn out to be a trap for their good faith? Would it, in other words, create the mutual confidence without which few Governments will take the grave step of agreeing to reduce their national strength?

In considering these questions, the first important point

concerns the means which there would be of ensuring by mutual control that no Government should secretly exceed its proper allocation by illicitly diverting to military uses monies voted in its budget for civil ends. The difficulty is discussed in another connection later on.[1] It is, of course, true, as is there pointed out, that in many countries the publicity of the budget and the vigilance of Socialist or other Parliamentary parties might suffice to check or to frustrate the schemings of a disloyal Administration. But it must be remembered that in some countries Parliamentary Government has been suspended, that in others it functions very ill. The control of budgetary appropriations destined to cover all " defence " expenditure of every kind, whether on military, naval or aerial forces, each Government retaining liberty to use its money exactly as it liked, whether on battleships, on the training of military recruits, on subsidies to fleets of quasi-commercial aircraft, or on any other form of preparation—control in such conditions would be most difficult; far more difficult, to say the least, than that of the limited appropriations for specific purposes proposed in Chapter IX. So great, indeed, would be the latitude of action which every Government would have, so immense would have to be the scope of any enquiry into any alleged violation of the undertakings given, that it may be doubted whether under even the most rigid system of mutual control faithful observance could be guaranteed. Indeed, it might well occur that excessive military expenditure on a considerable scale might pass, if not unsuspected, at least unproved. For these reasons it seems unlikely that any system based exclusively upon the reduction of budgets for national defence would be accepted. Such a system would require a measure of mutual confidence and trust which, unhappily at the present time, does not exist; the prospective signatories to the disarmament agreement would almost certainly consider that it would not give them sufficient guarantees for its observance; and those who themselves were of good faith might reasonably hold that the difficulty was greatest just in respect of countries whose faithful observance it would be most important to secure.

There is, moreover, a further difficulty which might deter

---

[1] Cf. chap. ix., pp. 160 *seqq.*

a Government which was asked to-day to accept a scheme based exclusively on budget limitation. It is this: that the whole balance established by such a scheme, the whole ratio of strength mutually agreed upon, might be suddenly and utterly destroyed, perhaps even without any infraction of the disarmament agreement, by the invention of some new and effective but cheap weapon of offence, which could be produced, it might be, at negligible cost, by one or by a few only of the parties. It was argued in Chapter IV. above that the secret invention of such a weapon is now quite possible.

Thus it may be concluded that a scheme based exclusively on budget limitation would, in theory, be unsound, that in practice it would be difficult to work, and that for these reasons —whether or not they ought really to prove conclusive—the Governments would in fact be most unlikely to accept it. Even the strongest adherent of the budget scheme would be obliged at the least to admit that the case against it is strong enough to make it necessary to discuss alternative plans by means of which disarmament can be secured.

There is, however, one way in which an exclusively budgetary limitation might be made of use. Although the Governments might be unwilling to bind themselves for any length of time to a scheme founded on what they would regard as an unstable basis, they might agree to do so as a preliminary measure for the period during which a more comprehensive and satisfactory plan was being prepared. It might be suggested, for example, that all the Governments intending to disarm should forthwith give a mutual undertaking, which they should embody in a simple preliminary agreement, to reduce their annual defence expenditure of every kind by a fixed percentage, on the condition that this arrangement should continue for a certain period of time, say perhaps three years, or until the Disarmament Treaty proper had been made and ratified. This plan would have advantages so obvious that they need hardly be explained. If a large initial reduction were agreed—for example, 30 per cent—it would secure, without the delay involved in the elaborate negotiation of a more comprehensive scheme, a great relief to national budgets. It would bind the negotiating powers to something concrete, and thus would constitute a mutual guarantee of their good faith. It would render less obnoxious and less dangerous the delay that might occur in general ratification of the disarmament treaty proper when it had been made. It would create a favourable atmosphere, not only for the negotiation of this treaty, but also for its discussion and approval in the national Parliaments of all the states concerned. Over so short a period, whatever risks it might involve could safely be neglected. Even if some countries, by skilful manipulation of their permitted budgetary appropriations, should succeed in making smaller reductions in their effective military strength than that made by their neighbours, that fact would hardly matter, since the whole system would be provisional, and any inequalities that might result would be readjusted when the disarmament treaty proper came into force.

It may be said that the plan could hardly be adopted unless the Governments were ready to accept a new standard model for their military budgets of the sort above proposed. It does not seem certain that this is true; but even if it were, such a standard model could be rapidly prepared by an international committee of budget experts, and its general adoption would be useful, not only for the purpose of the preliminary agreement, but also in drawing up the subsidiary provisions for budgetary restriction which may be needed as part of the disarmament treaty proper when it is made.[1] There seems, therefore, much to be said in favour of a provisional reduction by simple budgetary limitation as a first step towards the more comprehensive scheme that is required.[2]

[1] Cf. chap. ix., pp. 149 *seqq.*

[2] The proposal may be compared to that adopted in the following resolution of the Second Assembly of the League:

" That, subject to the conditions set out in the recommendation of the First Assembly, the recommendation that Members of the League should undertake not to exceed for the next two financial years following the present year the sum total of expenditure on military, naval, and air forces, provided for in the budget of that year, be again forwarded to all Members of the League, together with a statement showing the replies already received to this recommendation."—*Resolution* 8 *of the Third Committee of the Second Assembly.*

In view of the conditions of 1921 and succeeding years, this resolution was in fact of no great practical value.

The " conditions " contained in the recommendation of the Sixth Committee of the First Assembly were as follows:

" *Pending the full execution of the measures for the reduction of armaments recommended by Article 8 of the Covenant*, the Assembly recommends to the Council to submit for the consideration of the Governments the acceptance of an undertaking not to exceed, for the first two financial years following the next financial year, the sum total of expenditure on the military, naval, and air services provided for in the latter budget, subject, however, to account being taken of the following reservations:

1. Any contribution of troops, war material, and money recommended by the League of Nations, with a view to the fulfilment of obligations imposed by Article 16 of the Covenant or by treaties registered by the League;

2. Exceptional conditions notified as such to the Council of the League of Nations in accordance with the spirit of paragraphs 2 and 6 of Article 8 of the Covenant."—*Resolution and Recommendation adopted December* 14, 1920.

CHAPTER VII

OTHER UNSUCCESSFUL PROPOSALS

OTHER unsuccessful proposals for methods of disarmament must now be considered. There comes next in logical sequence the abortive scheme laid by Lord Esher in 1922 before the Temporary Mixed Commission of the League.

LORD ESHER'S SCHEME: PEACE-TIME EFFECTIVES

This scheme was designed to deal with land forces only; it resembled the budget scheme above discussed in that it sought to solve the problem by limiting one only of the various factors which make up military strength. It was founded, in other words, like the budget scheme, on the doctrine that there is one dominant factor, the reduction, limitation and control of which would solve the armament problem.

Although it failed, it included a number of features that are of enduring interest and importance; it is worth while, therefore, to reproduce the text:

" (1) That the size of standing armies in time of peace should be restricted on a numerical basis.

" (2) That the restriction should be fixed by ratio, following the naval precedent at Washington.

" (3) That the ratio should be confined to metropolitan forces, leaving each country to fix the forces required by it for colonial and overseas defence.

" (4) That within six months of the ratification of a treaty fixing the ratio, the High Contracting Parties shall reduce their standing military and air forces maintained within the metropolitan area in times of peace to the scale set forth in paragraph 9, and shall agree that the scale will not be exceeded for a period of ten years.

" (5) That the term ' standing military and air forces ' shall be held to include all military and air personnel of all

74

ranks serving either voluntarily or compulsorily in the metropolitan areas, with the regular military and air forces, all police forces permanently armed, and all permanent staffs of reserve or territorial forces, but shall not include the reserve or territorial forces.

" (6) That the Permanent Advisory Commission of the League shall be reconstituted and strengthened, under a Chairman to be appointed by the Government of the French Republic.

" (7) That it shall be the duty of the Permanent Advisory Commission to report to the League any infringement of the treaty embodying these agreements, and to prepare such plans as may be necessary for its enforcement.

" (8) That the Permanent Advisory Commission be authorized to nominate naval, military, and air attachés, who shall be given by the Governments to which they are accredited such facilities and information regarding armaments as may be from time to time required by the Commission.

" (9) That the fixed ratio of the standing military and air forces shall be as follows, taking 30,000 men of all ranks as the unit:

Belgium	2	Netherlands	3
Czechoslovakia	3	Norway	2
Denmark	2	Poland	4
France	6	Portugal	1
Great Britain	3	Roumania	3
Greece	3	Sweden	2
Italy	4	Spain	3
Serb-Croat-Slovene State	3	Switzerland	2

N.B.—The forces of Germany, Austria, Bulgaria, and Hungary to remain as defined in the Treaty of Peace."[1]

The principles on which this scheme was founded are simplicity itself. They are as follows:

1. Lord Esher proposed to deal with the forces maintained by signatory powers in time of peace. He made no attempt to limit the effort they would make or the forces they would build up if war should happen to break out. Equally in the scales

[1] Report of the Temporary Mixed Commission, 1922, A. 31, 1922, C.T.A. 173.

of peace-strength which he proposed he made no special allowance in his ratio for the greater war-strength of powers with industries suitable for the production of material of war.

2. He proposed to limit only the *effectives*—that is to say, the soldiers of all ranks actually in service in the standing armies. He neglected altogether the question of reserves for reasons which will be explained in a moment; for the same reasons, he neglected territorial forces of all kinds.

The reasons for this neglect of reserves and territorial forces are connected with the conception of what came in the debates of the Temporary Mixed Commission to be known as " Period A." This conception may be best explained by a passage from the 1922 Report of the Commission :

" In all questions connected with the reduction of armaments," says this Report, " it is essential to keep clearly in mind the distinction between the two periods into which a war, which resulted from an act of aggression occurring after a general and mutual reduction of armaments, would be divided. The first period, which may be called Period A, would be that in which each of the belligerents would put into the field only those forces which it had been able, under its reduction agreement, to prepare in time of peace. The second period, which may be called Period B, would be that in which steps would be taken to put into the field forces mobilized and trained after the outbreak of war. The first period would probably be of a few months' duration; the second would begin with the entry of the first war-trained troops, and would continue until each belligerent had mobilized its full national strength."[1] Lord Esher's purpose was to limit the forces which each signatory power would be able to put in the field during Period A. On general grounds he thought it would be absurd to attempt any limitation of the newly trained forces that would come into action in Period B. Moreover, he believed that with the new general security system of the League, it is Period A that matters; before that period is over the general guarantees of Article 16 will have become effective. And for Period A he thought he could achieve a just and equal limitation by fixing simply the

[1] A. 31, 1922, C.T.A. 172, p. 13.

peace effectives of the standing armies without troubling to restrict either territorials or reserves.

In respect of reserves—that is to say, of trained ex-soldiers used on the outbreak of war to dilute the existing units of the standing army—he held that, whatever recruiting or organization system an army might adopt, there was an automatic limit to the possible expansion of its standing forces during Period A. He based this contention partly on general doctrine, partly on the experiences of the war of 1914. Previous to that war every general staff had made the most minute study of the problem of mobilization, with a view to expanding to the utmost possible degree the forces which it could throw into action in the first weeks and months of war. In particular the German staff had concentrated on the point, having not only the most perfect military machine in history, but also almost unlimited reserves, at their command. Yet none of these general staffs, when hostilities broke out, could place in the field more than two and three-quarter times the number of troops they had maintained in time of peace. The French and German staffs both reached about this figure. The Russian and Belgian staffs did rather less; the British staff, with, of course, a voluntary system, mobilized one and three-quarter times their standing force.

According to certain military experts, the staffs were unable to improve on these results, because the coefficient of expansion is limited by two different factors: first, by the power of an existing cadre to provide at a moment's notice for newly mobilized troops the infinitely intricate organization of supply, transport, and command without which they cannot be effective in the field; second, by the power of any given number of soldiers in full training to absorb, without too great loss of efficiency, reserves who, although they have had experience in the past, are out of training at the moment when they are called upon to join. These experts, therefore, hold that the average mobilization coefficient upon which any general staff could dare to count would be about two and a half to two and three-quarters, and that making all allowances for special organization, and for a smaller total force to be manœuvred, as under a disarmament scheme there would be, it could not at the best be more than 25 per cent above what the German staff in 1914 achieved.[1]

Lord Esher proposed then to neglect reserves, because, however many reserves a Government maintained, it could not in Period A, with which alone he was concerned, make use of more than a certain proportion of them, and a greater strength in trained reserves would not, therefore, during that period give an undue advantage to one of two powers whose peace effectives had been proportionately reduced by a disarmament scheme. He did this because he desired simplicity and because, while every expert agrees that the size of *standing* forces can be easily controlled, the secret preparation of reserves is far harder to prevent. But, of course, he recognized that if freedom to organize unlimited reserves were thus allowed, Governments might not organize only those whom they could use in Period A, but a much greater number. The average total of organized reserves in conscription countries under present conditions is not two and three-quarter times, but about six times the numbers of the standing force. Freedom in this respect would therefore keep up the level of military expenditure, and thus *pro tanto* would defeat one of the purposes for which disarmament is desired.

Moreover, it would have the inevitable effect of shortening Period A. There is no agreed military opinion as to how long must be allowed before a staff can place in the field new formations created after mobilization has occurred. Six months is certainly too long; two months is probably too short. The French were only able to place their first new divisions in the field in January, 1915—nearly a full six months; but the Germans had at Ypres before the end of October, 1914, divisions

---

[1] The following calculation is kindly supplied by a military friend:

MAXIMUM DILUTION OF SERVING TROOPS WITHOUT TOO GREAT
LOSS OF EFFICIENCY.

Within two weeks of mobilization .. Serving troops 30 per cent, Reserves 70 per cent—*i.e.*, mobilization coefficient of $3\frac{1}{3}$.

Within six months of mobilization .. Serving troops 15 per cent, Reserves 25 per cent, Recruits 60 per cent—*i.e.*, coefficient of expansion within six months $6\frac{2}{3}$.

which had not existed in the previous July. But whatever is the minimum period that may be required, it will certainly be shorter for a staff with large trained and partly organized reserves than for a staff with less.[1]

Lord Esher deliberately neglected this fact, because for his purpose a Period A of two to three months was long enough, and because for at least this length of time a superiority of organized reserves would not mean any very great difference in the forces which a Government could actually use in action in the field.

3. For similar reasons he neglected militias or territorial forces, by which he meant forces whose members are " part-time soldiers " only. Such territorial forces are in one respect superior in military value to reserves; they are organized in their full war-strength, and have full war-equipment. They are therefore of great importance in a long war, as British experience in 1915 sufficed to show. But in Period A they can rarely if ever be used for active service. It is calculated by experts that they require an absolute minimum of six weeks' training before they can be used in war. The British " Territorials " are an excellent force, probably as good as any militia in the world. Yet not even their warmest admirer believes that they could have been used in France sooner than November, 1914—*i.e.*, four months after mobilization had occurred. " A Military Correspondent," writing in *The Times* on the lessons of the 1925 manœuvres,

---

[1] The following calculation is supplied from the source cited above:

Reserves which have had less than six months' training cannot be fit to take the field in modern war.

Reserves which have had six months' training only are of effective value four years later.

Reserves which have had one year's training only are of effective value six years later.

Reserves which have had two years' training only are of effective value ten years later.

Reserves which have had six years' training only are of effective value twelve years later.

The fact that longer service has a more permanent value has the obvious effect of limiting the total number of useful reserves that can be turned out by a system of intensive short-term training; while the fact that training " wears off," as shown in this table, has the further effect of limiting automatically the total number of useful reserves that can be turned out by a given standing force under a system.

spoke of the " statement, much criticized at the time, that the old (*i.e.*, the pre-1914) Territorial Force would require six months' training before being fit to take the field. We have no equally authoritative statement about the period which must elapse before the new Territorial Army can be ready. I have taken the opinion on this point of several General Officers who know Territorials well. Their opinions differ, as might be expected, . . . but my enquiries have led me to the conclusion that four months would be a safe average upon which to base our military policy, *provided that the numbers can be made up by war-trained veterans.*"

In view of this opinion, and particularly of its closing phrase, it is safe to conclude that territorial forces will not be used in Period A, and that therefore, if his premiss is accepted, Lord Esher was justified in excluding from his plan any restriction upon the liberty of Governments to organize territorial troops.

4. It is next to be noted that while Lord Esher excluded part-time soldiers, he included in the " effectives " to be limited all full-time soldiers of every kind. He expressly specifies not only "all military and air personnel of all ranks serving either voluntarily or compulsorily in the metropolitan areas," but also "the permanent staffs of reserve or territorial forces" (*i.e.*, the standing cadres upon which such forces are built up when mobilization takes place), and all classes of auxiliary full-time troops, such as "police forces permanently armed."

This, again, follows logically from his theory that any full-time troops in permanent service can be openly or secretly trained for active service during Period A, and that, therefore, they are an important element not only in the peace-strength of a country, but also in its war-strength in Period A—that is to say, of that strength which in a disarmament treaty he thought it essential to restrict.

5. It is also worthy of special notice that the only restriction which Lord Esher proposed for the air forces of the signatory states was the inclusion of all ranks of their personnel in the total number of effectives allowed to each. In other words, he lumped the effectives of the army and the air force together,

leaving to each state to decide for itself exactly as it liked
how great a part of its total man-power would be devoted to each
different arm.

6. In other ways Lord Esher likewise neglected altogether
the question of the tactical organization of the effectives he
allowed. He did not deny that one sort of tactical organization
might very well be superior to another, or that the careful peace-
time preparation of a highly trained cadre might enable one
power to achieve a somewhat greater expansion, and therefore
greater strength in Period A, than another power with equal
peace effectives could achieve. But he did not believe that the
various Governments would be willing to accept any control of
their tactical arrangements, still less that they would accept
a complete reorganization of their armies on a uniform and
standard model, and he held that to ask them to do so was
simply to interpose a dangerous and an unnecessary obstacle
to the realization of a disarmament plan. He proposed, therefore, to leave them full liberty to organize as they might each
desire, to let them do the very best they could with the
effectives they were respectively allowed, and to disregard
the inequalities that might follow from the superior results
which the wiser and more efficient general staffs might be able
to achieve.

These suggestions of Lord Esher's for freedom of tactical
organization and liberty to develop different arms with a fixed
total of effectives are not only novel, but also of great interest,
as will later on appear.

7. Lord Esher also proposed to neglect in his disarmament
plan other factors of military strength, in respect of which his
arguments are less easy to explain.

He proposed, for example, that his scheme should be " confined to metropolitan forces, leaving each country to fix the
forces required by it for colonial and overseas defence." He
held that the small number of countries with colonial responsibilities were in a quite special position; that they required a
certain number of troops to maintain order among the primitive
and sometimes savage peoples under their control; that since
such troops were expensive, and since their work was arduous
and distasteful, the Governments were certain voluntarily to

6

reduce them to the lowest point they safely could; that in any case such troops, often composed in great part of native levies, stood on a wholly different footing from those of the metro-politan armies; and that for these reasons they might be left altogether out of account.

The point will be discussed again, but it may be here observed that Lord Esher's argument, to be conclusive, ought to show that existing colonial forces are nowadays confined exclusively to their primary and legitimate purpose, that they do not exceed in strength what is required for this purpose, and that thus they do not add in any way to the military power of the mother country. It would be difficult to maintain any such contention.

8. Next, Lord Esher proposed to neglect altogether the factor of the armament with which his effectives were equipped. Again, he did not do anything so foolish as to deny that the efficiency of troops in modern war is largely dependent on the armament they use. But he defended his proposal by an argument very similar to his argument about reserves. He said first, what is obviously true, that it would be difficult to control the stocks of arms and ammunition which a disloyal Government might secretly maintain; that no Government would willingly accept a restriction of its liberty to develop or increase any weapon which its staff believed effective; that under his plan no doubt some countries by greater efficiency would so equip their standing forces as to give them greater proportionate military strength than others; but that during Period A this difference would be of small account, since the forces mobilized in Period A could not use more than a certain quantity of armament; that, therefore, to attempt to limit armament in his scheme would be simply to introduce a new and unnecessary obstacle to its success; and that, instead, the proper object to be striven for was the simple reduction to the lowest possible figure of the standing effectives to be maintained. The reduction of effectives would mean, according to this reasoning, an accompanying and automatic reduction of arma-ment and equipment, and thus a corresponding reduction of the total economic burden which the armed forces involved; though, no doubt, the relief thus afforded would be less than it

would be under a more rigid system which also directly limited armament as well.

9. So much for the factors of military strength which Lord Esher wanted to restrict. What does he suggest for the second of the technical problems which must be solved in a disarmament agreement—namely, the problem of the method of measuring and comparing the strength of different countries in these factors?

For him, of course, the answer is very simple. He only deals with peace effectives, neglecting all other factors; he can, therefore, measure and compare the strength of different countries by merely measuring and comparing the total man-power which they respectively maintain. He can write down in treaty form, and with what he regards as sufficient accuracy, the strength which he proposes to give to different countries by simply stating in the treaty schedules what total number of effectives they are each allowed. Once his ratio is settled, and the allotted man-power of any single state has been agreed, there is no further problem: all he has to do is a little multiplication or division of the simplest kind.

In fact, however, Lord Esher introduced another unnecessary and, as it proved, unfortunate complication. This was what he called the "unit." Instead of simply stating his proposal as follows:

Belgium	.. ..	60,000 men
Czechoslovakia	..	90,000 men
France	.. ..	180,000 men, etc.

he stated it thus:

" The fixed ratio of the standing military and air forces shall be as follows, taking 30,000 men of all ranks as the unit:

Belgium	..	..	..	2
Czechoslovakia	..	..		3
France	..	..	..	6," etc.

If his scheme had laid down a fixed tactical organization for the armies of the signatory powers, or if it had included a limitation of the amount of armament with which his fixed number of men, 30,000, might be equipped, then perhaps the conception of a "unit" of measurement might have been of value. As it was, it simply served to confuse the thought of those who had to consider and report upon his plans.

It should in justice be added that Lord Esher, in speaking of units, and in choosing a unit of 30,000 men, had no doubt in mind the army allowed to Austria under the Peace Treaty of St. Germain. It was perhaps reasonable to think that an easy method of comparison between the forces which he proposed to allot to every country, and the forces which had been granted to a disarmed ex-enemy republic, would be of value. Had he suggested the general application of the full Peace Treaty system, including limitation of reserves and armament, tactical reorganization, etc., no doubt then the adoption of the Austrian Army as the unit would have been of the greatest use. That, indeed, might be an excellent plan for solving the technical problem of disarmament;[1] but it was not the plan which Lord Esher put forward, and for that reason his "unit" was not of any value.

10. With regard to the third element of the technical problem of disarmament, that of the ratio, Lord Esher was no more fortunate.

Having settled his "unit," he proceeded to construct the table of coefficients which is reproduced above. In fact, the proportion between the different countries established by these coefficients corresponds to that between the peace-effectives which they respectively maintained before the war of 1914 began. It was therefore based on a principle, and was not wholly "arbitrary," as was alleged. And Lord Esher no doubt also thought that if the Governments were willing to accept so great a reduction of their forces as he proposed, they would not make difficulties about the minor inequalities or anomalies which his actual figures might involve. So far it may perhaps be held that his ideas were a contribution to the solution of the technical aspects of the ratio problem.

But the reception which his scheme received, and the universal and lively criticisms of his ratio that were made, clearly showed that it was an error at that stage to propose any figures at all. More will be said later about the ratio; it suffices for the moment

[1] Cf. p. 125, *infra*.

to say that to his so-called "artificial coefficients" was, above all other causes, chiefly due the non-success of Lord Esher's project.

11. Lastly, Lord Esher made provision, in the most elaborate of his clauses, for the mutual control by the signatory powers of the observance of their disarmament undertakings. The details of his proposals are no longer of any practical interest or importance; as for their principles, it is only necessary to note that Lord Esher considered some effective system of mutual control to be an essential part of a disarmament treaty.

THE REPORT OF THE TEMPORARY MIXED COMMISSION

Lord Esher's plan led to no practical results, but it served to provoke, both among military critics in general and in the Temporary Mixed Commission, to which it was submitted, discussions of some value. The Temporary Mixed Commission appointed a Special Sub-Committee of most distinguished men[1] to consider it, and this Sub-Committee drew up a Report, the main conclusions of which the full Commission subsequently decided to adopt. It is not possible here to give a full account of all the various points that were discussed, nor a description of the course of the debates. But an attempt may be made to summarize the more important views put forward, and the provisional conclusions that were reached.

It will be most convenient in this summary to follow the arrangement adopted in the above description of Lord Esher's plan.

1. The Temporary Mixed Commission, including, of course, its distinguished military advisers, agreed with Lord Esher's first principle that "the limitation of armaments must be imposed on the peace-time strength" of the contracting parties.

---

[1] Its members were Viscount Cecil (Great Britain), M. Janssen (now Minister of Finance in the Belgian Government), Lieut.-Col. Réquin (of the French General Staff), General Marietti (of the Italian General Staff), Col. Lohner (of the Swiss Army), General Inagaki (of the Japanese Army). Its Report is to be found in A. 31, 1922, C.T.A. 173, p. 73.

By this they meant that it would be absurd to attempt to limit " the effort made by a country should it carry out a national mobilization ";[1] and, indeed, no one has yet given a rational explanation of how a disarmament treaty could limit the forces or the armaments which a nation fighting for its life could use. But they did *not* mean that they accepted Lord Esher's view that in limiting peace-strength it was only necessary to limit factors which would affect war-strength during Period A; nor did they mean that it was necessary in making up the ratio to allow for such factors of war-strength as armament industries and so on. On neither point did the Temporary Mixed Commission express a view, while on both some of the military critics strongly differed from Lord Esher.

These military critics held that it was impossible to consider modern war at all except as the clash of nations in arms, of entire peoples making use of all the resources which the whole of their economic and industrial systems could bring into play. To confine attention, therefore, to factors which affect war-strength in Period A alone would be, they thought, to make of disarmament only a trap for nations of good faith. They held it essential to consider not only Period A, but the maximum *potentiel* of each signatory power—that is to say, the maximum military strength which each power could develop, measured by the maximum armed force and the maximum equipment of all kinds which, in the course of a prolonged war, and with every facility for thorough preparation, it would be able to throw into action; and they rightly observed that if this view is taken, if the purpose of a disarmament treaty is to secure equality of limitation upon the factors that constitute war-time strength in Period B, then it is not enough to deal with peace-effectives only; there must also be supplementary agreements about the peace-time organization of armament-producing industries, about peace-time stocks of arms and ammunition, about reserve and territorial forces. All these factors, these critics urged, can be dealt with by peace-time measures—*i.e.*, without an attempt to limit the effort made by a country should it carry out a national mobilization; and, if their premiss is accepted, if the object of disarmament is to affect the war-

[1] Sub-Committee's Report, Para. " (*a*)."

time *potentiel* after the end of Period A, the force of their contentions is quite plain.

Again, on the second point, whether in determining the ratio between different powers their respective maximum *potentiels* of war-strength should either be made the basis of the ratio or should at least be taken into account, some military critics repudiated altogether Lord Esher's principle of 1914 peace-effectives, and showed a disposition to substitute for it the principle of the *potentiel*. It was for this reason that the statistical enquiry of the Temporary Mixed Commission begun in 1921 was so largely devoted to the industry and to the maximum war capacity of the different countries.[1] The debates on the point, however, were distinctly vague, and its further discussion may be usefully postponed.

2. The Temporary Mixed Commission and the military critics all agreed with Lord Esher's next principle, that "the size of standing armies should be restricted on a numerical basis." But they did not agree that it was *enough* to limit the size of standing armies, neglecting all other factors of military strength.

On the contrary, there was general dissent from this proposition. On the question of reserves, no conclusion of any kind was reached. The Temporary Mixed Commission went no further than to say, as Lord Esher himself had done, that not only actual effectives, but also permanent cadres for reserve or territorial forces, must be included in the total troops allowed. The military critics likewise confined their attention to the standing cadres rather than to the reserves themselves. They suggested, somewhat vaguely, that the proportion of standing cadres to effectives proper might be established by a uniform agreement among the signatory powers—a suggestion not

[1] Cf. Para. 2 of the Report of the Third Committee of the Third Assembly: " What is required is an investigation (on statistics) carried out as a first step towards the preparation of a general plan for the reduction of armaments. This plan should be based upon Article 8 . . . which recognizes the primary importance of national security. . . . As may be clearly seen from the statements received from the different countries, the national security of each depends . . . on the *full* military strength of other countries," *i.e.*, . . . "the potential military strength, in which an important element is the industrial and economic power of each state."

without importance.[1]   But beyond this the question of reserves was not much explored, and the failure to produce counter-propositions might justify the claim that Lord Esher's neglect of the factor of reserves had not been seriously challenged.

3. The same might equally be said of his contentions about territorial forces of part-time soldiers. The military critics had urged in general principle that all factors which would affect the military potential in a lengthy war must be dealt with; and territorial forces are plainly such a factor. But they suggested no way in which a limitation could be made. Nor did the Temporary Mixed Commission deal with the question in its Report.

4. The same is not true of Lord Esher's proposals about colonial troops. No one agreed with his implied doctrine that existing colonial troops are in all cases confined to the task of maintaining order in overseas possessions, and protecting them against aggression, nor that they do not exceed in strength what is required for these purposes. On the contrary, everyone agreed that in some cases colonial troops are an important factor in the total military peace-strength of the mother country.

For these reasons the Temporary Mixed Commission decided that it was essential that colonial troops should be dealt with in a disarmament treaty. But they recognized that they stood on a different footing from metropolitan forces, that they had their own distinct and legitimate functions to perform, and they therefore proposed (i.) that "those acknowledged to be necessary for the occupation or defence of colonies," which would therefore "be unable to take part in the defence of the mother country," should (ii.) be "limited in a special agreement supplementary to the general reduction agreement."[2]   These principles may perhaps be a sound and sufficient guide to the solution of this matter. It is noteworthy that they were specifically agreed to by a French staff officer and by a Belgian minister of state.

5. Again Lord Esher's proposals about armament and equipment engendered lively opposition, and again counter-proposals of a kind were made. It was yet another point on which the

---

[1] Cf. pp. 137 *seqq.*, *infra.*
[2] T.M.C. Sub-Committee Report, Para. 3(c).   *Loc. cit.*

Temporary Mixed Commission and the military critics were all agreed. The former used emphatic language. "The Commission is of opinion that mere numerical strength *alone* does not express the military force of a state as, in modern warfare, in which man acts through war material, the combination constituting the armed unit is composed of certain proportions of men, of organizing staffs and of material." And one of the French military critics went so far as to assert that, in calculating the efficiency of a military force, French experts were accustomed to give only one point to their numerical strength, as against six points to the weapons and material with which they were equipped. Certain it is that in modern conditions, in which machine-guns, artillery, tanks, tractors, unlimited supplies of ammunition, aeroplanes, and gas, play now an ever-increasing part in warfare, a thousand well-armed men could probably defeat ten thousand armed only with the best equipment that was available, for example, in August, 1914. It is no less certain, as the Temporary Mixed Commission observed, that unless weapons and material are controlled by a disarmament treaty, these results will follow:

First, it will be much harder to secure agreement on the ratio on which the treaty must be built, for the poorer powers, and those especially without armament-producing industries, will suspect that any limitation of their effectives, in which they may be strong, will throw upon them an unjust and dangerous disadvantage. The seeming simplicity of Lord Esher's plan may thus only create another obstacle to be overcome before confidence can be engendered and a treaty made.

Second, it will allow, and indeed make almost certain, quite as intense a competition in rival development of weapons as there has been hitherto in the increase of total forces. The cost of armament per man is already growing fast; if total effectives were limited, every staff would concentrate its efforts on increasing to the utmost the mechanism of destruction which each man could use; the competition which would follow would create suspicion and fear, would inflate military budgets, and might thus defeat the main purposes of a disarmament treaty.

Third, if by any chance war were to happen after the disarmament agreement had been made, the unlimited quantities of armament that would be used would not only make warfare in Period A infinitely more terrible than it would be if the treaty had imposed a limit on all forms of preparation, but they might make the early operations of the war so destructive that it would not much matter what happened after Period A was over. Indeed, it is often said by experts that the next war will be very short; that there will be no Period B at all. If so, of course, the whole basis of Lord Esher's doctrine would be gone. And although it is true that Lord Esher proposes in his scheme very low numbers for the standing armies he allows, yet even these armies would be able to use a quantity of armament far greater than they could have used twenty or even ten years ago. The time is fast approaching, indeed, when effectives will no longer be in any sense the dominant factor in land warfare, and when material will have taken their place. This being so, it is plain that a disarmament treaty founded on the exclusive limitation of effectives might not only meet with opposition from non-industrial powers when it was first proposed, but that, if war occurred, it might also in actual practice involve, even in Period A, inequalities of military strength which it was intended to avoid.

For reasons such as this it was unanimously agreed that in this respect Lord Esher had gone seriously wrong; that no treaty would be worth the paper on which it was written unless it dealt with armament as well as men. Once more the military critics confined themselves to pointing out the difficulty; but the Temporary Mixed Commission with some hesitation put forward a tentative suggestion as to how the difficulty could be overcome. " The Commission recognizes," they said, " that if a limitation is to be effective, it is necessary that it should simultaneously affect the strength of the troops . . . and *material* either *directly or by an indirect method of financial limitation.*"

In making this suggestion the Temporary Mixed Commission were not unaware of the great difficulties of limiting armament either directly by writing down into the treaty the exact quantities of each weapon, etc., to be allowed to each signatory power, or indirectly by allowing to each signatory power a fixed sum of money per annum for the purchase and replacement of weapons. But although they knew the problem to be difficult, and although they had not worked out the details of their tentative proposal for its solution, they were convinced, and they had no hesitation in declaring, that it was essential to solve it by some means or other, if the disarmament treaty was to be of any use. The practical application of their suggestion for a financial limitation will be examined in Chapter IX. In the meantime, it may be taken as an accepted principle, established by all the discussions on Lord Esher's plan, that if a disarmament treaty is to achieve the purposes for which it will be made, it must limit not only effectives but the armament with which effectives are equipped as well.

6. Neither the Temporary Mixed Commission nor anyone else came to any firm conclusion concerning Lord Esher's proposals to include in his effectives permanently armed police forces and other auxiliaries, and to allow to his signatory powers full liberty of tactical organization.

On the former point there was hardly any discussion. The statistical enquiries of the League had indeed established the fact that the number of troops required by civilized powers for maintaining order within their frontiers was, according to the Governments' declarations, very small indeed;[1] auxiliary forces, therefore, were in all likelihood organized at least in part for defence against external attacks, and were almost certain to be available for that purpose.[2] It was therefore tacitly assumed that Lord Esher's proposal was right.

[1] In its statistical enquiry the T.M.C. had asked the Governments to establish " as far as possible a distinction between the forces intended for the maintenance of order and the forces whose purpose was to provide for defence against an attack from outside " (cf. A. 31, C. 631, C.T.A. 173, 1922, p. 8; vide *ibid.* for Government Replies). Commenting on the replies made by the Governments on this point, the Third Committee of the Third Assembly said in its Report: " The statements . . . show that the forces maintained by the various Governments for the purpose of the maintenance of internal order are relatively very small; that, in consequence, the military effort made by the various countries is almost exclusively intended as defence against aggression from without " (Para. 7, A. 124, 1922, iv., p. 8).

[2] This conclusion is certainly supported by the figures given in Para. 6, p. 8, of A. 31, C. 631, C.T.A. 173, 1922, and in the Government Replies. Cf. also pp. 132-3, *infra.*

7. On the point of tactical organization, the military critics made two observations: first, that divergence of tactical organization would make it almost impossible to measure or compare the strength of one army against that of another; second, that any suggestion of a uniform tactical unit or organization would be so much resented by the Governments that it would be a fatal obstacle to progress. But they only considered the point in connection with Lord Esher's unit, and they did not profess to have reached definite conclusions.

The Temporary Mixed Commission came no nearer to a verdict, though the language they used implies that they were disposed to take Lord Esher's view. In speaking of the method of calculating " the respective values of different armies " they expressly repudiate the intention of " imposing a standard unit on existing armies."

8. No part of Lord Esher's proposals was so vigorously discussed as the " unit " by which he proposed to measure and compare the forces allowed to different countries. It has already been said that, since he dealt only with effectives, his unit was for his purpose a useless complication; he could solve his technical problem by simply writing in his treaty the total man-power allotted to each state. But since his military and other critics had agreed that not only effectives, but also other factors, and in particular armament, must also be limited, it was for them necessary, or at the least it was desirable, to find some fixed unit by which the various factors of military strength taken in combination could be measured and written down.

Broadly speaking, the military critics held that it was impossible to find any such " common measure " of the military forces of different states in time of peace. They held, of course rightly, that when a measurement of comparison of strength was required for a disarmament treaty, it was the strength of troops *in use* that it was necessary to know. The question to be answered, therefore, was, Will two bodies of men, belonging to different states, each 30,000 strong in time of peace, be of equal or approximately equal strength after mobilization has occurred—*i.e.*, in Period A ? The answer would depend on very many factors: length of training of the men, tactical organization, dilution by reserves, armament, stocks of ammunition (a very important point), and so on.   In each of these factors very great variations of practice by different states must, they said, inevitably occur; these variations would necessarily affect the real strength of any unit of a *prima facie* standard size.   Since the variations could not be avoided or controlled (this without argument they assumed), no standard unit of measurement could be devised which would with any degree of accuracy serve as a basis for a comparison of different armies or which would provide a technical method of writing down in treaty form their allotted strength.

It was sometimes said that this contention, that no common unit of measurement could be devised, was equivalent to a denial that there was any technical form in which a disarmament treaty could be made.   But this, of course, is not so, as can easily be shown.   Assume, for example, that a disarmament conference decided now to limit all land armaments on the exact basis of the *status quo*.   It could be done by allotting to the various parties in the treaty schedules exactly that amount of every factor of military strength which they to-day maintain. No unit of measurement would be required.   The treaty would be difficult, but by no means impossible, to write down.

But suppose that, instead of limiting armaments on the basis of the *status quo*, the conference decided to make a 30 per cent cut in strength all round; suppose that it also decided to alter the ratio between certain powers from that which now exists; and suppose that it decided, as the military critics assumed that it must decide, that all factors could not be limited by treaty stipulation; how could the changes to be made then be represented in the schedules ?   Some way could probably be found to do it, though it might involve a negotiation only less complicated than that of the ratio itself.   Obviously it would be far easier if there were some comparatively small unit, arrived at by combining certain quantities of each of the factors to be limited and agreed as representing for each of the parties an approximately equal amount of military strength.

The Temporary Mixed Commission expressed a hope that such a unit might be found.   It did not arrive at any firm conclusion, but at least it did not endorse the wholly negative verdict of most military opinion. Its sub-commission, including of course, Colonel Réquin and his three soldier colleagues, suggested that " it might be possible to take as a unit of measure the combination of a certain strength (in effectives) and a certain fixed sum of money representing the remaining factor of armament." This reflected their other provisional decision that besides effectives, armament must also be dealt with by means of a financial limitation. They believed, in other words, that if a disarmament treaty could be made at all by limiting these two factors only, a fixed combination of these two factors would also serve as a sufficiently just unit of measurement for its negotiation.

At this point the problem of the unit may for the time be left.

9. It was said above that nothing did so much to spoil its chances of success as the proposals for the ratio which Lord Esher embodied in his plan. His principle of basing it upon the peace-effectives which the different states maintained in 1914 was wholly disregarded. The Temporary Mixed Commission denounced it as a system " based on co-efficients chosen in an arbitrary manner." Military writers equally objected to its crude assumption that, in their vital interests, Governments would accept a position of proportionate power so casually put forward. None of them, indeed, had any definite counter-proposals to put up. But they felt—it was a matter of feeling rather than of argument—that the matter should not be treated in that way; that it was one which would require long and arduous negotiations before it could be solved; and that such negotiations must lie in the hands of the Governments themselves.[1]

[1] This view was indicated in the T.M.C. Sub-Committee's report: " Under Article 8 . . . the calculation of the requirements of national safety constitutes one of the essential bases for the reduction of armaments. The first factor to be considered when drawing up such an estimate consists of the replies of the various Governments with regard to their requirements. . . . An estimate of the requirements of national safety of any country cannot be complete unless it is based on an appreciation of the dangers threatening that country—that is to say, unless it takes into account the forces of neighbouring states and their political tendencies, nor yet should such an estimate ignore the assistance that might be given by other states " (*loc. cit.*, Para. 1).

That their view, though unargued, was not unreasonable, will perhaps appear in Chapter XIII when the problem of ratio is discussed.

10. Lord Esher's proposals for a system of mutual control were another part of his plan that did not receive much attention. There was a strong tendency on the part of the military critics to repudiate any suggestion of mutual control as " inconsistent with the fundamental principle of national sovereignty." But neither the Temporary Mixed Commission nor the Governments of Members of the League took much notice of this objection, as is shown by the stringent provisions on the subject inserted both in the Draft Treaty of Mutual Assistance and in the Geneva Protocol.[1] It is worth noting that in both these documents the authors not only adopted Lord Esher's principle that mutual control is necessary, but also agreed with him that the machinery for exercising such mutual control must be established as an essential part of the treaty which brings disarmament into force.

Before the subject of Lord Esher's project is left, reference must be made to the reception given by the Third Assembly to the Report of the Sub-Committee of the Temporary Mixed Commission, from which numerous quotations have been made.

The Third Assembly discussed in general terms the principles provisionally enunciated by the Sub-Committee in that Report —the reduction of peace effectives on a numerical basis, the reduction of armament and material by means of a financial limitation, the making of a separate supplementary agreement for fixing the troops required for colonial defence, the adoption of a unit consisting of the combination of a given number of men and a given sum of money—and without entering into a detailed examination, it gave them " its general approval." It went on to say that it was " of opinion that these principles constitute a considerable beginning towards the task of preparing such a treaty [of general disarmament], and it considers that the Temporary Mixed Commission should be instructed to press forward without delay its investigations on this subject. It

[1] Treaty of Mutual Assistance, Art. 12 (vide A. 111, 1923, iv., p. 9. Geneva Protocol, Arts. 7 and 8).

believes that the Temporary Mixed Commission should work out its principles in more detail, should elaborate the method by which they can be applied in the framing of an agreement for reduction, and should then formulate as definitely as possible a scheme founded on these principles."[1]

THE MOSCOW CONFERENCE FOR DISARMAMENT, DECEMBER, 1922

The next unsuccessful proposals for disarmament which need discussion are those laid by the Russian Soviet Government before the Conference at Moscow in December, 1922, in which, besides Russia, there took part Poland (representing both herself and Roumania), Finland, Esthonia, Latvia and Lithuania.

It must be said at once that the whole atmosphere of this Conference was artificial. It was freely said afterwards by some of the delegates who were present that it had only been summoned for what they called " propaganda " purposes. From the first day of its meeting it was plain that its chances of success were slender. In fact, its rapid and ignominious failure was primarily a demonstration of the fundamental truth that disarmament cannot be achieved without the mutual confidence born of a sound and comprehensive scheme of security.[2] But apart from that political consideration, the whole Conference had been so ill-prepared that no one in reality expected any practical results.

But the proposals made by the Russian Government are not without technical interest, and will repay a brief examination. As will appear to the careful reader, some of them seem to show that the Soviet authorities had not failed to follow with attention the proceedings of the Temporary Mixed Commission. The scheme they put forward is as follows:

1. They proposed to deal only with the land forces of the various powers. Their objection to including naval armaments

[1] Report of the Third Committee to the Third Assembly, A. 124, 1922, iv., p. 10.

[2] It is true that the delegations all signed a somewhat anæmic Pact of Non-Aggression. But a close examination of the negotiations that took place shows, nevertheless, that the statement in the text is undoubtedly correct. For the text of the Pact of Non-Aggression, vide L.N. Document, C. 59, 1923, ix., C.T.A. 205.

was above referred to; it was a contributing cause to the failure of the Conference.

2. They confined their attention to the peace-time strength of the contracting parties.

3. They did not discuss in detail the factors to be limited, nor whether these factors should include those which affect war strength in Period B. They contented themselves with proposing a double limitation: first, upon the total effectives to be maintained in standing armies; second, upon the sum of money to be expended by each power for the equipment and maintenance of these effectives.

4. So far as effectives were concerned, they proposed the sweeping reduction shown by the following figures:

		Standing Armies, 1922.	*New Limits Proposed.*
Russia	..	800,000	200,000
Poland	..	280,000	70,000
Finland	..	28,000	7,000
Esthonia	..	16,000	4,000
Latvia	..	19,000	5,000
Lithuania	..	35,000	8,000

They proposed that this reduction, to a quarter of their existing strength, should be carried through in the course of the succeeding two years. It was to be done in four successive stages, a reduction of one-quarter being made every six months.

This suggestion is of interest, as it coincides with calculations made by Western military experts as to the rapidity with which disarmament measures could be carried through.

5. The Soviet authorities also proposed the mutual abolition of irregular forces. Apart from that, and apart from the financial limitation to be discussed in a moment, they made no proposals for dealing with reserves, or with auxiliary or territorial forces.

6. As for their proposed financial limitation, they suggested that the signatory powers should all agree upon a fixed " rate of expenditure for each man under arms." This rate was to be a maximum, which the Governments were to undertake not to exceed, and it was to be equal for all the signatory powers, no allowances being made for the special position or circumstances of any of them.

7

When the rate per man had been fixed, it was to be multiplied by the totals of the effectives allotted to the various Governments, and the results were to be the maximum military budgets which they would respectively expend. No extra additions to these budgets were to be allowed for any purpose; on the other hand, the sums allotted could be used by the Governments in their full discretion in any way they wished.

It was intended, of course, that this financial limitation should serve as a restriction upon the cadres and the reserves maintained, and the armament and equipment built up by the various powers. It was, in fact, a generalized application of the Temporary Mixed Commission's proposal for limiting *armament* by a fixed budgetary appropriation proportionate in amount to the number of the effectives allowed. So far it was certainly superior to Lord Esher's project. But its generalization laid it open to many of the objections which are inherent in the " budget " method of reduction, and which were discussed in Chapter VI. Nor did the Soviet authorities propose any reorganization of budget procedure or standardization of budget schedules and legislation—changes which would have done something at least to meet the more obvious of the objections. In consequence, this promising principle met with a disappointing reception from the other delegations. They were not slow to point out that although the figure per soldier allowed to each Government was nominally to be equal, in fact this nominal equality would involve the gravest injustice. For, in practice, although all the Governments represented had conscription systems, yet the cost of maintenance per soldier, nevertheless, differed widely in their respective countries. Moreover, as was pointed out above, a great part of the cost of maintaining Russian soldiers was met by taxation in kind which never appeared in the budget, and part of their supply of arms and ammunition was provided by a similar system; thus under the plan proposed Russia would have had a large surplus to expend on extra armament which the other countries would not have had.

Unfortunately, the negotiations did not last long enough to show whether or not the Conference could have cleared up these difficulties, nor long enough even to throw further light on the technical application of the interesting principle which the Russian Government proposed. On the contrary, its proposal merely served to increase the suspicion of the other weaker powers, and to hasten the untimely end of the proceedings.

7. The Russian Government made no further proposals for restricting weapons or equipment, but they did propose to supplement their disarmament treaty by the establishment of neutral zones along the frontiers between the parties. Again, unfortunately, this interesting suggestion met with so cold a reception that its technical application was not discussed.

8. On their side, however, the Russian Government also strengthened the suspicions of the other powers by refusing to listen to suggestions for the limitation and control of the manufacture of, and traffic in, arms and ammunition. As the Russian armament industries are strong, this was naturally resented, and no doubt it helped to cause the rupture of negotiations. The incident is noteworthy because for the first time in practical negotiations it demonstrated the essential and vitally important connection between voluntary disarmament and the restriction of production of, and traffic in, arms and ammunition.

9. The other technical aspects of the Russian proposal are also of interest.

They solved the problem of the " unit " by adopting virtually as it stood the suggestion made by the Temporary Mixed Commission. Their unit was to be the *man-under-arms plus a fixed annual sum for his maintenance ;* and in terms of these combined factors their respective forces were to be compared and measured, and their treaty obligations written down. The fact that the Temporary Mixed Commission proposed that the annual sum of money should cover only armament, in the strict sense of the word, and not all the rest of the military budget, was for this purpose an irrelevant detail.

10. For the ratio, their solution was still simpler. They proposed to adhere to the exact ratio of the *status quo*, and to carry out the reduction of armaments by abolishing an exact three-quarters of the existing forces of the different powers.

The other parties objected strongly to this suggestion, holding that it took no account of the specially favourable position of Russia and of her armament industries, etc., by reason of which, they held, they should have been allowed substantially greater strength in peace-effectives. Without analysing these contentions in the light of the general doctrine of the ratio, it may be observed that their justice is not universally accepted, and that they merely serve to illustrate the inherent difficulty of any disarmament negotiations which are confined to a single geographical region, particularly when the powers in that region are of most unequal strength.

11. Lastly, it may be noted that the Russian Government proposed an international machinery of mutual control for supervising the actual execution of the reduction agreement, but did not supplement this by suggesting any kind of permanent control or supervision after the first reductions had been made.

The Moscow Conference formally broke down on the differences that arose concerning the exclusion of naval armaments, the exclusion of armament production, and the arbitrary character of the suggested budget limitation. As the two latter questions were largely technical in character, Poland, Finland, Esthonia and Latvia jointly proposed, before the Conference ended, " to form a Committee of military experts to enquire into the establishment of a basis for the solution of the technical disarmament question."[1] The whole of the proceedings had shown that this was exactly what was needed, and, with the minutes of the Conference to work on, the Committee, if it had been formed, would have had some solid ground from which to start. Unhappily the Russian Government did not agree to the proposal, and what might have been a valuable investigation did not take place.[2]

THE FIFTH PAN-AMERICAN CONFERENCE, 1923: THE LEAGUE OF NATIONS NAVAL CONFERENCE AT ROME, 1924

This is the logical place in which to discuss the other unsuccessful attempts to prepare disarmament treaties made at

[1] Vide L.N. Document, C. 59, 1923, ix., C.T.A. 205, p. 6.
[2] For further information concerning the Moscow Conference vide *ibid.;* also C.T.A. 227; C.T.A. Minutes of Fourth Session; " La Conférence de Moscou pour la limitation des armaments." Commissariat du Peuple pour les Affaires Étrangères, Moscou.

Santiago and Rome in 1923 and 1924. They can be quickly disposed of.

The Fifth Pan-American Conference at Santiago had as Item XII on its agenda:

> " Consideration of the reduction and limitation of military and naval expenditure on some just and practicable basis."

Little or no preparatory work was done, however, before the Conference met. Some sporadic proposals for extending the Washington Naval Treaty to Central and South America were put forward by Argentine, Honduras, Chile and Brazil, but none of them was accepted, nor did they even serve to provoke really serious debates. For the rest the Conference discussed security, arbitration and other political aspects of disarmament, and never got near enough to the real substance of Item XII— which was, after all, the reduction of military and naval expenditure—to throw any light on the technical problems under consideration in this book.

The debates at Santiago, indeed, served principally to show that no practical results on disarmament can be hoped for from an ordinary diplomatic conference, nor even from such cumbrous quasi-permanent machinery as that of the Pan-American Union.[1]

The so-called " Conference " summoned to Rome in February, 1924, by the Council of the League, was not really a conference at all. It was a meeting of experts for the preparation of a programme for a conference to be subsequently held. It was exclusively concerned with proposals made by the Temporary Mixed Commission for the extension to the rest of the world of the principles of the Washington Naval Convention. Its discussion was based on a draft treaty prepared jointly by the Temporary Mixed Commission and the Permanent Advisory Commission. This draft treaty did little more than reproduce in a generalized form the provisions of the Washington Naval Convention, with such changes of form and substance as were made necessary by the fact that the intending signatories were

[1] Cf. Report of Secretary Hughes to the U.S. Senate on the Fifth Pan-American Conference, Washington, 1924.

all (or nearly all) of them members of the League. Some of these changes were of considerable technical and political interest, but they will be more conveniently discussed after the Washington Naval Treaty has itself been dealt with.

The Rome meeting was remarkable because it was attended not only by the expert naval representatives of the principal Members of the League concerned in the new treaty which had been proposed, but also by a Russian admiral representing the Soviet Government of Moscow.[1]   It did not lead to any definite agreement even on the limited subject-matter with which it dealt, because it became plain during the course of the proceedings that nothing could be done without decisions on matters of major political importance, which the naval experts were neither qualified nor authorized to take.   The main lesson of the meeting was, indeed, that it is useless to ask staff and government experts to carry on preparations for disarmament until their political objective has been categorically established for them by their Cabinets or by the responsible heads of departments whom they serve.[2]

[1] Admiral Behrens.   The other representatives present were the Naval Sub-Committee of the P.A.C. (*i.e.*, naval representatives of the ten states Members of the Council), together with naval experts from Argentine, Chile, Denmark, Greece, the Netherlands, and Norway.

[2] Cf. Report of the P.A.C. on The Rome Conference, C. 76, 1924, ix.

CHAPTER VIII

SUCCESSFUL DISARMAMENT TREATIES (LAND AND AIR FORCES)

Various unsuccessful attempts to make disarmament treaties having been considered, attention may now be turned to successful attempts. They are of two kinds: treaties of reciprocal disarmament, voluntarily accepted by a number of different powers, and treaties of unilateral disarmament, imposed on defeated states by their conquerors. There are some examples of both kinds of comparatively ancient date, but conditions have so changed that it is better to confine attention to those that have been made since the end of the war in 1918. As there are great differences in the problems presented by land and naval disarmament, it is more convenient to deal with them in separate chapters.

The Central American Disarmament Convention of 1923

In 1923 the five republics of Central America, Guatemala, Honduras, Salvador, Nicaragua, and Costa Rica agreed upon a treaty for mutual and reciprocal reduction and limitation of their armed forces.

The clauses of this treaty do not require any elaborate examination. They are of a simplicity that corresponds to the simplicity of organization of that section of international society with which they had to deal. It is a section of international society which occupies, as nearly perhaps as any small group of nations can be said to do, a distinct geographical region of its own. It consists of states too small and too poor to afford the great armaments which European nations have built up, even if their peoples desired to have them. They are states without commercial aircraft, without the industries that produce armaments and the machinery of war, and without chemical industries or plant of any kind. Although they have the system of obligatory service, they have never built up large conscript armies with unlimited numbers of reserves by training for long periods all the recruits of every annual class. They are virtually, therefore, in the condition of those eighteenth-century states among whom, according to the military critic referred to in Chapter V above, disarmament would have been a relatively simple thing.

For these reasons there is little in the Central American treaty that has any bearing upon the complicated problem of European armaments to-day. But nevertheless it is worth while to glance briefly at some of the technical features which it presents.

1. It is a " general " treaty in both senses of the word.

First, it includes all the powers of Central America among its signatories: it only comes into force when ratified by four out of five of them; it would lapse if more than one of them denounced it.

Second, it covers in a single instrument all their armaments of every kind, land, sea, and air forces alike.

2. Its purpose is restricted to limiting peace-time strength, and its provisions lapse if peace is broken. Indeed, on this point it has a definition far looser than would be accepted by other countries. The signatory powers undertake to observe its terms " except in the event of civil war or threat of war from another state." In such cases " the right of defence shall not be limited except in so far as is laid down in existing treaties."[1] Presumably—though the treaty is not explicit on the point—after the danger is past the parties are obliged to return to the treaty scale of armament; but even so this is too great a degree of liberty to receive acceptance in parts of the world where mutual confidence is less and where armaments are greater and more dangerous than they are in the Central American republics.

---

[1] Art. 4. Vide A. 35 (Part II), 1923, ix, p. 12.

3. The main basis of the limitations imposed consists in the restriction of peace-effectives to the following totals:

Guatemala	..	..	..	5,200 men.
Honduras	..	..	..	2,500 ,,
Salvador	..	..	..	4,300 ,,
Nicaragua	..	..	..	2,500 ,,
Costa Rica	..	..	..	2,000 ,,

4. These totals are to include the " permanent army and the national guard," *i.e.*, the auxiliary forces used for maintaining order internally and on the frontier. They also include, presumably, officers, staffs, and cadres (if any). No mention is made of reserves.

5. No provision is made for the limitation in any way of the ordinary armament and other material with which the effectives are to be equipped. Presumably the contracting parties have no fear of the amount of material which could be used by such very small forces as are allowed, or else they rely on the poverty of their respective exchequers to prevent any great expansion of the armaments that actually exist.

6. But there are various and severe restrictions placed upon the class of weapons that may be used. The Central American republics have no affection for the new means of destruction which have changed the character of war, and which perhaps if suddenly developed by one among their number might mean a military hegemony dangerous to the rest. Thus the treaty provides that no signatory power may possess more than ten military aircraft;[1] that none of them shall ever make use in any way of poison-gas or other asphyxiating substances;[2] and that none of them shall acquire any vessels of war except the armed coast-guard vessels necessary to the maintenance of order on their coasts.[3]

These restrictions no doubt will serve to prevent new forms of dangerous and costly rivalry, and it may be that in them will lie the chief value of the treaty to the states that made it.

---

[1] Art. 4.   [2] Art. 5.   [3] Art. 4.

7. Article 3 of the treaty imposes an absolute prohibition of the traffic in " arms, munitions, or other military stores" as between the different Central American republics. It makes no mention of the traffic with the outside world, and it is difficult to see what value the mutual prohibition of export among these republics can have, if each of them is free to import as many arms as it desires from the outside world.   But the clause is of interest as a recognition, though a curious one, of the fact that the arms traffic is intimately related to the execution of a disarmament agreement.

8. Lastly, the treaty institutes a rudimentary form of mutual control over the observance of its clauses.   It consists in the exchange, at six-monthly intervals, of reports drawn up by each Government " on the measures adopted in execution of the present Convention."   Again, it is a system that demands a mutual confidence among the parties which in other parts of the world does not exist.

The treaty thus described is an almost exact application, with some additional restrictions of weapons and some extra compensating elasticity, of the principles which Lord Esher proposed.   Those principles were adequate for Central American society; it does not follow that they are adequate for the world at large.   But the fact that the treaty was made at all is a valuable proof that even in the less highly developed portions of the world, where international relationships are less embittered than in Europe and the militarization of society is less extreme, a policy of reciprocal reduction and limitation of national armaments is recognized to be a necessary condition of peace and social progress.

The Disarmament of Germany: Treaty of Versailles, Part V (Land and Air)

Part V of the Treaty of Versailles constitutes the principal modern example of the second class of disarmament treaty— *i.e.*, treaties of unilateral disarmament imposed on defeated states by their victorious neighbours.   Its clauses are of particular interest and importance, because they were designed to deal with the greatest national army and the most perfect military machine which history has seen, and because, if they are successful, they will achieve for the most militarized of modern nations precisely that demilitarization which every civilized people now desires.

Moreover, as their analysis will show, these clauses give guidance of great value concerning some of the technical problems to be faced in the making of a general treaty of disarmament. They do not cover the whole ground, for the simple reason that by the Treaty of Versailles only *one* power was affected; the unilateral disarmament of one single state only was carried out. Thus no attempt was made to establish a given relation between the armaments of Germany and those of the rest of the world, nor even, as it happened, between the armaments of Germany and those of the other three ex-enemy states disarmed by the treaties of St. Germain, Trianon, and Neuilly. Part V of the Treaty of Versailles, therefore, has no light to shed on the problem of the ratio and how it can be established among a large number of powers of widely different strength and size. But, on other problems, on the factors of military strength which it is desirable to limit, on the detailed ways in which their limitation can be effected, even on the methods by which a unit of measurement could be established, Part V and the corresponding parts of the other Treaties of Peace have much to teach.

They furnish, indeed, a model which, if it were followed, would render comparatively simple the task of a disarmament conference. Once the conference had agreed by negotiation on the ratio to be established between the different states, it could proceed to make its treaty by the general application of the method of Versailles, with the certainty that, so far as it is humanly possible by a disarmament treaty to do so, the scales of armament allotted in its schedules would *faithfully reproduce the adopted ratio*.

It is true that Part V does not deal, as probably no treaty of disarmament can directly deal, with some modern factors of military strength. But, apart from this consideration, it is as nearly perfect an attempt to limit by treaty the strength

of a given country as any that could be made. It was indeed
carried out in the most favourable possible conditions. The
supreme difficulty in disarmament negotiations is bound to be
the reluctance of the Governments to accept reductions, or to
give up their liberty of action in various ways. But at Versailles this difficulty did not exist. The Allies supplied for
Germany all the goodwill she may have lacked. The method
has its drawbacks when it comes to execution, but for the writing
of treaty clauses it is pure gain. The military experts of the
Allies thus had full liberty to make the perfect model treaty,
and it must be remembered that for months a great gathering
of distinguished soldiers devoted their full attention to the
task.[1] We may be sure, therefore, that nothing of importance
was forgotten or passed over that could be of use in restricting German strength to the nominal level which the Allies
fixed.

If the Governments were altogether whole-hearted about
disarmament, if they had no *arrière-pensée* of any kind, they
would, no doubt, accept for themselves at least the system
which they imposed on Germany, if not proportionately equal
scales of strength. In practice, however, though we may desire
it, we can hardly venture to expect, as has been said above,
that other Governments will voluntarily accept the rigid system
of Versailles. But even if they will not accept it all, parts of
that system, and the principles on which it was founded, may
be capable of adaptation to a general treaty. It is with this
conception of it, therefore, with the idea in mind that its provisions may be taken as a model, that the Treaty of Versailles
must be discussed.

It will be convenient once more to follow the general arrangement of the subject adopted for the discussion of Lord Esher's
plan.

1. *Object of the Disarmament effected.*—Part V of the Treaty
of Versailles differs from Lord Esher's project in that its purpose
is not merely to limit peace-time strength, allowing suspension
of its provisions if war should happen to break out. On the
contrary, it assumes that Germany will never be allowed to go

[1] The work was done under the personal supervision of Marshal Foch
and Sir Henry Wilson.

to war again. It even goes so far as to define the purpose for which the German army shall exist: it " shall be devoted exclusively to the maintenance of order within the territory and to the control of the frontiers."[1] The limits laid down in the treaty can never be exceeded, even after Germany has become a Member of the League, unless and " until they are modified by the Council of the League," acting—since there is no stipulation to the contrary—by unanimous vote.[2] Even this power of the Council to modify the limits laid down applies only to the arms and ammunition with which the German army is equipped, *not* to the numbers of the German army itself.

This being so, there is no attempt to limit merely those factors of military preparation which are of importance during Period A. Every factor which can be limited, whether it affects Period A or Period B, is brought into the system. The whole is designed to ensure that the military strength of Germany shall *never* be greater than that which the treaty allows.

2. *Effectives*.—Germany is permitted to maintain a maximum army of 100,000 strong. This figure includes the staffs, officers and men of all ranks, the staffs and instructors of the few military schools that are allowed, and even the officers serving in the Ministries of War in the different German states. This is a rigid and all-embracing limitation of effectives " on a numerical basis "—*i.e.*, by the establishment of a total maximum number of men that may not be exceeded.

3. *Tactical Organization*.—The organization of the army is laid down in detail. It must consist of not more than seven divisions of infantry and three of cavalry,[3] grouped under not more than two army corps headquarters staffs.[4] It is precisely stipulated in elaborate tables exactly how the headquarters staffs of divisions and army corps shall be composed.[5] The strength of every unit of every kind—regiment of infantry, trench-mortar company, divisional squadron, field artillery regiment, signal detachment, divisional medical service, parks and convoys, etc.—in both officers and men, is laid down in

---

[1] Art. 160, § 1.   [2] Art. 164, § 2.   [3] Art. 160, § 1.
[4] Art. 160, § 3.   [5] Art. 160, § 2, and Table I.

exact numbers, which are maxima that must not be exceeded.¹
It is provided that only certain units—an infantry regiment,
a cavalry regiment, a regiment of field artillery, a battalion of
pioneers—may have a depot of their own. The Great German
General Staff is to be dissolved, and must not be reconstituted
in any form.² The "maintenance or formation of troops
differently grouped or of other organizations for the command
of troops . . . is forbidden."³

In other words, the whole German army is to be reorganized
from top to bottom on a new plan laid down in an international
treaty to which Germany, under compulsion, has agreed. This
is to be done in order to enable the Allied Governments to
estimate more exactly the military strength which Germany
maintains; to enable the control of her army arrangements
and of her total effectives to be more easily carried out; and to
prevent her army from being so organized that it could be
easily and rapidly expanded to a much greater size. Among
other things, it has, of course, the effect of depriving Germany
of all liberty as to the use of her permitted man-power, as to
the arms she will develop, or the proportionate effort of different
kinds which she will make. It imposes on her a stereotyped
and unalterable system, which does not allow for changes in
the nature and conduct of modern war.

We are entitled to assume that these provisions have a
genuine military value; that they do really help to limit the
strength of the German army, to render control over that
strength simpler and more effective, to prevent its diversion
to new and more dangerous methods of war, and to make its
rapid increase harder for the Germans to carry out. If this
were not so, the Allied military experts would not have given so
much thought to the preparation of these clauses, and so much
thankless labour to securing their observance in the past six
years.

4. *Reserves.*—Besides the provisions for a uniform and
stereotyped tactical organization, there is much more in the
treaty which is designed to prevent the expansion of the German
army beyond its permitted strength. Its clauses deal in detail
with the formation of cadres, the maintenance of reserves,

¹ Art. 160, § 2, and Table I.   ² Art. 160, p. 2.   ³ Art. 160, p. 3.

and the training and practice which the army is allowed to have.

(*a*) It is provided, in the first place, that the officers of all grades, including all the staffs of every kind, and the instructors at military schools, may not exceed in number 4,000—one-twenty-fifth of the whole permitted strength.[1]

The purpose of this restriction is, of course, to prevent the permitted force from being organized as the cadre for a much larger army. If there were a very high proportion of officers the staff would obviously be able to mobilize a greater force on the basis of the prescribed effectives than they will with this rigid limitation on the number of their skilled persons capable of organizing work.

(*b*) With the same purpose it is provided that even the army administrative services consisting of civilian personnel, and therefore not included in the number of precribed effectives, " will have such personnel reduced in each class to one-tenth of that laid down in the budget of 1913."[2] But for this provision much of the organizing work of the army might have been done, and a great skeleton administration might have been built up, by unenlisted but highly trained civilian personnel.

(*c*) Another supplementary clause, inserted with the same intention of limiting the skilled organization of the German army, appears a little later in the treaty: " In no case must formations, administrative services, or general staffs include supplementary cadres."[3]

(*d*) Next, and most important of all, the conscription system is abolished in Germany, both for officers and men. None but volunteers must be enlisted. All officers must be professionals, and must undertake to serve on the active list for twenty-five years at least, or until the age of forty-five.[4] Other ranks must be recruited for a period of service of not less than twelve consecutive years.[5]

Further, the number of either officers or men discharged in any year before the expiration of their term of service,

[1] Art. 160, § 1.   [2] Art. 161.   [3] Art. 178, § 2.
[4] Art. 175.   [5] Art. 174.

for any reason whatever, must not exceed more than
5 per cent of the total strengths fixed respectively for
officers and men—4,000 and 96,000.[1]

Conscription was abolished in Germany largely because
the British Government of the day believed it to be a
dangerous cause of militarism and of inflated armaments.
Most of the continental allies, afraid of its abolition as a
possible precedent for themselves, would have allowed
Germany to keep it. But the British Government prevailed;
and the effect of its success is to prevent the German staff
from building up the big reserves which conscript armies
always have. Indeed, so stringent are the provisions
about replacement and discharge, that the German staff
will not be able to form even such reserves as are possessed
under the voluntary system by the British army. The
clear intention of these provisions is to prevent any reserves
of any kind from being formed by the organized passing of
well-trained men out of the service into civil life.

(e) Further, it is laid down that ex-officers who previously
belonged to any formation whatever in the army, and who
have now gone into civilian life, must not take part in any
military exercise of any kind, whether theoretical or
practical, and must not be under military obligations of
any kind.[2]

This, of course, is again a provision designed to prevent
the formation of reserves—its importance lies in the existence of great numbers of veterans of the world war, and
is therefore temporary.

(f) With the same purpose of preventing the training of
any men beyond the 100,000 prescribed effectives, and particularly of preventing the training of officers or organizers,
the number of military academies and similar institutions
is cut down to the absolute minimum essential to an army of
100,000 men, and the number of students admitted to them
is so limited as to correspond exactly to the number of

[1] Arts. 174, § 2, 175, § 4. In the Treaties of Trianon, etc., an additional clause appears under which it is provided that if, in any year, a
greater number than 5 per cent leave the service, their places may not be
filled by new enlistments.

[2] Art. 175, § 3.

commissions vacant in the service.[1]   The previously existing schools for non-commissioned officers are abolished altogether.

Here again the supply of possible reserves or of supplementary cadres is cut off at source.

(g) In the same order of ideas it is provided that no German military missions may be sent abroad, and that German nationals shall not be allowed to take service in foreign armies.[2]   Yet another way in which trained reserves might be made available is thus closed.

(h) Lastly, it is laid down, in rigid terms, that " all measures of mobilization or appertaining to mobilization are forbidden."[3]

The German staff are to have no opportunity of any kind for practising the expansion of their standing forces, nor even, indeed, for putting those forces themselves on to a war footing.   There can be no doubt that this must make far more difficult any attempt to prepare effectively for the use of large numbers of reserves in time of war.[4]

It is fair to conclude from the above provisions, when they are thus taken all together, that the Allied military experts attached a great importance to the question of reserves; that they determined to prevent the German staff from maintaining or organizing any reserves whatever with which to augment their prescribed effectives; that to this end they put in every clause they could devise for prohibiting the open or secret training of supplementary civilian organizers, officers, or men;

---

[1] Art. 176.   [2] Art. 179.   [3] Art. 178, p. 1.

[4] The importance of actual manœuvre practice, particularly on a large scale, as an essential part of the preparation for the operations of war, is perhaps well illustrated to the civilian by the following remarks of *The Times'* " Military Correspondent," who has already been quoted above.   Speaking of experiments in the lorry transport of infantry in the British Army manœuvres of 1925, he writes: " The Third Division has now specialized for two years in practising these ' bus-column ' movements—last year by battalions, this year by whole brigades. The Eighteenth Brigade carried out some very good night work of this nature. . . .   New lessons are learned every time such movements are attempted, the chief one being the need for forethought, mastery of detail, and *practice*."—*The Times*, October 20, 1925.

and that, as a result, if the Treaty of Versailles is observed, Germany, if she were involved in war, would only be able to mobilize on its outbreak the standing forces which she is allowed in time of peace.

5. *Auxiliary Forces.*—The Treaty of Versailles does not follow the simple plan adopted by Lord Esher of including in the prescribed effectives which are allowed all such auxiliary forces as armed police, and so on. But it does limit those auxiliary forces strictly by other supplementary clauses, and it includes among them not only police but all permanently employed state officials who might, owing to the nature of their work, by any possibility be trained as soldiers.

Thus it provides that all such officials as customs officers, forest guards, and coastguards—*i.e.*, services whose members are in many countries armed—must not exceed in number the officials functioning in the same capacities in 1913—an absolute restriction to a maximum figure that must never be exceeded.

For the gendarmerie and police—services whose duties do not depend, like those of forest guards, etc., on an invariable factor, that is, on the extent of territory to be looked after, but on a variable factor, the numbers of the population—it is laid down that they may only be increased to an extent corresponding to the increase of population since 1913 in the various districts in which they are employed.

Lastly, it is stipulated that none of these officials may ever be assembled for military training.[1]

There can be no doubt that the authors of the treaty were right in imposing these restrictions on all the Government services whose whole-time employees may in the pursuance of their ordinary duties require to be armed, who can be secretly organized under the direct control of Government departments, and who might therefore be converted without difficulty into auxiliary troops of great military value. It is said by experts that, in spite of these restrictions, the German armed police are, in fact, an effective military force. It must be remembered, however, that they are at present composed almost exclusively of war-trained veterans, which cannot continue indefinitely to be true; while the prevention of mass-training must, in the

[1] Art. 162.

nature of things, make it every year more difficult for the German staff to handle them efficiently enough to make them of value in an actual war.

6. *Militia and Territorial Forces.* — Again the Treaty of Versailles is more rigid than Lord Esher's plan, in that it absolutely forbids the organization or training of any sort of militia or territorial force—that is to say, of any " part-time soldiers " —whether voluntary or conscripted.

This prohibition is, of course, included in the wider prohibitions above referred to, by which any training of any persons beyond the prescribed effectives is forbidden. But these wider prohibitions are also supplemented by special clauses under which absolutely every form of voluntary association— universities, schools, societies of ex-service men, shooting or touring clubs, and so on—are prevented from occupying themselves with military matters in any way, from giving any instruction or exercise to their members in " the use and profession of arms," and from maintaining connection with the Ministry of War or other military authority.[1]

Again, therefore, it may fairly be said that the Allied experts thought it worth their while to exhaust their ingenuity in devising provisions of every kind to prevent Germany from building up anything in the nature of territorial forces.

7. *Colonial and Air Forces.*—The question of colonial forces does not arise in the Treaty of Versailles, as all Germany's colonies were taken from her and given to other countries to administer under mandate.

There is equally little to be said about air forces. The only provision of more than temporary effect on this subject is that the " armed forces of Germany must not include any military or naval air forces."[2] As this provision raises the whole problem of the value of restricting warlike preparation in the air, comment may be deferred to the chapter where that subject is discussed.[3]

8. *Armament, Munitions, and Material.*—With this matter the Treaty of Versailles deals as exhaustively and thoroughly as it does with the formation of reserves. Its authors had no idea that, if the effectives of Germany were reduced to a very

[1] Art. 177.   [2] Art. 198.   [3] Cf. chap. xii.

modest figure, it would not matter with what armament and material they were equipped. On the contrary, with their minds full of the conception of the " war of guns " and of the decisive value of an " overwhelming weight of metal," they once more inserted in their treaty all the restrictions which they could devise.

(*a*) To begin with they started by prohibiting Germany altogether from using or possessing certain of the more dangerous modern means of war. The prohibition of military and naval aircraft has been already mentioned; to them were added " poisonous or other gases and all analogous liquids, materials, or devices," armoured cars, tanks, and all similar constructions suitable for use in war.[1] No guns of any kind of a calibre greater than 105 mm. (4 inches) are allowed at all, except for the defence of the fortified works and fortresses which Germany is permitted to retain.[2]

Thus the German army is entirely deprived of all the most effective modern weapons, and is restricted to the relatively simple armament of the later nineteenth century.

(*b*) Of those weapons which she is allowed to use, Germany is only granted a comparatively small number. Each weapon is dealt with in detail in the schedules attached to Part V; the numbers allowed per unit, and the totals for the whole army, are both laid down. Thus, in this list of prescribed weapons it is provided that she may have per infantry division (of a maximum strength of 10,830 men) 12,000 rifles, and for the whole army 84,000; for the infantry division she may also have 108 heavy machine-guns, 162 light machine-guns, 24 3-inch field guns, 12 4-inch howitzers, and so on.[3]

The whole of her armament is thus prescribed, even to the last rifle, in an elaborate treaty list, and on a scale much lower than that which every other modern army now possesses.

(*c*) To the totals just mentioned, which are given in the schedules to Part V, the German Government is, however, free to add an optional increase for replacement purposes, up to one-twenty-fifth part for small arms and one-fiftieth for guns. The figure is modest enough to be of small account.[4]

[1] Art. 171.　　　　　　　　　[2] Art. 164, and Table II.
[3] Art. 164, and Table II.　　　[4] Art. 164.

(*d*) In addition to the limitations of weapons, the amounts of ammunition which Germany may keep are also rigidly restricted. Again, there is a schedule laying down the stocks that may be retained for each permitted weapon. For each rifle there may be 400 rounds, for each machine-gun 8,000, for each field gun 1,000, for each howitzer 800.[1] That these totals are not excessive is shown by the fact that the annual peace expenditure of ammunition for a field gun is, at a high average, about 400 to 500 rounds, in an army whose practice-ammunition is not restricted by treaty.

Moreover, these stocks of ammunition, which are maxima in no case to be exceeded, must be stored at points to be notified to the Allied powers, and no other stocks or depôts of any kind may be created.[2]

The Allies cannot have been unaware how difficult this part of their system would be to supervise, and, in fact, there can be little doubt that so far it has not been well observed. But there can be equally little doubt that it has enormously reduced the quantities of ammunition which Germany possesses, and the amount which, if she were involved in war, she would be able to use during Period A. This fact is of general importance.

(*e*) It should be added that for the fortified works and fortresses which she was allowed to maintain—*i.e.*, those on her coasts and on her southern and eastern land frontiers, such as they were in 1919—Germany is permitted to keep the number of guns of all calibres with which they were then equipped. This number, however, constitutes a maximum which cannot be exceeded, and the stock of ammunition with which the guns are furnished is reduced to 1,500 rounds for light guns and 500 rounds for heavy guns.[3]

(*f*) All guns, weapons, ammunition, and material possessed by Germany in 1919 in excess of the permitted quantities had to be handed over to the Allies to be disposed of or destroyed under their control. It was part of the function of the Allied Commissions, whose task will be later on discussed, to receive and deal with all consignments of weapons and munitions so delivered by the Germans.[4]

---

[1] Art. 169, Table III.   [2] Art. 166.
[3] Art. 167.   [4] Art. 169.

9. *Production of, and Traffic in, Arms and Ammunition.*—As an adjunct to their provisions concerning arms and ammunition, the Allied experts included in their treaty very stringent measures concerning the production of arms and ammunition in Germany, and the traffic in them between Germany and other countries. It was, indeed, obvious that if they were to be able seriously to hope for the observance of their other limitations, they would be obliged to institute a control over the commerce and industry of armaments, for unrestricted production and freedom of trade would have made it virtually impossible to detect fraud, to discover secret hoards, or to check the quantities legitimately in the possession of the German army. In consequence the Allies insisted on the following provisions:

(*a*) The manufacture of arms, munitions, or war material of any kind is only to be carried out in a restricted number of factories where the Allies specifically permit it. Every other arsenal, armament factory, or other establishment for the making or designing of arms, is to be shut down and its plant destroyed. (It was in pursuance of this provision that the Krupp works, the greatest armament factory in the world, which employed more than 100,000 men, were converted to exclusively peaceful uses.)

The Allies only allowed sufficient plant to be retained to supply the prescribed quantities of arms and ammunition given above.[1]

(*b*) The manufacture in Germany, for export to foreign countries, of arms, ammunition, or material is absolutely forbidden.

(*c*) Similarly, importation from abroad is forbidden. Thus, there can be no commerce of any kind whatever between Germany and the outside world in weapons or material of war.

10. *Fortifications,*—Little need be said about fortifications. The arrangements for the coasts and for the eastern and southern frontiers of Germany have been already mentioned.

---

[1] Art. 168.

On her western frontier Germany was obliged to create a broad demilitarized zone, in which no fortifications of any kind may be maintained.[1] The significance of this zone can be more usefully discussed in a later chapter.[2]

11. *Allied Supervision and Control.*—A whole separate section of Part V is devoted to defining the rights and powers of the Allied Commissions of Control which were entrusted with the task of ensuring the faithful execution and observance of the provisions above described.

Again the Allied experts omitted nothing which they thought could help them to achieve their aim. They organized two separate stages of control: first, that during which, within the various time-limits laid down, the initial reductions would be made, the effectives brought down to 100,000, the surplus armament handed over, the armament plant destroyed, and so on; second, the permanent maintenance of the reductions which had thus been made. For the first stage they set up special Allied Commissions with the widest possible powers; for the second they provided that the Allies could hand over their responsibilities, when they felt it right to do so, to the League of Nations. But the League was not in any case to take charge until it had been agreed by the Allied Governments that the prescribed reductions had all, in fact, been made.

The Allied Commissions were empowered to go to any point in German territory as often as they liked, to make their headquarters at Berlin, to procure through qualified representatives all documents or information which might be required, to receive delivery of all the arms and material which Germany was to hand over, etc. The German Government on their side were obliged to grant every possible facility to the Commissions, to furnish to them all the information they might demand, and in other ways to help them in their task. Again it will be more convenient to postpone discussion of the working of the Allied Commissions, and of the arrangements made by the League of Nations for the second stage of the control, until a later chapter.[3]

---

[1] Art. 180.   [2] Vide chap. xv.   [3] chap. xvii.

The Disarmament of Austria, Hungary, and Bulgaria: Treaties of St. Germain, Part V, Trianon, Part V, and Neuilly, Part IV.

Germany's three allies, Austria, Hungary, and Bulgaria, were also disarmed by the Treaties of Peace. The provisions applied to them were so very similar to those imposed on Germany that little need be added to the description that has been given of Part V of the Treaty of Versailles. The few differences of importance may be briefly dealt with.

1. *Tactical Organization.*—Much the most important of them consisted in the granting to Austria, Hungary, and Bulgaria of a greater measure of freedom than had been allowed to Germany in the tactical organization of their armies. In the German army not only were the permitted kinds of units specifically laid down, and the maximum strength of each prescribed, but it was also stipulated that Germany must have not more than seven infantry and three cavalry divisions. Since it was also prescribed of what units a division must consist, her whole tactical organization was thus imposed upon her in a rigid system. There are no corresponding clauses in the other three treaties. Certain kinds of unit are forbidden altogether; but for all permitted units not only a maximum but also a minimum strength is laid down in the schedules, and, subject to the observance of these maxima and minima, liberty is left to the various staffs to decide for themselves what kinds of unit and what tactical formations they will create.[1]

This leaves them free to decide for themselves, for example, whether they will have cavalry units at all, and if so in what proportion, whether they will combine cavalry and infantry in mixed brigades or not, and so on. It also leaves them free to settle the main lines of their own army organization. There is thus on this point a much greater measure of elasticity than there is in the Treaty of Versailles.

On the other hand, there is no sacrifice of the main purposes which were sought in the corresponding clauses of Versailles. Those purposes were to facilitate control over the numbers of

[1] *E.g.*, Art. 104 of Treaty of Trianon.

the German army, to prevent the diversion of its forces to new and more dangerous methods of warfare, and to prohibit its organization into numerous skeleton cadres which could be much expanded if mobilization should ever happen to occur. These purposes are all secured by the prohibition of certain kinds of weapons and by the establishment of maximum and minimum strengths for each permitted unit. For, of course, the variation allowed in any unit was relatively small, as these figures show:

Unit.		Maximum Effectives.		Minimum Effectives.	
		Officers.	*Men.*	*Officers.*	*Men.*
Infantry division	..	414	10,780	300	8,000
Cavalry division	..	259	5,380	180	3,650
Regiment of infantry	..	65	2,000	52	1,600
Battalion of infantry	..	16	650	12	500
Cyclist group	.. ..	18	450	12	300[1]

Margins such as this give the Staff a certain freedom, but they do not make it possible for them to use the prescribed effectives to build up the skeleton cadre of a much greater army than it is intended they should have.

It is also to be particularly noted that these schedules of maximum and minimum strengths are uniform in all the Treaties of St. Germain, Trianon, and Neuilly. They have thus established a standard system common to three armies.

2. *Limitations of Weapons.*—As a necessary consequence of this elasticity of tactical organization, a modification of the method of limiting weapons had to be adopted. If an infantry division might consist of anywhere from 8,300 to 11,194 men, it was not possible to allow it a fixed number of, say, 12,000 rifles without running the risk that it might have a considerable and an undesirable surplus. The obvious course was therefore adopted—that of establishing a fixed relation between a given number of men and the maximum amount of armament which they might have. In order to avoid errors and to facilitate measurement of the permitted totals, the number of men selected as the basis of calculation was small, to wit, one thousand; and for each thousand men, whether cavalry, infantry

---

[1] Vide, *e.g.*, Table IV, part v, Treaty of Trianon.

or other troops, the following amounts of arms and ammunition were allowed :

	Weapons.	Rounds per Weapon.
Rifles *or* carbines	1,150	500
Heavy *or* light machine-guns ..	15	10,000
Light trench mortars }	2 {	1,000
Medium „ „ }	{	500
Field *or* mountain guns *or*		
howitzers	3	1,000

N.B.—No gun, mortar, or howitzer over 105 mm. (4 inches) calibre is allowed.

It must be noted that once again slightly more liberty of action is permitted to the staff, but that, none the less, a very stringent limitation is achieved. Again the arrangement is common to the three treaties, and thus there is produced a standard unit of measurement and comparison by means of which the respective strengths of the three disarmed states are, in fact, described and written down in the treaties, and by means of which these strengths can, with all the accuracy that is humanly possible, be compared.

As the question of the unit of measurement will arise again, it is worth pointing out how this unit of the Treaties of St. Germain, Trianon, and Neuilly is obtained. First, a great number of factors of potential military strength are altogether forbidden : reserves, territorials, aircraft, gas, and all the other more powerful kinds of weapon. Then the outline of a standard tactical organization is imposed. All this having been done, a fixed relation is then established between a given number of effectives and the maximum quantities of every kind of permitted arm and ammunition with which that number of effectives may be equipped. And it is important to note that what matters is this fixed relation—the proportion established between man-power, weapons, and ammunition. The use of the word " unit " may indeed be misleading. For it does not matter in the least whether the proportion be established on the basis of Lord Esher's figure, 30,000 men, or of 10,000 or 1,000 or 1. The number of 1,000 happened—given the size of the three armies reduced by the treaties now in question— to be a convenient basis for the arithmetic required. But a larger number might be more convenient for larger armies.

That is a minor point; the essential thing in the clauses now being discussed is the fixed relation between man-power, weapons, and ammunition which they set up. This relation provides a satisfactory means of measuring the respective strengths of the armies in question because, as a result of the other restrictions upon the states concerned, it covers all the factors of their strength that really matter, and constitutes a standard combination of these factors common to all three treaties. As has been said above, it would no doubt be possible to make a disarmament treaty without adopting any standard unit, nor even any standard proportion between the various factors of military strength which it was desired to limit. But no one can read through the disarmament clauses of the Treaties of St. Germain, Trianon, and Neuilly without realizing how very much the drawing up of these clauses is simplified by the existence of a standard unit, and how much greater still would be the value of such a standard unit, or at the least of a standard proportion between different factors of military strength, in the preparation of a general treaty.

The remaining points of interest in the Treaties of St. Germain, Trianon, and Neuilly require no more than the briefest mention.

3. *Reserves.*—In addition to the Versailles restriction upon the proportion of officers (in fact, the proportion allowed is one-twentieth instead of the Versailles one-twenty-fifth of the total effectives), the three treaties limit the number of non-commissioned officers to one-fifteenth of the whole. This again, of course, is with the purpose of limiting the skilled organizing power of the armies,[1] and it is a most important addition.

4. *Mobilization.*—A special provision is inserted forbidding preparatory measures for the Government requisition of animals—in some countries, particularly in the Balkans and in mountainous districts, a most important part of army mobilization.[2]

---

[1] *E.g.*, Art. 104, Para. 2, of Treaty of Trianon.
[2] *E.g.*, Art. 106, Para. 3, Treaty of Trianon.

5. *Police.*—In the Treaty of Neuilly, Bulgaria is given a special right to organize, in addition to her gendarmerie and police, a frontier guard, not exceeding 3,000 men in number. They may be armed with rifles, but the number of rifles, for all auxiliary services combined, must not exceed the total of 13,000.[1]

6. *Manufacture of Armaments.*—The three treaties all provide, in identical terms, that the manufacture of armaments may for the future only be carried on in a single factory in each country, which must be the property of the state and under its control, and the production of which must be strictly confined to supplying the prescribed requirements of the army in arms and ammunition.[2] Thus all the very difficult problems of private manufacture are solved by the simple method of cutting the Gordian knot. It is another example of the great advantage in making a disarmament treaty of not having to depend on a limited measure of Government goodwill.

A number of different plans for land disarmament have now been discussed, some unsuccessful, some embodied in the treaties which are the foundation of the European system. Wearisome though the process of description and analysis may have been, it will be found of value in the attempt that will be made in Chapter IX to suggest the principles upon which a general scheme of land disarmament can be built.

---

[1] Art. 69, Para. 4, Treaty of Neuilly.
[2] *E.g.*, Art. 115, Treaty of Trianon.

CHAPTER IX

LAND DISARMAMENT: SUGGESTED PRINCIPLES FOR A GENERAL SCHEME

THE purpose of the present chapter is to suggest, in the light of what has hitherto been said, the principles upon which plans for a general treaty of land disarmament may be drawn up. The points discussed will relate to two only of the technical problems involved in the making of such plans: first, to the factors of military strength which must be taken into account and limited by the terms of the disarmament treaty; second, to the method of measuring the strength of different countries in these various factors when they are combined.

Nothing will be said about the ratio to be established between the states to be disarmed. As was previously argued, the question of the ratio is primarily a political problem, and one which is better dealt with separately and last. For the present purpose it will be assumed (though this would certainly be the reverse of the actual order of events) that the Disarmament Conference has agreed upon a ratio, and that it is faced simply with the problem of transferring its agreement on to paper in such a way that no injustice will be done, and that the military strength allowed to each party will really correspond to that which the Conference has decided it should have.[1]

There is a Balkan saying that "the best is always best." If it is seriously desired to reduce and limit the military strength of the countries which have not yet disarmed, if it is decided to establish among them for the future an agreed balance or ratio of strength, there can be no better method for the purpose than to follow the most perfect model in existence, and to apply the reduction and limitation system of the Treaties of Peace. The first guiding principle of all, therefore, ought to be, if the Governments were sincere, that the closer

---

[1] Cf. *supra*, chap. v.

they adhere to the system of Versailles and Trianon, the better will be the disarmament treaty which they make.

There is, moreover, a special reason why it is desirable that the Disarmament Conference should apply the Peace Treaty system. The disarmament plans are to be League of Nations plans, the disarmament treaty a League of Nations Treaty; among the Members of the League are now included all the four states which have already been disarmed; can any general scheme be satisfactory as the basis of future relations among the Members of the League, unless it is founded on an absolute equality of treatment for them all ? The keynote of current foreign policy happens at the moment to be that of reconciliation between the enemies of the war, and the reinstatement of Germany in a position of legal, political and moral equality with other powers. But apart from that perhaps temporary consideration, is it really to be expected that four Members of the League will indefinitely endure a system which places them in a position of material and moral inferiority ?

It is, of course, possible that equality between Germany and other Members of the League should be established by a relaxation of the Versailles system in favour of Germany and her allies, instead of by the imposition of that system on the other Members. But it is improbable that such a course would in practice be allowed by France; and it is most undesirable that it should be. For in the question of disarmament there is another special reason why the best is much the best. It is this: that the more rigid the disarmament which is agreed, the more comprehensive the scheme adopted, the more factors of military strength with which it deals, the simpler is the technical problem to be solved. This may look at first sight like a paradox, but that it is true every sentence of the present chapter ought to show. It can be proved to be so by simply conjuring up the vision of a conference at which all the parties present had agreed beforehand to apply to themselves the whole system of Versailles. The task of such a conference would be confined to reaching an agreement on the ratio which its Members should respectively accept. And once they had reached that agreement, they would have absolute confidence that their disarmament treaty would give them each, as nearly as any written instrument could give them, the relative strength upon which they had reciprocally agreed.

But in spite of these powerful reasons—they *ought* to be powerful, whether or not in practice they will be so—not even the most optimistic can hope with any confidence that the other Members of the League will thus voluntarily accept the whole system of Versailles. It becomes necessary, therefore, to consider what alternatives to that system can be devised. But none the less the guiding principle above referred to still holds true; in this consideration of alternative plans, it is still right at every moment to remember that the closer the Governments stick to the Peace Treaty system, the better will be the work they do.

In addition to that general introductory principle, two others like it may be mentioned. The first relates to Lord Esher's doctrine of " Period A." It is no doubt desirable in a disarmament treaty to limit not only factors of military strength which affect Period A, but also, as is done in the Treaty of Versailles, those which affect Period B as well. No treaty which does not limit both can be completely sound. But it may occur that the limitation of factors which only affect Period B—for example, great numbers of reserves, Militia or Territorial forces, armament factories and plant—may create great or even insuperable difficulties at the Conference. If that should happen, such factors may be neglected with less reluctance than they could be if they affected Period A. For it is a plain principle of the matter that while Period B is important, it is far less important than Period A. This is already true; and the relative importance of Period A is all the time increasing. The last big war, indeed, was very long, and only in the later stages did fighting reach a high pitch of intensity. But that will not be so in the next big war, if there should be one. All the new large-scale weapons, and especially bombing aircraft, gas, and the newer types of tanks, have much increased the chances that a belligerent might secure a rapid victory by sharp decisive blows.

Equally from the point of view adopted by the Temporary Mixed Commission, Period A is of chief importance. If the Covenant and the various supplementary security plans are a success, the League of Nations should be able during Period A either to settle by peaceful intervention any quarrel out of which war might arise, or to organize a joint resistance to the aggressor which should bring about his speedy downfall and defeat. While, therefore, it is desirable to bear in mind the risk of a protracted war, that risk is much less serious than the risks of Period A, and, if we cannot deal with all, it is on the factors that make armies strong during Period A that we must concentrate.

The other general principle of which something must be said has been already mentioned. It is that it is desirable to limit in a treaty only those factors over which it is possible afterwards to exercise a fairly adequate control. If mutual obligations to reduce a certain weapon are given and taken, and if in violation of them some disloyal state is able treacherously and secretly to increase its stock far beyond the accepted limit, those obligations become a trap for nations of good faith. It may be better to make no limitation than to risk disaster by such an unfortunate result.

But of course this principle is not simple in its application. There is no *a-priori* rule as to what can be controlled and what cannot. It all depends on the measure of freedom which the Governments are willing to give up. Almost any warlike preparation can be discovered, however carefully it may at first be hidden, if expert and impartial investigators from abroad are given full powers to make the researches that may be required. Thus we come again to the question of goodwill—the question in which lies so great a part of the whole problem. If the Governments really mean to make the changes in their general policy which a programme of disarmament ought, if it is serious, to entail, if they are prepared to sacrifice their sovereign liberty of will, not only as regards the kind and amount of armament they have, but also as regards their present right to keep their preparations secret, then almost any kind of armament or weapon can be controlled. But if they wish to retain their present power of secret preparation, if they restrict the right of impartial international enquiry, then in many ways the agreed reduction of armaments may involve unfair risks to loyal states. Since we cannot know beforehand how much goodwill the Governments will bring to the Disarmament Conference, whether their sacrifice of present freedom will be small or great, the present examination of its programme must be made with a double hypothesis in mind.

There are, then, three general introductory principles which are agreed: the value of the Peace Treaty system as a model, the primary importance of Period A, and the need for adequate control over every factor with which the Disarmament Treaty will be made to deal. To them we must add certain other modifying considerations.

The first is that in the Treaty to be made the Disarmament Conference cannot limit the purpose of the Contracting Parties' armies as the purpose of the German army was limited by the Treaty of Versailles. They cannot lay down that these armies " shall be devoted exclusively to the maintenance of order within the territory and to the control of the frontiers," for they have to bear in mind the stipulations of Article 8 concerning " the enforcement by common action of international obligations," and the general undertakings of the Covenant and of various special treaties which may oblige the Members of the League to take a share by military action in the international policing of the world. For this reason it may be impossible, for example, to forbid the signatory states to practise the mobilization of their forces and to make general preparations to that end; there must be provision for the suspension of disarmament if joint international action should be required; and other similar changes from the system of Versailles may perhaps result.

Next, whether we like it or not, we must count on the virtual certainty that the continental powers, whose armies we most desire to reduce and limit, will stubbornly refuse, for reasons above discussed,[1] to give up the principle of universal and compulsory short-term service. This evidently involves a vital and a drastic alteration in the Versailles plan.

Again it is only too probable, though of this happily we cannot be so certain, that many Governments will refuse to give up their liberty to develop whatever arms they please, and to

---

[1] Cf. chap. iv., *supra.*

9

choose for themselves, with all or almost all the freedom which they now possess, the weapons with which their troops shall be equipped.

If these predictions should prove to be correct, various problems of much complexity will obviously arise. Can army reserves, for example, be dealt with by treaty in any way at all ? Can armament as a whole be limited ? Can individual weapons be restricted, and if so, how ? Or must all these factors simply be neglected ?

These discouraging prospects, together with the difficult questions which they raise, and together also with the introductory principles above discussed, form the starting point from which the detailed consideration of the technical problems of disarmament may be begun. These technical problems, it may once more be repeated, are two. What factors of military strength shall be dealt with ? How can these factors be so combined as to permit comparison between the strength of different states ? The solutions to them, and the answers to the riddles which they involve, will be sought in the examination of the various factors one by one.

1. *Standing Effectives.*—Everyone is agreed that the effectives of the standing armies must be reduced and limited, as they were both in Lord Esher's scheme and in the Treaty of Versailles, " on a numerical basis." That is to say, each state must not be allowed so many divisions or brigades, but a fixed maximum number of men, which its effectives in time of peace must never exceed. This fixed maximum number must include all ranks of its army: staffs, officers, men, instructors and cadres.

This limitation of peace-time effectives will no doubt not only in itself be the most important element in land disarmament, but it will also be the basis upon which, as in the Treaty of Versailles, other limitations will be built. If other factors of military strength are also dealt with, the number of men allotted to each signatory party will correspond exactly to the ratio co-efficient which it is allowed. This initial and fundamental limitation is not only a prime necessity, but it has the advantage that its observance is easily controlled. The effectives of a peace-time army cannot be hidden; even in present conditions they are always known to the military attachés of other powers.

2. *Auxiliary Forces : i.e., Armed Police, Forest Guards, Coastguards, Customs Officials, etc.*—There can be no doubt that auxiliary forces, the members of which are armed and are in the full-time service of the state, must in some way be limited by the disarmament agreement. If Governments were left entirely free to maintain as many of such forces as they liked, they might be able, if inspired by disloyal motives, to build up a dangerous supplementary army which would bring their real military strength above the level which they were allowed, and thus disturb or totally destroy the balance of the ratio on which the treaty had been based.[1]

Fortunately, the Peace Treaties provide logical and satisfactory principles by means of which the numbers of such forces to be allowed to each signatory power might be decided. Such forces, broadly speaking, are of two kinds: first, those charged with the execution of certain definite duties, such as collecting customs, guarding forests, and so on, for the execution of which the number of men required varies with certain fixed unchanging factors, such as the number of ports and frontier stations, the area of forest land, the length of coast-line, and so on; and second, those charged with the general maintenance of order, whose numbers, *ceteris paribus*, must vary with changes in the numbers of the population. For each kind the Peace Treaties provide a satisfactory basis of limitation. For the former they lay down that the number of officials or employees of the various services, customs officers, and so on, " shall not exceed that of the employees or officials functioning in these capacities in 1913." This is an absolute restriction to a figure that may never, without change of the treaty, be exceeded. The year 1913 was chosen as a basis because it was in 1919 the last normal year of peace, because no state was then disarmed, and none, therefore, had endeavoured to increase its services of this kind beyond the numbers necessary for the efficient execution of their proper duties.

For the second kind, gendarmerie and police, it laid down that their numbers might only be increased beyond those

[1] Cf. chap. viii., *supra*.

enployed in 1913 " to an extent corresponding to the increase of population," 1913 again being taken as the basic year for the reasons explained above.

It would seem possible to apply these same principles in a general treaty to all the states whose land armaments are dealt with. There is no valid reason why any Government should object to their application to itself; 1913 might even be taken as the basic year, if there were thought to be advantage in so doing. Probably, however, it would be better to adopt the figures of the *status quo* in some post-war year. There have been so many great territorial changes since 1913, and so much movement of population, that complicated calculations would be needed if that year were taken. These calculations could, of course, be made, but since there is nothing abnormal in the post-war numbers of the gendarmerie and police, at least in the vast majority of countries, there would seem to be a balance of advantage in taking some such year as 1925.

But if this were agreed, there would remain the question whether any limitation should be placed upon either the armament with which these auxiliary forces may be equipped, or the training which they may be given. It would, of course, be possible to impose such limitations, and, if the system of control is adequate, fairly easy to ensure their observance. Moreover, most states would certainly be willing to accept limitations—*e.g.*, to arm such services only with revolvers or rifles, never to assemble them for mass military training, and so on—which would in no way alter their present invariable practice, nor in any way diminish the efficiency of the services for their proper functions.

But such limitations as these on numbers and equipment would obviously be an alternative to the other policy, which Lord Esher proposes, of reckoning such whole-time auxiliaries as an integral part of the total peace effectives to be allowed to any state. For if such auxiliaries are to be counted as equivalent in military value to the regular troops of the standing army, if they are to be included in the total force for which the agreed ratio coefficient of any state provides, that state must plainly have full liberty to train them as it trains its regular troops. And the point thus raised is not an easy one. In some states to count the armed police as equivalent to the army would clearly be unjust; in other states, it would be equally unjust not to do so. Italy, for example, had in 1923 at her disposal a force of 120,000 men (carabinieri, *i.e.*, gendarmerie, Royal Guard of Public Safety, and customs officials)—a force which is not only armed, but which is so organized and trained that the Italian army, in fact, used them in the field in their war of 1915–1918. Poland in the same year had a force of 60,000 men similarly armed, trained, and organized; Latvia a force of 5,000—a large figure proportionately to her size; while a number of states, for example, Finland, Lithuania, and Bulgaria, make no distinction whatever between their police and military forces.

To meet this difficulty two alternative plans are possible. The first is to secure a general agreement on Lord Esher's principle, and to count the members of the auxiliary services among the peace effectives to be allowed, giving liberty to every state to train them, if it so desires, as it trains its other forces. The second is to secure general limitations like those of the Peace Treaties on the armament and training of these services, not to include them in the permitted ratio total, and to make some special supplementary arrangement in the ratio negotiations for those states, like Italy and the others mentioned, which normally maintain an exceptionally large number of men in these services, and normally train them virtually as a military force. This arrangement no doubt would have to allow these states to continue the training they now give to their auxiliary forces, in compensation for which there would have to be a reduction of the number of ordinary effectives they would otherwise have been allowed.

The second plan at first sight seems more complicated than Lord Esher's simple principle, but, in fact, it might more easily secure general acceptance.

3. *Tactical Organization.*—The question of prescribing in a general treaty of land disarmament a uniform system of tactical organization raises some difficult points. It was observed above in the discussion of the Peace Treaties that the Allied experts attached a real importance to tactical organization as an element in limiting the military strength of the ex-enemy states, and that

they hoped by prescribing a fixed system to facilitate control over the numbers of the German and other armies, to prevent the diversion of their forces to new and more dangerous forms of warfare, and to prohibit their organization into numerous skeleton cadres which could be much expanded when mobilization took place.

Apart from its effect on the question of control, therefore, the question of tactical organization is thus related: first, to the restriction of certain weapons and methods of warfare; second, to the formation of reserves. If there are to be no general restrictions of weapons, similar to the prohibition of military aircraft, of tanks, and of poison-gas, imposed upon Germany and her late Allies, and if every power is to remain free to prepare all the reserves it pleases, the importance of regulating tactical organization will be much reduced, and the difficulty of doing so much increased. But if weapons are restricted by the general treaty, and if some attempt is made to deal with the question of reserves—and it must be hoped that something will be agreed to on both matters—then, no doubt, it is desirable that some effort should be made to regulate the tactical organization of the prescribed effectives.

But, though this may be desirable, it is a point on which resistance from the Governments may be expected. At the most nothing more than the acceptance of the comparatively elastic system common to the three treaties of St. Germain, Trianon, and Neuilly can be hoped for, with its maximum and minimum strengths for an agreed list of permitted sorts of unit. Against even that it is probable that the general staffs would unanimously rebel. They will all be most reluctant to abandon the various organizations which they have worked out for themselves, and to which by habit and by tradition they are attached. They will be no less reluctant to give up their freedom to develop as they wish whatever arms may seem to them at any moment most effective. Some staffs may fix their hopes on aircraft, some on tanks, some on other weapons, according to their national aptitudes or the geography of the frontiers they must defend. Any prescribed tactical system, even the looser system of the three later Treaties of Peace, would obviously limit their freedom to organize their permitted

forces as they like, and it is certain that the staffs will fight
against it.

How far would it be wise for those who draft the plans for
the Council of the League to insist upon the adoption of the
Trianon system ?   Probably it would be worth an effort to
secure it; certainly it would *not* be worth risking for this the
whole success of the general proposals which they make.   If
this system or something like it is not adopted, it will no doubt
be a serious departure from equality with the ex-enemy states
which have already been disarmed; but it will not be a departure
which, *in itself*, and apart from the restriction of weapons or
reserves, can lead to grave disturbance of the balance of military
strength which is established.

4. *Reserves.*—There comes next the important question of
reserves.   Here again it was evident, in the discussion of the
Treaties of Peace, that the Allied experts attached great importance to a rigid limitation.   A long list of different clauses
was given in the last chapter, all of them designed to prevent
the maintenance of reserves and the formation of supplementary
cadres, or to restrict the kind of training which the ex-enemy
armies might receive.   In the light of the Allied experts' work,
what should be done about reserves in the general treaty ?
How many of their clauses ought to be, or can be, generally
applied ?

No doubt, again, it is desirable to reproduce in the general
treaty the whole or almost the whole system of reserve-control
which the Peace Treaties imposed upon the enemy states.   Not
to do so would involve once more an inequality in the general
scheme, and an inequality of the most serious kind.   But, on
the other hand, there are some parts of the Peace Treaty system
which *cannot* be generally applied, and others which, as we have
seen, will not be generally accepted.   The Peace Treaty prohibition of all preparation and practice for mobilization cannot
be imposed on Members of the League who may be called upon
to undertake joint action under Article 16; conscription will
almost certainly be retained in deference to the wishes of the
Continental powers.   Is there, in view of this, anything of value
which can be done in a general treaty on the subject of reserves ?

Certainly nothing can be done that will give results corresponding in rigidity and effect to the treaty system. If compulsory short-term military service is to be retained, the staffs will always have at their disposal large reserves, and no other measures that can be taken will prevent these reserves from being organized and used. If conscription is allowed, then, and reserves are in consequence allowed, under the general treaty, the looser kind of disarmament that will result can only be defended by Lord Esher's doctrine explained above. He held, it will be remembered, that there is a maximum co-efficient of expansion for any army when its mobilization is carried out; that no troops in training can absorb more than a certain proportion of reserves; and that no staff can organize and handle a force more than a certain number of times greater than its peace-time army. It will also be remembered that the maximum coefficient of expansion achieved by the most efficient armies at the beginning of the late war was $2\frac{3}{4}$, and that experts have calculated the highest possible figure to be 4. However many reserves may be on the national roll-call, held Lord Esher, not more than four times the number of the effectives of the standing army can possibly, during Period A, be used, and probably not more than three times will be efficient troops. And since it is Period A that matters, he went on to argue, the factor of reserves should be neglected, and attention concentrated on reducing to the lowest figure that will be accepted the standing peace-effectives which the Governments retain; such reductions will not only mean greater economies in time of peace, but will mean a consequent and automatic reduction of the total forces which could be used in Period A, and thus the two chief purposes of disarmament will be achieved.

This is, no doubt, a policy easily acceptable to conscription Governments, relatively simple in execution, and, since it would leave to all the staffs the same liberty of action, not unjust except towards the disarmed ex-enemy states. It would certainly be possible, if Lord Esher's whole doctrine were accepted, to make a general treaty of land disarmament, omitting every single clause of the Peace Treaty system of reserve-control discussed in Chapter VIII; and to make such a treaty would certainly be far better than to make no treaty at all.

But, in fact, it is not necessary either to accept or to reject the whole of Lord Esher's doctrine. There are certain parts of the Peace Treaty system which are not inconsistent with conscription, which could be applied quite simply in a general treaty, which ought to be easily accepted, which, indeed, would strengthen the working of Lord Esher's doctrine, and would tend to ensure the results for which he looks. They are measures, short of the total prohibition of reserves, which would help to prevent a great expansion of the standing forces by restricting the number of trained and organized personnel capable of doing the skilled staff work upon which successful mobilization must depend.

Thus, for example:

(*a*) It would obviously be quite simple, even if complete liberty of tactical organization were allowed, for all the parties to a general treaty to agree that the number of their officers should not exceed a fixed proportion (either one-twenty-fifth as in the Treaty of Versailles, or one-twentieth as in the other three treaties) of the total effectives which they were respectively allowed. This number should, of course, include all officers of every rank or grade, and all the various sorts of staffs and cadres. The observance of this undertaking could be quite easily controlled.

(*b*) It would be equally simple for them to agree that the number of their non-commissioned officers should be similarly restricted, perhaps to one-fifteenth of the total effectives, as in the three later Treaties of Peace. This, again, would be a clause of obvious value, the observance of which could be controlled.

(*c*) Again, it would be possible, and indeed quite simple, for the treaty to lay down what military academies and schools each country should possess. Probably the easiest method of so doing would be to provide, first, that the staffs and students of such academies should all be included among the total officers allowed to each country under the restrictions above provided, and second, that the total places in these academies of every kind should not exceed a certain fixed proportion of the total effectives allowed. This would make a standard limitation, uniform for all countries, of the training staffs and military students whom they might maintain.

These three limitations, since they refer to the standing enlisted forces of a country, would be quite easy to control, and they would have the evident effect of reducing and limiting the skilled personnel upon which a staff could count, either for organization or command, when it wished to mobilize. They would thus, *pro tanto*,[1] equally reduce the mobilization coefficient of all the armies, and would frustrate attempts by any given state so to increase by special measures the staffs and cadres of its standing forces that they could be expanded more rapidly than those of neighbouring countries. They would therefore be well worth while, as a simple means of limiting reserves and the forces which would take the field in Period A, even in a general treaty in which the system of conscription was retained.

Others of the Peace Treaty clauses would be, in such a general treaty, of more doubtful value. Thus:

(*d*) The restriction upon the civilian administrative personnel employed in the whole-time service of the army might be much more difficult than the other limitations to control. Otherwise no doubt it would be desirable to include it in a General Treaty, though perhaps its importance is not great.

(*e*) Similarly, the prohibition of the part-time training of ex-officers is not only difficult to control, but is definitely inconsistent with the short-term conscription system, under which some reserves must inevitably be allowed. If conscription is retained, therefore, this clause must be allowed to drop, important though otherwise it might be.

[1] Some military experts believe that these limitations on the proportion of officers and N.C.O.'s are the most effective of all ways of limiting the mobilization coefficient, and they hold that the experience of German disarmament (under which N.C.O.'s were *not* limited with unfortunate results) confirms this view.

(*f*) The prohibition of the discharge of *officers* above a fixed percentage (*e.g.*, 5 per cent in the Peace Treaties) every year, and the supplementary prohibition of their replacement if they *are* discharged, stands on a different footing. This would not be inconsistent with the conscription system, if it were stipulated in the General Treaty that officers must serve a certain minimum term, and no doubt it would be desirable to introduce a limitation that would prevent an abnormal increase of the skilled organizing personnel. But it would not be easy to control, it might be regarded as vexatious, and there is in any case the automatic safeguard that the great proportion of an army's officers must be long-term professionals, unless its whole efficiency is to be destroyed. This, therefore, if it were resisted, might be allowed to drop.

(*g*) Similarly, the Peace Treaty prohibition of all "supplementary cadres" attached to "formations, administrative services, or general staffs," would be very difficult to control, unless a standard regulation of the whole tactical organization of the various armies had been agreed. Indeed, its general adoption would seem to depend necessarily on whether such a standard regulation were or were not accepted. In any case, its importance is not great, if, on the one hand, reserves are to be allowed at all, and if, on the other hand, the total number of officers bears a fixed maximum proportion to the effectives which are allowed.

(*h*) There remains the Peace Treaty prohibition of foreign military missions and of foreign enlistment. The purpose of this prohibition was twofold: first, to cut off at its source a supply of fully trained reserves; second, to prevent close military relations between Germany and other states. There can be no doubt that its acceptance in a general treaty, if supported by an undertaking by all the parties not to receive foreign military missions or to make enlistments of foreign subjects in their respective armies, would be of value. It would have a slight importance as a restriction on reserves; it might be more useful as a means of preventing military groupings and the evil results of military hegemony and tutelage to which they lead—results which otherwise might be liable to lead to violations of the terms of a disarmament agreement, and to destroy the spirit of confidence on which it ought to rest.

Such a prohibition of military missions and of foreign enlistment would, therefore, be a useful part of a general treaty. But it is not a vital part, nor one the abandonment of which, if it were much opposed, would mean disaster.

It may be concluded, therefore, on the subject of reserves, that the general application of practically the whole system of the Peace Treaties is to be desired; that since, however, short-term compulsory service will almost certainly not be abolished, much of the remaining Peace Treaty clauses must as a result be given up; that three of its limitations—on the proportion of officers, of non-commissioned officers, and of military schools to the total of prescribed effectives—would, none the less, remain of value, and should certainly be inserted in the general treaty; and that some others of its limitations, less easy than these three to control effectively, would be worth while, though they are not vital if they should happpen to be opposed. A general treaty of land disarmament, which dealt on these lines with the subject of reserves, would be less satisfactory than one which gave a general application to the Peace Treaty clauses, but it would work; apart from the inequality of treatment for the ex-enemy countries, it would not be unjust; and, if the reduction of peace effectives involved a drastic all-round cut, it would achieve much of the purposes for the sake of which disarmament is so urgently desired.

5. *Limitation of the Period of Compulsory Service.*—There remains the question of the limitation of the period for which conscription countries should be allowed to make their soldiers serve. Is it worth while to place any limitation upon this period, and if so, what period should be desired?

The point might perhaps have been considered under the heading of reserves, but it is so important that it needs a separate discussion by itself. It does affect, of course, the question of the reserves that will be available, not in Period A, but in

Period B. That this is so is very simply shown. If the total standing effectives are limited in number, the longer the period of service, the fewer the reserves; it is for this reason that the German private is now obliged to serve twelve years. On the other hand, the maximum period that could possibly be fixed would be, under a conscription system, say, three years at the very most, and with a three-year period of service the general staff will always be able to build up all the reserves which it can mobilize in Period A. But with so long a period as three years the third-line troops, the reserves who can be re-trained for use in Period B, would be much restricted, if the number of the standing force were small. A long period of service would therefore have this desirable effect in respect of Period B.

On the other hand, the longer the period of service the better the fighting qualities of the standing force. Troops trained for three years would be far better material for a smashing campaign of attack designed to secure a victory in Period A than troops who had only been in service, say, six months. While, therefore, a short period would greatly increase the number of partly trained third-line reserves who could be brought into action in Period B, it would reduce and perhaps would much reduce the aggressive power of the various states at the moment when fighting first began.[1] On the general principle, therefore, that it is more important to limit military strength in Period A than in Period B, that it is the temptation to sudden aggression that must be removed, it would seem right to try to secure in the general treaty a limitation of the length of service to a short period, if possible to something like six months.

There is, moreover, the consideration that such a limitation would be immensely popular in every conscription country, and that for that reason it would produce a profound psychological effect. No single other measure would so much reduce the real burden of militarism upon the common man, or mobilize so powerfully his general support for the policy of the League.

It may well be impossible to secure agreement for such a drastic change, or, indeed, for any common period of service. If so, the general system of land disarmament proposed in this

---

[1] The Swiss army, which is virtually organized as a national militia, provides the most striking illustration of this argument.

chapter will not break down. Limitation of the period of service is not an essential element in that system; but it is emphatically a desirable addition.

It may be added that whatever reduction of service is agreed to should be made, if possible, all at once, and not in a series of instalments. Every such reduction means virtually a complete reorganization of the army, and a series of successive reductions would therefore involve general inconvenience which it would be better to avoid. The recent discussions in Belgium on the point have been instructive.

It is probable that if, in fact, any general agreement were to be secured, it would be at first for a period of not less than a year. Even such an agreement would be worth while. It would not secure all the benefits of a shorter period; but it would mean a great relief in a number of countries; it would establish the principle of general limitation of the length of service by international treaty; it would thus prepare the way for greater reductions at a later time; and there is no reason to fear that the maximum period so established would become a minimum. On the contrary, states which are even now disposed to make a greater reduction than that would not be deterred from so doing, but would actually be encouraged to press forward by the reductions in many other countries which the general adoption of such a period would mean.

6. *Militias and Territorial Forces.*—There comes next the question, important in Great Britain but not in most conscription countries, of militias and territorial forces; that is to say, of forces composed of part-time soldiers—usually volunteers who receive a short annual training, enough to teach them the elements of the use of arms and how to work together—which are organized and equipped on the basis of their full war-time establishment, and which often are available for use either in foreign service or for home defence. What should be done about them in a general treaty?

The answer depends entirely on the view that is taken of Lord Esher's doctrine of Period A; on whether, that is to say, attention should be devoted principally to the opening stages of a possible war, or whether an attempt should also be made to limit factors which affect the potential strength of a national army after Period A is passed. There are few, if any, militias better trained than the British Territorial Army; yet, as was seen above, British experts hold that they could not take the field without at least four months' full-time training after mobilization had occurred. They are, therefore—and no doubt all militias are the same—troops for Period B, which will in no way affect the fighting strength of any army during Period A. Thus, if the purpose of a disarmament treaty is simply to limit strength in Period A, such forces may be altogether neglected in its terms.

But, on the other hand, it is held that Territorial forces, when they have had six months' full-time training and six months' experience of actual war, are then of equal fighting value with the regular troops of the standing army. If, therefore, the purpose of the Treaty is to limit potential strength in Period B, they must be dealt with no less than the peace-effectives which are allowed. Those indeed who build mostly on the lessons of the last war, and who expect the next war also, if it comes, to be a long one, have suggested that Territorial forces should be thrown in together with the regular army as part of the peace-effectives which each country may maintain.

But it is plain that this policy would impose during Period A a severe handicap on those states which keep a high proportion of Territorial forces, and whose regular effectives would thus be much reduced. Since, as has been so often urged, Period A is of primary and of continually increasing importance, this policy, at least, must be rejected unless it is supported by other supplementary arrangements to meet the objections that would be raised.

Equally, Lord Esher's policy of taking only Period A into consideration, and in consequence of leaving Governments unrestricted freedom to build up as many Territorial forces as they like, is one that it is difficult to accept. It would leave open a dangerous path to rivalry and competition, it would afford excuse for the almost indefinite expansion of weapons and equipment, and it would make the observance of other parts of the treaty harder to control. This, therefore, can also be rejected.

The best plan would probably be to treat Territorial forces as

—what in fact they are—a sort of reserve to the regular army which cannot be used in action during Period A, and to limit them on this basis. To this end two stipulations would be necessary in the general treaty. First, it would have to be provided that such forces should not be given more than a certain maximum period of training every year, to prevent them being converted by protracted annual service into Period A forces, and thus virtually increasing the prescribed number of regular effectives. Second, a fixed maximum proportion between prescribed effectives and Territorial forces would have to be agreed. This proportion would, in principle, be uniform for all countries; but for those who do not have conscription, and who have not therefore got the large number of reserves for use in Period B which conscription countries have, an exceptionally large proportion could, no doubt, by negotiation, be arranged. This would be obviously just, since Territorial forces correspond exactly to those classes of conscripted reserves whose previous service is of a certain value, but who require some months of continuous training after mobilization before they can be thrown into action.

The proposed arrangement may seem complicated. But only a few countries are much affected by the Militia question, and the necessary exceptions from the standard proportion could probably, therefore, be negotiated without much difficulty, while, if there is a sound system of mutual control, observance of the agreement could be supervised reasonably well. The lower the proportion between effectives and Territorials which was fixed, the greater, of course, would be the economies in the cost of the latter which would be made. The proposal has the further advantage that every reduction of regular effectives would entail a corresponding and automatic reduction of Territorials too.[1]

[1] It has been suggested by Señor Cobian, the distinguished Spanish member of the Committee of the Council of the League on Disarmament, that it might be possible to deal with the limitation of standing effectives, with the question of the varying lengths of service in different countries, and with Militias and Territorial forces, by allowing to each country a certain fixed number of " man-days " per annum; a force of Militia serving for two months would thus be counted as equivalent to the sixth part of a force of the same size consisting of soldiers serving for a year.

7. Armament and Ammunition.—There can be no question that no general treaty of land disarmament will be much use unless it deals not only with the number of troops that are maintained, but also with the armament with which they are equipped. This was the opinion not only of the Temporary Mixed Commission, but of everyone who seriously discussed the proposals which Lord Esher made. No one was more insistent than the military experts that his plan of omitting any limitation of armament at all would not work in practice, even if it were ever accepted, which they did not believe it would be.[1] Some way, therefore, it is generally agreed, has got to be devised for limiting armament unless the attempt to reduce land forces is to be given up.

This is, indeed, one of the capital points in the whole discussion of disarmament, for not only is it of vital importance to find a solution for the problems which arise, but it will also be very difficult to do so unless the Governments give up more liberty of action than it can be expected at this moment that they will. It furnishes, perhaps, the most striking example of the general truth, that rigidity of limitation means real simplicity, while apparent simplicity, like Lord Esher's, which left wide liberty of action to the Governments, means technical and political difficulty of many kinds. If the Governments were willing to make great " sacrifices " of their present freedom, if they were willing to apply to their own armies the system which the Peace Treaties have imposed upon the enemy states, there would be no problem to be solved. It is only because we are

---

The idea is ingenious, and is not wholly inconsistent with the calculations given in a footnote to p. 79 concerning the period of time during which military training of varying length remains of value. It would be well worth while investigating whether the Governments were willing to entertain it. On the one hand it would give a maximum of elasticity to the system of limitation of effectives; on the other hand it might be difficult to control, and it has an artificial air which is against it (vide L.N. Document C.P.D. 1, p. 34).

[1] Cf. Major-General Sibert, U.S. Army, in foreword to *Chemical Warfare*, by Fries and West: " Men are nothing in modern war unless they are equipped with the most effective devices for killing and maiming the enemy's soldiers, and are thoroughly trained in the use of such instruments."

obliged to doubt that the Governments will do this that we must face the difficult questions which are now to be discussed.

But the fact that we must doubt, and must therefore speculate upon alternative plans, does not make it less desirable to press for the general adoption of the principles which the expert Allied staffs worked out at Paris; for we know that from the adoption of these principles a practicable, just, and effective treaty would result. Nor will it in the least degree diminish the grave responsibility which the Governments will bear, if, through their intransigence upon the point of armament, the whole negotiations for a general treaty should break down or otherwise should fail of their effect.

With this plea for the serious consideration of the Allied experts' system, the various elements in it may now be dealt with one by one.

(a) The first, and an essential, part of this system is the restriction which it places upon the kinds of weapons which the ex-enemy states may use. Military aircraft, " poisonous or other gases, and all analogous liquids, materials or devices," armoured cars, tanks, and all similar constructions suitable for use in war, are all forbidden; they are not simply limited in size or in amount, they are excluded altogether from the weapons with which the ex-enemy armies may be equipped. Likewise no guns, or trench-mortars of any kind, of a larger calibre than 105 mm. are allowed. By this means the ex-enemy armies are totally prevented from making preparation either for attack or for defence by all the modern methods of conducting war. In chemical and aerial warfare, in tank warfare, in large-scale bombardment by heavy guns—in other words, in all the forms of attack by means of which a decision in modern war can be obtained—the ex-enemy armies quite simply do not exist. Will the other Governments agree to place upon themselves the same restrictions, or will they insist upon retaining their liberty to use these new and devastating weapons ?

The question is a large one, which requires special consideration at a later stage.[1] A subsequent conclusion may be

---

[1] Cf. chap. xv., *infra*.

anticipated to the extent of saying that it is *possible* (though improbable) that some of these means of warfare—for example, tanks—will, by general agreement, be given up, but that in regard to others the most that can be hoped for, at any rate when the disarmament treaty is first adopted, is some measure of agreed reduction in the quantities which the various Governments now possess.

(*b*) This conclusion has a great though indirect effect upon the next question that arises, that of the ways in which *permitted* weapons can be limited in amount. For if modern methods of warfare are altogether excluded, if the list of permitted weapons is a relatively small one, the Governments which have agreed to such restrictions will, no doubt, also agree to accept the same system of limitation of weapons " on a numerical basis " which the Peace Treaties have imposed. That is to say, they will agree that for every thousand of their prescribed effectives (assuming they adopt, as no doubt on this hypothesis they would, the basic " unit " of the three later Treaties of Peace)[1], they will have not more than a certain maximum number of weapons of each permitted class. Thus the general treaty would contain lists or schedules of the weapons allowed to every signatory power identical in nature with the " Tables " which the Treaties of Peace contain. The figures in these schedules would, of course, include not only weapons in actual use, but also those for mobilization purposes and for replacement; and thus the whole question of armament would be solved.

Whether the details of these schedules would also be identical with the details of the Peace Treaty Tables is a question of comparatively secondary importance. Indeed, since they must presumably allow a surplus of weapons for use when mobilization occurs, which the Peace Treaty Tables of course did not, the actual figures cannot be the same. The proportion between weapons and men laid down in the three later treaties must be increased, and a higher figure—perhaps a much higher figure—per thousand men must be allowed. Likewise the list of permitted weapons itself might not be the same as that of the Peace Treaty Tables; guns of larger calibre,

[1] Cf. *supra*, chap. viii.

some military aircraft, or other additional weapons might be allowed.

If such changes from the Peace Treaty system were required, it would be necessary to have a new and perhaps a difficult negotiation on both the points involved—what additional sorts of weapon, and what quantities of each should be retained. On both it would be the duty first of the Preparatory Committee and then of the Council of the League to make proposals in the plans which they prepare; and on these proposals the negotiation between the Governments would be based. But when the negotiation had been concluded, when agreement on both points had been reached, the system of armament limitation which would result would be the same in nature as that which the Peace Treaties have set up. Like that system, it would be radical, equal in its operation, and relatively easy to control. Since it would embody the same uniform standard of armament per thousand men for all parties (except the ex-enemy states), and since it would include the same standard proportionate combination of the most important factors of military strength, it would permit the Disarmament Conference to make the approximately accurate comparison and measurement of forces which it will need to make. It would be, in fact, in almost every way by far the most satisfactory system which the Conference could adopt.

It is therefore much to be desired that the Governments should agree to an application of this list or schedule system of the Peace Treaties, in which all the quantities of permitted weapons of each class are set out in detail, changes being made if necessary by negotiation, both in the sorts of weapons and in the quantities of each sort which are allowed.

(c) But if, on the other hand, modern methods of warfare are not excluded, if the Governments insist on retaining full liberty to use whatever means of war they like, they will further insist on full freedom to experiment as they think right, to develop this arm or that, to increase this kind of weapon or that, to alter the character of their whole military preparation in accordance with the changes in the science of attack and of defence which new inventions cause. Nor will it be possible to object to their demands. While they are still liable to treacherous attack by new and unknown weapons, while they still have to depend at least in great degree upon themselves for safety, they will be justified in wishing to adapt their preparations to their individual needs, and to increase those arms which, in changed conditions, or in view of their special geographical and tactical requirements, may, from time to time, seem to them to be the most effective.

In this case—and it has been said that unfortunately it is only too likely to arise—the schedule method of limiting armament plainly cannot be adopted. If the Governments want continually to change the sorts of weapons with which they arm their troops, if they want to change the proportions of the different sorts of troops, if they want to develop now a tank corps, now an air force, now a chemical brigade, now their heavy guns, above all if they wish to keep their various preparations, as at present, secret, or nominally so, then it is not possible to hope that any schedule can be devised which will lay down the exact quantities of all permitted weapons which each of them will be allowed to have. It will not even be possible to make a list of the sorts of weapon which are allowed, if every Government is free to add to any possible list whenever it may desire; still less will it be possible to establish the proportion given to each weapon in the list. Some other system, some system of greater elasticity than any schedule can possess, must be devised if there is to be a limitation of armament at all.

Of what nature can such a system be ? Only one proposal on the subject has so far been made—that of the Temporary Mixed Commission in its Report, above discussed, upon Lord Esher's plan. The Commission suggested, with the concurrence of Colonel Réquin, of the French general staff, and of his distinguished military colleagues, that " material " might be limited " either directly or by an indirect method of financial limitation." They further suggested as the " unit of measure " a certain strength in effectives " and a certain fixed sum of money representing the remaining factor of armament."[1]

In what way can this tentative suggestion be worked out ? How can " a fixed sum of money " be made an effective limita-

[1] Vide L.N. Document A. 31, 1922, C.T.A. 173, p. 73. Cf. chap. vii.

tion upon the total armament with which Governments equip their armies? The Temporary Mixed Commission give no further indication in their Report of what they had in mind, but an attempt may perhaps usefully be made to construct a reasonable scheme upon the basis of the phrases which they used.

(*d*) If Governments are not willing to agree upon a schedule of fixed quantities of permitted weapons, it might, nevertheless, be possible to get them to agree upon the total quantity of armament which they each will have, lumping together for this purpose in a single block all the weapons of every kind which they possess. But if this is done the only way in which to measure and compare the total blocks possessed by different states is to give them a financial valuation. A rifle cannot be measured against an aeroplane, or a gun against a tank, nor can any rational proportion be established between the military value of different weapons. But suppose that every state were allowed to spend each year a certain fixed sum of money upon the armament with which it equipped each thousand of its permitted effectives; suppose that instead of laying down in a schedule, as the Peace Treaties do, the exact number of rifles, guns, etc., which might be possessed for every thousand men, the general treaty permitted the expenditure for their armament of, say, £10,000 per annum; is there any hope that by this means an effective, just and workable scheme could be devised?

(1) It was evidently the intention of the Temporary Mixed Commission that their "fixed sum of money" should cover only the cost of armament proper—*i.e.*, of weapons of all classes and of the munitions which they require. They had not in mind the system proposed at the Moscow Conference by the Russian Government of a fixed appropriation for each effective which should cover all the army cost of every kind. In this way they met the most obvious of the objections that are made to the budget method of limiting armed forces. For by restricting their appropriation to armament proper, the Temporary Mixed Commission excluded from it those factors in military cost which vary most between different countries, that is to say, the maintenance of personnel, the construction of fortifications,

etc., the level of which varies with the standard of living of each country. Indeed, they restricted it to material the price of which is approximately equal throughout the world. It is true that a gun to-day costs more in the United States than in Japan, because the labour cost of its production is higher— though *not* higher by the amount of the difference in wage-rates, because the better-paid American labour is more efficient. It is also true that, in a recent competition for a Balkan naval contract, French capitalists made bids for submarine construction at a price 40 per cent less than the lowest British offer.[1] But, broadly speaking, the labour costs in armament production are relatively low; the cost of guns, etc., depends largely on the cost of raw material, that is to say, principally of steel. And the price of steel, calculated in gold values, is a world-price, varying little (except for the cost of transport from places where it is produced to those where it is not) between any two countries in the world. Thus an armament appropriation of a fixed sum per annum, calculated in gold values, would give *approximately* the same return in quantities of armament to every country. As has been said already, the variations of output due to differences in the standard of living will be less than might be expected, because high wages almost always go with a greater efficiency of labour; and in any case such variations as do occur will not in practice greatly matter, because the standard of living does not often vary widely as between countries that are neighbours, and it is against neighbour countries that land armaments are made. Thus, for example, if Japan were able to produce 20 per cent more weapons than the United States for a fixed sum of money, the difference would in no way alarm the American public, while as between Japan and China the cost of production ought to be approximately the same.

A fixed annual appropriation for the arms and ammunition required for land armies, which alone are being now discussed,

---

[1] This occurred in November, 1925, and in large part, of course, was due to the wholly abnormal depreciation of the franc, and to the recent return by the British Government to the gold standard. The scheme under consideration can only be fairly considered on the hypothesis that the foreign exchanges of all countries are stabilized, as no doubt they shortly will be.

would thus adequately fulfil the first condition that is required of any armament limitation, that it shall give an approximately equal return per unit to all the signatory powers.

(2) In other ways, also, it seems to meet the requirements of the case. The exclusion from the annual appropriation of the cost of the maintenance of personnel and of such equipment and other charges as clothes, barracks, etc., clearly does not matter, for the factor of personnel has been already dealt with in another way; since the number of effectives to be kept by any country is fixed " on a numerical basis," it is of no military importance, and therefore, for the present purpose, of no account, how much or how little the Government of that country may spend upon their general upkeep. Similarly the exclusion of the cost of fortifications—apart, of course, from the guns with which they are provided—does not matter, since fortifications are only a factor of military strength for purposes of defence; they cannot be of use in aggression, and it is with the means of aggression that a disarmament treaty must be made to deal.

(3) Moreover, the method under discussion would give the Governments all the elasticity which they could possibly require. They would be free to spend the money exactly as they liked; what arms they chose to develop, what weapons they might buy, would fall within the province of their absolute discretion, provided only they did not exceed the total fixed appropriation for each thousand men. It is true that in the exercise of this freedom some general staffs might display a greater ability than others, that they might produce a greater military strength for their appropriated sums; in this respect the parties would take a risk which by the schedule method of the Peace Treaties they would avoid. But, apart from the chance invention of some new, cheap, and highly destructive weapon—a danger which under any system will exist—the risks they take are not abnormal and need not prevent agreement by the generality of states. They are no doubt greater than they would be under the Peace Treaty system if it were generally and integrally applied; but they are greater not so much because there will be freedom of choice as to whether more of one weapon than of

another shall be purchased, but because the range of permitted weapons will be wider.

(4) But, of course, the proposed system could be applied even if a very great restriction of permitted weapons had been previously agreed. Suppose, for example, that tanks and military aircraft and big guns and gas were altogether forbidden, and that only the classes of weapons prescribed by the Peace Treaties were allowed, the limitation of these classes could still be done by a total financial appropriation for every thousand men. There are thus two variations of the suggested method, involving greater and lesser sacrifices of the present liberty of action which Governments possess; or to put it in another way, the method is capable of application either to any list of permitted weapons that may be agreed, or without any such list at all, if no weapons of any kind are to be forbidden.

(*e*) But there remain a number of difficult questions to be answered, before it can be said that the method is practical or sound. In the first place, there is the question of putting it into operation at the beginning. How can this be done ? How can the armaments which states actually possess be dealt with ? Must there not in the nature of things be an initial list or schedule of what states are allowed to retain, and a destruction, under international supervision, similar to the destructions ordered by the Peace Treaties, of all armament above what is allowed ?

There must, in all probability, be an initial list as a starting point. In theory this is not absolutely essential. It *could* be agreed that every country should be allowed to retain for each thousand of its troops armament to the value of a fixed standard sum, which could either be a certain number of times its annual appropriation or a lump sum arranged by arbitrary negotiation. But this, of course, would involve making an agreed valuation in terms of gold of the price to be given to each weapon, and for this and other reasons it would probably in practice be even more complicated than drawing up a general schedule of what each state retained. It may be taken as almost certain, therefore, that it will be desirable to draw up such a schedule of all the arms which the parties respectively maintain, the schedule being the starting point by reference to

which it can be subsequently determined whether any state has
or has not exceeded its annual appropriation for addition or
replacement.

How then should this initial schedule be drawn up? It
depends entirely, of course, upon the general and particular
limitations of armament that are accepted.

If it is agreed that some classes of weapons, such as tanks,
etc., shall be abolished altogether, and that others shall be
much reduced in total quantity, then there must first be a
destruction under international supervision such as the Peace
Treaties imposed, and the initial schedule will consist of the
allotted numbers of a relatively short list of permitted weapons.

But if there are no particular limitations of armament agreed
to, if no weapons whatever are abolished, if the Governments
retain the freedom to spend their annual appropriations exactly
as they like, then the schedule must contain either the whole
of the armament which at present they respectively possess, or
else a fixed proportion of that armament, the retained weapons
being chosen by themselves. Probably in this case the simplest
plan would be to allow the Governments to retain all the armament they now possess, the whole of it being listed in the
schedule and constituting the amount of armament with which
they may respectively be equipped on the day when the disarmament treaty comes into force. If this were done, it
would not, of course, involve the permanent stereotyping of
the *status quo ;* for a certain period the existing scales of armament would be maintained, but as time went by, and weapons
became obsolete or went out of use, the scales would come to
depend upon the replacement allowed by the annual budgetary
appropriations. The first period would last a considerable
time, because the weapons used in land warfare do not become
obsolete or decay with great rapidity; and during this period
the quantities of armament which the contracting powers
respectively possessed would depend not upon the ratio among
them to which the Disarmament Conference agreed, but upon
the scales of armament which they possessed when the treaty
first came into force. This is an obvious disadvantage, but it is
temporary in its effect, and it is probable that it will be outweighed by the practical simplicity of the suggested plan.

It may thus be concluded on this difficult point of the initial schedule of permitted armament that the arrangements adopted in the treaty must depend on the general agreements about the restriction of weapons that are made. The initial schedule may register either the whole or a fixed proportion of the armament possessed by each contracting power when the treaty is drawn up. Probably, on the ground of simplicity, it will register the whole. If, however, it is agreed that it shall register only a fixed proportion of the whole, the remainder being forthwith destroyed under international supervision, then there must be a negotiation as to how large this fixed proportion ought to be. Obviously in this case the totals allotted to different states should correspond with the agreed ratio among them, and should accordingly bear a direct relation to the prescribed effectives which they are respectively allowed. Probably the most logical plan would be to allow to each country the armament which it would require if it mobilized—*i.e.*, as a maximum the armament needed to put in the field four times the number of its peace effectives. But, of course, this assumes an agreement as to the armament allowed per thousand men to the peace effectives themselves—and, as said before, this amount, which is the basic element in the limitation of armament, can only be agreed upon by means of a negotiation by the Governments on the basis of whatever detailed suggestions the Preparatory Committee or the Council may make.

(*f*) The next difficulty for consideration is whether the plan proposed for the limitation of armament could be made to cover not only weapons, but also the munitions with which those weapons are supplied.

It is obviously very desirable that it should do so; there could be no more effective way of reducing the temptation to an ambitious staff to go to war, for every military expert was convinced by the last war of the vast importance of the " weight of metal " doctrine. Moreover, a rigid limitation of munitions would, both by delaying decisions to go to war, and by rendering less destructive the opening stages of any hostilities that might begin, give the League of Nations the necessary time either to intervene by pacific means, or, if that were not enough, to make its coercive intervention more effective. It would also, if generally agreed to, make possible important economies in military expenditure, and would prevent another form of competition in military preparation.

There seems to be no insuperable difficulty in the plan of limiting munitions by means of a fixed budgetary appropriation, every contracting power agreeing that it will not spend upon them more than a certain permitted sum per thousand men per annum. It would no doubt be a less satisfactory form of limitation, and one that would be harder to control, than the Peace Treaty limitation " on a numerical basis " of the total rounds of ammunition allowed for every weapon. But the Peace Treaty method is only compatible with the general system of all-inclusive schedules, and the plan now being discussed is an alternative to that system, admittedly inferior, but necessary, if the Governments are unwilling to give up their present liberty in various important ways.

If, then, an attempt is to be made to limit munitions by a budgetary appropriation, there are two different ways in which this might be done. There might be a separate appropriation for the munitions allowed for every thousand men, supplementary to the fixed appropriation for weapons, the Governments being free to spend this supplementary appropriation on whatever forms of ammunition they might wish to make; or, alternatively, there might be a single appropriation for both weapons and munitions, the Governments being free to spend the whole on either weapons or munitions, or on any combination of the two, exactly as they liked. This second alternative has, of course, a greater apparent simplicity, though its faithful observance might be more difficult to control; probably, however, on the ground of its greater elasticity and the greater freedom it allows to general staffs, it would be preferred.

But, again, under either plan the budgetary limitation of munitions, like the budgetary limitation of weapons, must begin with an initial schedule of what the states are allowed to have when the disarmament treaty first comes into force. Otherwise there can be no means of knowing whether the quantities allowed to different Governments have been exceeded. And again, there must be a decision as to whether the whole of their existing stocks may be retained or whether part of them—and, if so, what part—must be destroyed under international supervision. Probably on this point it will be agreed, on grounds of practical convenience, to allow each state to retain the stocks of munitions which it possesses when the Disarmament Conference meets. The verification and destruction of part of the existing stocks would be a complicated business, and the objections to the maintenance of existing stocks are less strong in respect of munitions than in respect of weapons, because munitions become obsolete in a shorter time. The life of a shell is roughly ten years; after ten years from the time the treaty comes into force, therefore, the stocks of serviceable munitions of the parties will be those which they have made by the expenditure of their annual appropriations, and the quantities which they respectively possess will thus correspond directly to the ratio of strength agreed between them. This result will probably in fact be brought about within less than ten years, owing to the specially favourable circumstances of the present time. Every big army is now furnished with the stocks of munitions which it built up during the Great War, and which it had on its hands when the war came to a sudden end. These stocks were so vast, and the financial difficulties of the Governments ever since the war have been so serious, that no replacement of munitions, no new production on a large scale, has yet been begun. But the war stocks will be virtually useless by 1928—*i.e.*, within a very short time after the disarmament treaty, however quickly it be made, comes into force. Unless, therefore, there is a great new production of munitions between now and the date when the Disarmament Conference meets, which seems most unlikely, a reduction and limitation of munitions can be effectively brought about by the method of budgetary appropriation, even if the initial schedule permits the maintenance of the whole of the then existing stocks.

There remains the question as to the scale of the annual replacement of munitions which should be allowed, or in other words, of the total stocks which Governments will be permitted at any given moment to retain. After the early stages, this will depend on the size of the budgetary appropriation which is made for every thousand men. What standard should be kept in view when the size of this appropriation is decided ?

The civilian will be inclined to answer that the smaller the appropriation the better the results, and no doubt a strong case could be made for this view. But the military expert will probably hold that the point should be settled on the basis of the principles already agreed to. Since mobilization may be permitted, or even required, on behalf of the League of Nations, staffs must be allowed the munitions which they need to carry it out; and if the quantity of their armament has been already fixed on the rough basis of an annual sum of money, military experts will easily be able to agree on the quantity of munitions needed for this armament when mobilization occurs. Thus a technical negotiation between military experts of different countries will give without great difficulty the desired result.

It is quite likely that in practice this will be the way in which in fact the budgetary appropriation for munitions will be fixed. But as to the principle involved, there is no reason why the Preparatory Committee or the Council of the League should, unless they want to, adopt in their proposals the suggestion made above. An army can be mobilized with a greater or a lesser amount of ammunition. There is nothing sacred in the current practice of general staffs, who of course desire, and have always desired, to have available the maximum quantity of material which their troops can use in the early stages of a war. There is, indeed, no reason why the budgetary appropriation for munitions should not be fixed at some figure which in the light of past military experience might seem quite arbitrary, but which, since it would be the same for all countries, would serve the purpose quite as well as a figure based on some " scientific " elaboration. And unless there is ground for fearing that a disloyal power might be able to build up vast secret stocks of munitions so much greater than those possessed by loyal powers that the latter would be virtually at its mercy, there is every advantage in setting the munitions appropriation at as low a figure as the Governments can be persuaded to accept. But, of course, in this as in all questions connected with this vital matter of limiting weapons and munitions, the essential question is that of the faithful observance of the limitations that may be agreed. Whether the plan now being discussed would be satisfactory in this respect will shortly be considered.

(g) Another difficulty which must first be dealt with and which is inherent in the proposed method (as indeed in every method) of limiting armament and ammunition arises from the fact that some countries have great colonial responsibilities in backward parts of the world, and that in the discharge of their duty to keep the peace in their colonial possessions they are sometimes obliged to take warlike action on a greater or a smaller scale. The fact may be unpleasant, but it must be faced if any limitation of arms or munitions is to be secured. No colonial power would agree to any scheme that did not make allowance for its needs in this respect. Colonial powers must be given special increases over and above their normal allowance for the defence of the mother country whenever they are obliged in their colonies to take extraordinary punitive or preventive action.

How can this be done ? It is obviously not possible on this account to allocate to every colonial power a special additional appropriation every year. That plan would be essentially unjust to non-colonial powers; it would never be accepted by them, and since the scale of colonial expeditions cannot be foreseen, it would not even in many cases meet the requirements of the colonial powers themselves. Some other scheme must, therefore, be devised for dealing with this important and recurring need.

It may be suggested that no previously established treaty allocation can possibly meet the requirements of the case; that it is equally impossible to leave full liberty of discretion to the contracting powers to make whatever increases in their arms or ammunition they may wish to have whenever trouble breaks out in their colonial possessions; and that therefore the only satisfactory system must involve impartial decision by an international body concerning the extra increases that shall be allowed. There seems to be no reason why the Council of the League should not be charged with the task of deciding both when such increases should be permitted and what their extent should be. It would have no difficulty in securing the technical advice necessary for this purpose from its Permanent

Advisory Commission on military affairs. It is true that asking for such increases would not be a very pleasant business for a colonial power, for the reason that wars against subject peoples always bring a certain odium upon a Government that undertakes them. This fact, however, might act as a healthy check upon the colonial powers, and might stimulate their efforts to prevent unnecessary or unjust military action. And when such action is genuinely necessary, as no doubt it sometimes is, for the maintenance of peace and order, there is no reason why a colonial power should have any sense of shame in asking the Council of the League to allow a special increase in its armament, nor any reason why the Council should hesitate to grant it. It would, indeed, afford to the colonial power an admirable opportunity of defending its policy before the opinion of the world; and if its case were sound, the increase allowed by the Council would correspond in nature exactly to the suspension of the disarmament treaty that would be needed if the Members of the League were called upon to co-operate in joint military action against an aggressor state. The making of such decisions would no doubt be yet another difficult and thankless task imposed upon the Council, and one that might expose it to bitter and widespread criticism. But there seems to be no satisfactory alternative plan for dealing with the unpleasant but important problem raised by colonial wars.

Increases allowed by the Council would, of course, as a rule be retrospective; they would simply allow an abnormally large sum of money for replacement purposes in any given year when colonial operations had taken place.

(*h*) It is now necessary to return to the fundamental difficulty of controlling the observance of any limitations of armament and munitions that may be made by the method of budgetary appropriation now being discussed. Is the plan proposed satisfactory in this respect ? If it is adopted, will the contracting powers have any confidence that their neighbours, and it may be rivals, are faithfully observing the undertakings they have given ? And if, in fact, some state is disloyal to its pledges, if it builds up in secret excess stocks of arms and ammunition, can it be hoped that these excess stocks will be discovered before it is too late to stop the criminal attack for which they are intended? It has been said above that the answers to these questions are vital to any scheme of disarmament that can be devised, and to every part of any scheme.

They are questions not only of great importance but of great difficulty, so far as the limitation of armament and ammunition is concerned. This limitation will no doubt be the most difficult part of any disarmament treaty to control. Excessive numbers of effectives cannot be efficiently organized in secret; but secret hordes of weapons and of shells can be built up and are far harder to detect. The experience of the Allied Commissions of Control in Germany has shown that not even the rigid and comprehensive system of Versailles is sufficient to prevent breaches of a disarmament treaty in this respect, if the Government authorities of the disarmed country are not animated by a spirit of goodwill. Indeed, in this matter of armament and ammunition general goodwill without doubt will be the essential factor in the satisfactory working of any plan, and unless and until mutual confidence and goodwill have been created, there will be breaches of the treaty on a certain scale, whatever scheme of supervision may be drawn up.

But there is no reason to think that such breaches would be unduly great under the suggested limitation by budgetary appropriation. The additional elasticity of the system, the additional freedom which the Governments would retain, would no doubt make it more difficult than it would be under the system of Versailles to detect whether any given Government was spending more upon armament and ammunition than it was legitimately entitled to expend. But although it would be difficult, it ought by no means to be impossible, if the necessary supplementary arrangements were accepted.

The most important of these supplementary arrangements is the adoption by all the contracting parties of a common model for their military budgets. The whole essence of the scheme of armament limitation now being discussed lies in the rigid separation of military expenditure into different chapters—Maintenance of Personnel, Construction and Maintenance of Fortifications and other Works, Provision of Weapons and Ammunition—one of which is to be separately limited and controlled. It is most desirable, therefore, if the control of this one chapter is to be efficient, that the whole method of accounting for military expenditure of every kind should be identical in every signatory country, and that the present divergences of practice, discussed in Chapter V above, should be removed. This is not necessarily indispensable to the success of the present proposal, but it would, in obvious and important ways, facilitate control. And there seems no valid reason why the contracting powers, if they seriously desire to reduce the burden of their armaments, should not agree to adopt a common model budget and common methods of accountancy for their expenditure on national defence.

But even if this were done, there would still remain a double danger: first, that the civil Government of a country should secretly divert part of its ordinary budget for civilian purposes to the purchase of arms and ammunition; second, that the military authorities, possibly in some countries without even the knowledge of the civil Government, should divert sums voted in other chapters of the military budget to this purpose.

Against these dangers there would be safeguards of two kinds.

First, the general staff of every country, knowing, as it would, through the League of Nations Exchange of Information, through its military attachés, and through its secret service agents, the general organization of the armies of its neighbour states and the sources from which they procure their supplies of arms and ammunition, would be able to calculate with very little error the quantities of armament of different kinds which each of them ought to be able, with its allotted budgetary appropriation, to provide. If, therefore, on information from these sources any general staff had reason to suspect that any of its neighbours was purchasing more armament than could be paid for by its appropriation, it could then demand an investigation by the League of Nations. The system of mutual control to be set up will be discussed in a later chapter; it is enough to say here that no system could be adequate which did not ensure the right of full investigation into the armament expenditure and accounts of any state by the impartial and expert agents of the League, on the demand of any other contracting party which could make a *prima facie* case for holding that a violation of the agreed armament limitation had occurred.

Second, there is the safeguard that practically every civilized country in the world is now governed by ministers dependent on the support of freely elected Parliaments; that these ministers have to secure sanction for their expenditure of every kind from their Parliaments; that they would therefore have to explain and defend in parliamentary debate the whole of their military budgets; that this would give the opportunity in every country to socialist and other Members in whose eyes the strict fulfilment of international pledges is the first element in patriotism and national honour, to examine these budgets in the fullest detail, to decide, often in the light of their own administrative experience, whether the treaty obligations in respect of armament had been observed, and, if they were not satisfied, to demand fuller information on the point. It is true that there are still countries where at the present time budgets are not submitted to full parliamentary discussion and control;[1] but to cover such cases it might well be provided in the treaty that every signatory power should undertake to publish its whole military budget and to submit it to public debate in its legislative or other national assembly. No Government could refuse such a proposal at the Disarmament Conference without throwing itself under grave suspicion of bad faith.

It may be objected to this argument that no Member of Parliament would, in fact, be able in this way to discover breaches of the treaty obligations unless they were on the greatest scale. But it must be remembered, first, that in most countries the budget is submitted to most searching examination and criticism in parliamentary committees composed largely of the political opponents of the Government of the day; second, that any Member who accused the Government of bad faith would not have to rely only on his own resources in finding out the truth. He would, in all civilized and democratic countries, be supported by a great body of citizens who, in the normal pursuit of their daily avocations, would obtain information that would enable them to assist him on the point. It would, for example, be difficult, to say the least, for any Government to

[1] Italy, Spain, Greece, Japan, Russia.

build up secret stores of shells or weapons without working men of many categories being " in the know." All armaments, indeed, of every kind are made and handled at every stage by working men, and the Trade Unions to which these working men belong would not hesitate to help anyone who was seeking to oblige a disloyal Government to observe the pledges it had made. Anyone familiar with the attitude of the German workers towards the disarmament of their country in 1919 will know that this is true, and that it is a factor of the first importance in the whole question of armament control. The fact that the goodwill of the German workers was rapidly destroyed by the continuation of the Allied blockade and by other parts of the Allied policy towards their country does not invalidate the point.

To overlook the power of the organized workers to help in carrying out armament restrictions would, therefore, be a grave mistake. It would be no less foolish to neglect the factor of the general goodwill that will be created in every country by a disarmament treaty. The body of opinion in every democratic state favourable to the honest execution of armament limitation will be a great and growing power, and its influence on both Parliaments and Governments must be taken seriously into account when an attempt is made to estimate the chances of the successful working of the budgetary appropriation plan now being discussed.

There is, moreover, another way in which the working of the plan proposed could be made both simpler and more effective, if the Governments were willing to accept the restrictions which it would involve: the insertion in the disarmament treaty of provisions for the full publicity of the accounts of all armament firms or other establishments, public or private, in which arms and ammunition are produced. This suggestion will be considered in more detail when the general subject of the private manufacture of, and traffic in, arms comes to be discussed.[1] For the moment it is enough to say that it would again be very difficult for any country to resist this proposal if it were put forward at the Disarmament Conference, and that, if it were agreed to, it would much facilitate the control of the

[1] Cf. chap. xvi., *infra.*

limitation of armament and ammunition by the system of budgetary appropriation.

It may be concluded, then, that there are reasonable grounds for hoping that this system of budgetary appropriation would prevent any large-scale violation of treaty restrictions on arms and ammunition. In some countries where the sense of national honour is rudimentary or perverted, minor breaches would probably occur, but if they were on any considerable scale their neighbour states would not hesitate to demand a League investigation, from which budgetary diversion or other disloyal manœuvres could only be concealed by a measure of good fortune on which no Government, however reckless, would dare to count.

A few words may conveniently be said at this point on the chief advantage of the plan of armament limitation that has been proposed. It is this : that by attaching to the factor of armament a fixed money appropriation that must be voted every year, it would focus on it the attention of the tax-payers and of the representatives of the tax-payers in national Parliaments. It would thus create the maximum degree of parliamentary pressure, not only for the strict observance of the limits first laid down, but also—what is even more important—for subsequent and increased reductions in those limits. Moreover, by its very elasticity it would make it easier to secure such subsequent reductions as the years went by and general confidence increased. In many ways, as was said above, this method is less satisfactory than the Peace Treaty system of schedule limitation of the actual weapons and munitions allowed for every thousand men. But it has this advantage over the Peace Treaty system, that it would no doubt be simpler to secure general agreement for a 10 per cent or a 25 per cent reduction in a standard money sum than it would be to get such agreement for, say, an equivalent reduction in the number of permitted tanks and guns.

In addition, the proposed system has this further advantage, common both to it and to the more rigid Peace Treaty system, that the smaller the standard appropriation that is allowed, the more efficiently will it work. Not only will greater economies be obtained, not only will the risk of competition in various kinds of armament be removed, not only will the dangers of incipient hostilities, if they should happen, be much less, but with every reduction that is effected, the whole thing will become easier—and much easier—to control. This is plainly so; the less money there is in the annual appropriation, the less the arms and ammunition that ought to be in existence, the more easily will excessive production be found out.

Again, and in a similar way, the prohibition of any class of weapon—tanks, gas, big guns, etc.—would *pro tanto* make mutual supervision and control easier and more effective under the system of limitation that has been proposed. This system thus fits in with all the main objectives which it is the purpose of a disarmament treaty to secure. Although, therefore, it may be less satisfactory than would be the general application of the Peace Treaty system, it may fairly be said that it might be an adequate second best.

8. *Limitation of Total Army Budget.*—It may be asked why, if it is expected that the limitation of armament by budgetary appropriation would work so easily and well, the same plan should not be applied to army budgets as a whole. The answer is that the limitation of armament will only work easily and well if the budgetary appropriations are relatively very low, that the limitation of total budgets is a more complicated and difficult affair, but that none the less, if certain conditions are fulfilled, there is no conclusive reason why it should not be attempted, and some reasons why it should.

The limiting conditions are two.

First, it is essential that the financial limitation of the total army budget should be made *in addition to*, and not instead of, the limitation of armament above proposed. In other words, there would be laid down in the treaty two separate budgetary appropriations, one, as above, for arms and ammunition alone, the other for remaining army costs. This is necessary, because otherwise there will be virtually no way of controlling the amount of armament which countries may possess, and without such control, it has been argued, no disarmament system can inspire the general confidence that is essential to success. But if the double appropriation were laid down, then of course the limitation of the total budget could only help to make the limitation of armament yet more effective. For obviously a control of the total budget would make it easier to detect the diversion of money from its proper purpose to the secret production of excessive armament.

Second, it is essential that no attempt should be made, like that of the Soviet Government at the Moscow Conference in 1922,[1] to lay down a fixed standard appropriation per man or per thousand men, which every country would be asked not to exceed. It has been explained above that, owing to differences in army organization and in the national standards of living, a given sum of money gives very different quantities of military strength in different countries. An attempt, therefore, to impose a standard appropriation per thousand men would meet a double difficulty; if it were calculated on the costs of a country with a *high* standard of living, it would achieve little or no general result; if it were calculated on the costs of a country with a *low* standard of living, it would involve grave injustice to the richer states. For this reason, it is necessary that if total budgets are limited, the limitation for each country must be based on the average expenditure per thousand men which —apart from the cost of arms and ammunition—the upkeep of its own army has in the past involved. The calculation for each country could either be made on its budget figure for the last year before the disarmament treaty came into force, or for some year before the Great War—*e.g.*, 1913—or on an average of the figures over a given period of years. Before the calculations could be made at all it would, of course, be necessary to redraft all the budgets in accordance with the kind of standard model above referred to; this would be the only way to get rid of the misleading differences in methods of accounting described in Chapter VI. The process of thus redrafting the budgets of past years would be a heavy and complicated task, but one that it would, no doubt, be possible to carry out.

If this plan were followed, therefore, each country would be allowed to spend upon the upkeep of each thousand of its permitted effectives, for all purposes other than the purchase of arms and ammunition, a fixed percentage—the same for all

[1] Cf. chap. vii., *supra.*

the signatory powers—of that which it had previously spent in some given year or years.[1] A supplementary provision would, of course, be needed to the effect that if a country changed its military system—for example, from a voluntary army to conscription—if it lowered its rates of army pay, or if in some other way it altered the previous standards of its costs, a corresponding change would then be made in the appropriation which it would thereafter be allowed. The actual percentage of previous expenditure to be permitted would be settled by a negotiation at the Disarmament Conference; again it would be true that the lower the rate of expenditure allowed, the more easily could its observance be controlled.

It has been said before that if the effectives of an army and its armament and ammunition are limited by treaty, additional expenditure upon its upkeep will not give an increase in its *aggressive* power. For this reason the limitation of total army budgets on the plan described is not an essential part of a disarmament scheme. But, though not essential, it may be none the less desirable. It would fit in well with the general plan of the treaty which has been proposed; it would be elastic in the restrictions which it would impose on the liberty of Governments; it would concentrate parliamentary attention on another aspect of the cost of armed forces; it would provide an easy mechanism for other repeated and progressive reductions in the economic burden which they cause; it would render more effective the control of the budgetary appropriation for the vital factor of arms and ammunition; it would *pro tanto*—and if the total appropriations were much reduced it would to a great degree—prevent the building up of large and well-trained reserves in addition to the standing peace-effectives that are prescribed. Being supplementary to the system of Versailles— for that has no such budget limitation—it would in part at least make up for and replace some of the more rigid limitations of

---

[1] An alternative to this proposal would be to work out some general standard appropriation per thousand men applicable to all contracting powers, subject to allowances made in accordance with the average standard of living, rates of army pay for officers and men, etc., in the different countries. On the whole the plan proposed in the text seems much simpler, and, since the factors of man-power and armament are to be dealt with in other ways, equally effective.

the Peace Treaties which other Governments will not now accept.

For these reasons it may be hoped that the limitation of total army budgets by some such scheme as that proposed will at least be considered with proper care before it is rejected.

9. *Vehicles.*—One other factor in the military strength of land forces must be mentioned—the means of army transportation. There is no doubt that vehicles of various kinds—animal transport, motor transport, tractor and caterpillar transport— play a great part in the efficient organization and manœuvring of a modern army. Of two opposing forces, equal in all other ways, that with the better transport would have a great and perhaps, in circumstances that can be conceived, a decisive advantage in the field. Is it necessary, then, to include in the disarmament treaty some special limitation of the amount of transportation which the various armies may respectively maintain ?

It would, no doubt, be theoretically desirable to do so. But on practical grounds it may be wiser not to try. Transport, in spite of its increased importance, is still only a factor of the second rate; so much so, indeed, that it is neglected altogether in the Treaty of Versailles. Moreover, it would be included in the general limitations of man-power and also of the army budget, if the plan suggested in the previous paragraph were carried out. Modern means of transport are costly in the extreme both in men and money; if total army funds were limited, there would be no danger that great transport systems would be built up. It may be concluded, therefore, that no special limitation of vehicles need be inserted in the disarmament treaty.

10. *Colonial Armies.*—It was said above that there is general agreement that some limitation must be devised for the strength and equipment of colonial forces.[1] Lord Esher's system of leaving to colonial powers freedom to maintain as large colonial armies as they like could only be justified if such armies did not add in any way to the military strength of the mother countries. In fact no such justification could be made for the colonial forces which some states to-day maintain.

This being so, the Temporary Mixed Commission laid down

[1] Cf. chap. vii., *supra.*

the principles by which they suggested that the question of colonial armies might be solved.[1] They proposed first that, since colonial forces have their own distinct and legitimate functions to perform, they should be dealt with in " a special agreement supplementary to the general reduction agreement." This supplementary agreement would no doubt be very similar in form to the general treaty, if not indeed identically the same; it would contain a limitation of effectives and of armament; it would establish the same fixed proportion between the two; it might be signed either as a distinct international instrument by the colonial powers alone, or as a separate but integral part of the general treaty, signed by all the contracting countries.   Probably the latter would be the better course, as the existence and the strength of colonial forces of course concern not only those countries which possess them, but every country which is intending to disarm.

As for the strength of the colonial forces which would be allowed, the Temporary Mixed Commission's principles are again important. They defined colonial forces as those " acknowledged to be necessary for the occupation or defence of colonies," and which would therefore be " unable to take part in the defence of the mother-country." It is true that these principles are somewhat vague, and that a negotiation would be required both between the colonial powers themselves and between the colonial and the non-colonial powers to settle the actual scale of the forces to be allowed.   But there are many colonial possessions throughout the world where, for the reasons mentioned in Chapter VII, the armed units have been kept down to the absolute minimum essential for keeping the peace and protecting the frontiers.   There would therefore be no lack of previous working standards by reference to which the Temporary Mixed Commission's principle could be applied.

It must be admitted that the application of these principles to the reduction and limitation of British colonial forces, and of that part of the British army which is devoted to policing colonies, seems at first sight to present a complex problem. But in fact the strength maintained in most British colonies is fairly near the minimum required for keeping peace; there is

[1] Cf. chap. vii., *supra*.

very little margin, as was shown at the outbreak of war in 1914, for ordinary international warfare, whether of aggression or defence. Even including those parts of the standing British Army proper which are maintained in fact for colonial defence, we should probably have no difficulty in satisfying the demands whether of other colonial powers or of other ordinary states participating in the Disarmament Conference. India, of course, which is now virtually a Dominion in international status, would have to be dealt with as a separate signatory of the general treaty, and not as a colony at all.

There is no need to point out the great advantages that would follow from an agreement on these lines about colonial forces. Such an agreement will not be easy to obtain; but if it were obtained, it would at one blow wipe out one of the great dangers of Imperialism, and would put an end, among other things, to the use of Black armies in European affairs, and to the militarization of the African native which is so grave a menace at the present time.

11. *Summary.*—A summary may now be made of the suggestions for a scheme of land disarmament put forward in this chapter.

On the assumption that the general application of the Peace Treaty system would not be accepted, it has been proposed that a treaty including the following provisions should be made:

(i.) The peace-time effectives of the standing armies should be limited " on a numerical basis." This limitation should cover all ranks of every branch of the army and its services.

(ii.) Auxiliary forces (armed police, forest guards, Customs officials, etc.) should be limited in accordance with the principles of the Peace Treaty system, special arrangements being made for those few countries which maintain particularly large and well-trained forces of that sort.

(iii.) An attempt should be made to secure general acceptance for the scheme of tactical organization contained in the three later Treaties of Peace. This attempt is unlikely to be successful; in any case, the point is not essential to a workable scheme.

(iv.) For the purpose of limiting reserves, the maximum proportion of officers should be limited to one-twentieth of the permitted effectives, of non-commissioned officers to one-fifteenth; and the number of military academies and training schools should be restricted in a fixed proportion to the total prescribed effectives of each state. The general prohibition of foreign military missions and of foreign enlistment should, if possible, be obtained.

(v.) The length of service in conscription countries should, if possible, be limited to the shortest period for which agreement can be obtained, but this again, while most desirable, is not essential to a workable scheme.

(vi.) The strength of Territorial forces and Militias should be limited first by an agreed restriction on the annual training which they may be given every year, second, by fixing an agreed proportion between the number of prescribed effectives and the number of permitted Territorials. Special arrangements should be made to increase the proportion of Territorials allowed to non-conscription countries.

(vii.) For the limitation of the arms with which the permitted troops may be equipped, either the system of the Peace Treaties should be applied, or, if that is impossible, as it almost certainly will be, a fixed annual sum of money should be allowed every year to each signatory power for the equipment of each thousand of its men.

In addition an attempt should be made to secure general agreement for the prohibition of as many as possible of the modern weapons of war, such as tanks, etc., which add greatly to the destructiveness of warfare and to the cost of preparation for it.

The annual budgetary appropriation per thousand men allowed for the provision of arms should cover ammunition as well as weapons.

(viii.) In addition to fixing a maximum annual appropriation for arms and ammunition, it may be desirable—though again it is not essential—also to limit the total army budgets of the signatory states. This limitation should be based on the past expenditure of each state, in order to allow for the varying factors of army organization and national standards of living.

(ix.) For colonial armies a special supplementary agreement should be made, if possible as part of the general treaty.

These are principles by the application of which it should be possible, if the Governments have serious intentions in the matter, to make a general treaty of disarmament on land. Such a treaty, if not perfect, would yet achieve a great part of the purposes for which disarmament is desired.

But it is plain that these principles do not cover the whole problem even of land armaments. There are other questions of which nothing has yet been said—the manufacture of armaments, their sale at home and abroad, mutual control over the observance of the treaty—questions evidently vital to the successful working of any limitation of any kind. But these questions affect not only land armaments, but also naval and aerial armaments in an equal if not in a greater degree. Their consideration may, therefore, usefully be postponed until naval and aerial disarmament have been discussed.

It is also true that even if everything suggested in this chapter were wholly carried out, there would still remain to be dealt with other grave dangers connected with the use of armaments on land. There would remain above all the question of chemical warfare—a danger so grave that a distinguished expert has said that the whole military clauses of the Treaty of Versailles are irrelevant to the real problem of the future. Chemical warfare will be discussed at a later stage. In the meantime, it is enough to say that up till to-day it has been upon the factors of military strength discussed in this chapter that the powers have lavished their treasure and their organizing skill. Unless and until these factors are reduced and limited by some such plans as those put forward here, there can be no disarmament worthy of the name. They are the first objective, whatever else may lie further on behind.

CHAPTER X

NAVAL ARMAMENTS—EXISTING TREATIES

THERE is a prevalent idea that the problem of naval armaments was disposed of by the Washington Conference of 1921. That idea is false. There is at the present moment a naval competition going on almost as intense and almost as costly as that which was ended by the Washington Conference. It is among the Great Powers that this new naval competition has become particularly keen, but it is not only they who are concerned. Among the smaller powers as well some could be named which are imperilling their future economic prosperity by a policy of naval expansion, without adding to their national safety in any way. A new treaty of naval disarmament, therefore, is required— a treaty which shall be " general " in both senses of the word, which shall cover every class of fighting ship, and include among its signatories all naval powers, actual or potential, throughout the world.

The making of such a general naval treaty ought, for two reasons, to be much easier than the making of a treaty of land disarmament. First, there are already in existence two model treaties, one of each kind—one, that is to say, of unilateral disarmament enforced by victor states upon a vanquished power, the other of mutual disarmament voluntarily accepted by the five naval leaders of the world. Second, naval disarmament is, in itself, a simpler technical problem than the disarmament of land or air forces—simpler, because, in naval armaments, the doctrine of the " dominant factor " comes so near to being true that a treaty which limits warships and the guns they carry, neglecting all other factors of naval strength, will virtually solve the problem. A few words will show why this is so.

First, a warship can only use a limited number of men. It may not maintain its full establishment in time of peace, but if its crew are to be efficient for purposes of war, it must main-

tain a great proportion of them. And, once its full war complement has been made up, it has no need of any more reserves.
If some of its crew are killed or wounded in action, their vessel
will almost certainly be damaged also, and reserves for replacement will therefore not be needed. In short, a navy has little
need of trained reserves to replace or to augment its fighting
crews in time of war.

Second, a navy can only use in time of war the weapons with
which it is equipped in time of peace. Ships are always fitted
with all the guns which they are built to carry, and additions
to them mean structural changes, which, if they are possible
at all, would put a vessel out of action for a lengthy period of
time.

Third, the fighting ships which a state can use in time of war
are those and those only which it has in time of peace. Their
numbers cannot suddenly be increased by the construction of
new units. Even the smallest fighting craft take many months
to build, and every important unit of attack takes so long that
a war would almost certainly be over before it could be finished.

Fourth, a Government cannot build or keep in secret fighting
ships which under a disarmament treaty it is not allowed to
have. The construction or existence of a fighting ship of any
kind cannot be successfully concealed.

Fifth, naval ships and weapons, unlike some important
weapons of land and air warfare, have no peace-time use.
Thus there are not in existence, if war breaks out, large
reserve supplies which can be suddenly diverted from civil to
military use.

It may be concluded, therefore, that the war-strength of a
navy is to all intents and purposes the same as its peace-strength,
and that its peace-strength cannot be concealed. From that it
follows that the signatories to a treaty of naval disarmament
may be certain that its clauses will in fact secure the result
which they are intended to secure. And this is not doctrine
only, as the Treaty of Versailles has shown. While innumerable
difficulties have arisen in the execution of the land clauses of
that treaty, there has not once been a dispute about the naval
clauses. In this way also, therefore, a naval treaty is simpler
than a land treaty, that it will inspire full confidence in those

who sign it, that its terms will be faithfully observed, and that they cannot lead to any unforeseen or dangerous surprise.

Again, it may be simpler for the further reason, already mentioned, that various factors—for example, reserve personnel and reserve weapons—can, if necessary, be neglected. Whether in fact it may be wiser to neglect them will be later on discussed.

Similarly, the problem of naval disarmament is comparatively simple in its second technical aspect—*i.e.*, in the measurement and comparison of the naval strength of different countries. Navies can be measured and compared with great exactitude by the guns and tonnage of their ships, for on these two factors their effective fighting strength depends. These factors, moreover, permit measurements which can quite simply be written down in the schedules of an international treaty.

It must be added, however, that there are two points that are of much more importance in connection with naval than with other kinds of armaments: first, the international traffic in arms is obviously so, since the sudden and unrestricted sale of fighting ships from one power to another might make a disarmament treaty no better than a dangerous farce; second, fortifications and naval bases, which plainly have a particular importance in the offensive power of naval forces. But there is no reason to doubt that if a general agreement can be made about ships themselves, it will be quite easy to deal also with these questions of traffic and bases. It is therefore fair to say that, apart from the negotiation of the ratio of naval strength between the different contracting parties, there is no other question which should be of much difficulty or which should greatly complicate the negotiation of the schedules in which the ratio agreement will be written down.

Of existing treaties of naval disarmament, only the two mentioned above need be described. Between them they should furnish adequate guidance for the drafting of a general treaty. The Treaty of Versailles may be taken first; both chronologically and logically it ought to come before the Washington Convention.

The Treaty of Versailles.—The authors of the naval clauses of the Treaty of Versailles followed the example of their army colleagues in limiting, so far as it was possible to do so by treaty, every factor of German naval strength, and in inserting every provision which they believed would help to keep that strength permanently and effectively at the limit which was allowed. It follows from the arguments above that there are in naval warfare no " Periods A " and " B "; but if there were, the treaty clauses could no doubt be fairly said to limit German naval strength in both.

A brief analysis of these clauses may be useful.

1. *Limitation of Fighting Ships.*—(i.) The naval section of the treaty begins by a list of the fighting units which the German navy is permitted to retain. It includes four classes only:

(*a*) Six battleships of the Deutschland or Lothringen type.
(*b*) Six light cruisers.
(*c*) Twelve destroyers.
(*d*) Twelve torpedo boats.

The individual ships may be replaced, on certain conditions, which will be considered in a moment, but the total strength must never exceed that shown above. Limitation, it may be noted, is not made by tonnage, but by a definite schedule of permitted units. Since, however, in the replacement clauses there are rigid limits on the size of the ships that may be built, the point is one of form and not of substance.

(ii.) All the other fighting ships in the possession of the German Government were handed over to the Allied powers for disposal. The treaty gives a list by name of the battleships and cruisers handed over; for destroyers and torpedo boats it simply provides that forty-two and fifty units respectively of these two classes, to be chosen by the Governments of the Allies, should be surrendered.[1]

As is well known, the warships that were handed over were, in fact, sunk by their German crews. There is little doubt that in any case they would have been destroyed.

(iii.) All the ships of war under construction for the German Government when the treaty came into force were broken up. This, of course, was only a necessary consequence of the limitation of Germany's total naval strength above referred to.[2]

[1] Arts. 184 and 185.   [2] Art. 186.

(iv.) It was next provided that the German auxiliary cruisers and fleet auxiliaries—a list of thirty-two is given by name—should be disarmed and treated for the future as merchant ships.[1] Fleet auxiliaries did not need to be destroyed, for, of course, they were not really ships of war at all. They were only merchant vessels taken over by the navy and fitted with guns enough to enable them to fulfil the duties of fleet supply in time of war.

2. *Restriction of Weapons.*—Naval weapons are restricted by the treaty almost as stringently as land and air weapons. Thus, the German fleet is deprived of all its modern ships; it may not for the future possess any unit that could live for a single hour with the great fighting ships of the other navies of the world.

(i.) As has been said, only four classes of ships are allowed: battleships (that is to say, armoured ships), light cruisers, destroyers, and torpedo boats.

(ii.) Every unit in these four classes must be far smaller and less powerful than the ships now built for other navies. The displacement limits laid down are as follows:

Armed ships	10,000 tons.
Light cruisers	6,000 ,,
Destroyers	800 ,,
Torpedo boats	200 ,,[2]

(iii.) In addition to these general restrictions the German navy may possess no submarines of any kind, nor may any under-water unit be constructed or acquired by Germany " even for commercial purposes."[3]

(iv.) The German navy must have no aircraft of any kind. The aeroplane has already made so profound a difference in all questions of naval strategy and tactics that this restriction alone imposes a fatal handicap upon the German fleet.

3. *Armament and Ammunition.*—(i.) The treaty further provides that the ships of war which Germany has been allowed to keep may have on board or in reserve only that allowance of arms, ammunition, and war material which the Allied powers

---

[1] Art. 187.   [2] Art. 190.   [3] Arts. 181 and 191.

may fix. It is clear, therefore—and this is the point which matters—that the Allied experts thought it worth their while not only to limit the German ships, but to limit also the arms and munitions with which those ships might be equipped. These provisions apply, of course, to mines and to torpedoes of all kinds.

(ii.) All such arms, munitions, and war material over and above what the Allied powers allowed Germany to retain were " destroyed or rendered useless."

(iii.) All stocks, depôts, or reserves of arms and ammunition not specifically permitted by the Allies are strictly forbidden by the treaty.[1]

These provisions follow very closely those of the land disarmament clauses, and the arguments in their favour are the same. Of course, the amount of ammunition with which a navy is supplied, and the reserves which it maintains, may be as important to its offensive power during Period A as are munitions to the attacking strength of an army operating on dry land. For this reason the limitation of munitions must be carefully considered in connection with a general treaty.

4. *Ships in Reserve.*—It is plain from the general provisions already dealt with that Germany may not have ships in reserve which she could place in service if war broke out. To make assurance doubly sure, the general limitations are supplemented by a clause prohibiting the use of all " articles, machinery, and material, arising from the breaking-up of German warships of all kinds," from being used except for purely industrial or commercial purposes.[2]

5. *Replacement of Ships.*—The replacement of permitted ships is, of course, of great importance in a naval treaty. Warships, like other weapons, become obsolescent; after a period of years, they may need to be replaced. The replacement permitted by the Treaty of Versailles allows Germany to substitute, after a fixed interval of time, new vessels of a certain size for those of the various classes shown above. Thus, after *twenty years*, she may replace her six battleships of the Deutschland or Lothringen type, and her six light cruisers, by new units which, as said above, must not exceed respectively 10,000 and 6,000

[1] Art. 192.   [2] Art. 189.

tons. Similarly, *after fifteen years*, she may replace her destroyers and torpedo boats by units that must not exceed respectively 800 and 200 tons. In every case, the period of fifteen or twenty years shall be counted from the date at which the ship was launched. It is worth noting that the Allies thus imposed upon Germany the same period of obsolescence for armoured ships which they themselves accepted in the Washington Convention.

It should be added that if a ship is lost by accident, it may be replaced forthwith by a new unit, not larger than the standard size laid down.

It should also be noted that new ships, which replace obsolete units of the German navy, come under the general stipulations of Article 192, which limit the armament, munitions, and other war material of every ship to that which is allowed by the Allies.

6. *Naval Personnel.*—The man-power permitted by the treaty to the German navy is limited to a total of 15,000 men, who must include not only the staff and crews of the fleet itself, but also the personnel of coast defence, signal stations, administration, all the land services of the fleet, and all officers and men of every grade and corps.[1]

7. *Reserves of Man-Power.*—The provisions of the treaty about reserves of man-power for the German fleet are as elaborate and stringent as those about reserves for the German army, and, indeed, *mutatis mutandis*, they are almost identically the same.

(i.) To begin with " no naval or military corps or reserve force in connection with the navy " may be organized which is not included as part of the total effectives of 15,000 men.[2]

(ii.) Next, conscription for the navy is, of course, abolished, as it is for the army. Officers must serve a twenty-five-year period, and seamen twelve years. The strength of officers and warrant officers together is limited to 10 per cent of the total personnel, that is, to 1,500. Likewise, as in the military clauses, not more than 5 per cent of either officers or men may be discharged in any year, and if more are discharged they may not be replaced. There are the same restrictions upon the

---

[1] Art. 183.   [2] *Ibid.*

raining of ex-naval men who are now in civil life. Lastly, no one in the German mercantile marine, officer or man, shall receive any naval training of any kind.[1]

Why was it necessary to insert these elaborate restrictions upon the man-power of the German navy when, as was said above, additional man-power, even if it be unlimited in amount, can do little or nothing to increase the offensive power of a given naval force ?

The authors of the treaty no doubt had three main reasons in mind. The first is shown by the use of the word "military" in Paragraph 4 of Article 183.[2] The disarmament clauses of the treaty limit not only the navy, but, above all, the German army. Had there been no restriction upon the reserve corps which might be formed for the service of the German navy, there might have been built up under the disguise of a naval reserve a large and well-trained military force, capable of taking part, with the German army, in land operations. This the Allies had obviously to prevent, unless they wished their main purpose to be defeated.

Second, the existence of a reserve force which has had some naval training is of great value for the organization of auxiliary naval forces, such as supply cruisers, mine sweepers, and the like. Such services may possibly, on occasion, add directly to the offensive power of a navy, and there is no doubt that to improvise them at the last moment would be inconvenient.

Third, the Allies desired to protect themselves against the risk that Article 190 might not be observed, and that at a crisis Germany might buy from foreign powers a great number of additional fighting ships. If she had no trained reserves to man them, such a manœuvre could not help her.

For these reasons, therefore, and in accordance with the general principles of the disarmament clauses, all the restrictions were placed upon the Germans' right to raise naval reserves which the Allied experts were able to devise.

8. *Manufacture of, and Traffic in, Naval Armaments.*—The same restrictions as in the military clauses were placed upon the

---

[1] Art. 194, Para. 5.

[2] "No naval or military corps or reserve force in connection with the navy may be organized. . . ."

manufacture of all articles of use in naval warfare, and upon their export from, or import into, Germany.[1]

These restrictions, it may be repeated, are of particular importance in connection with naval armaments.

9. *Fortifications and Naval Bases.*—Fortifications also have a special importance in naval warfare. On land they are purely defensive, but at sea the operations which fighting ships can carry out depend in great measure on the naval bases from which they work, and the protection from shore fortification which they receive; such bases and fortifications, therefore, are a considerable factor in the offensive power of any given naval force. For this reason the treaty deals with the naval fortifications which Germany may possess.

(i.) First, Germany may erect no fortifications and install no guns of any kind within a defined area, the shores of which dominate " the maritime routes between the North Sea and the Baltic." The fortifications previously existing in this area were destroyed and the guns removed.[2]

(ii.) All the fortifications, military establishments, and harbours on the islands of Heligoland and Dune were destroyed and they may never be reconstructed in the future.[3]

(iii.) Other fortifications within 50 kilometres of the German coast or German islands are to be " considered as of a defensive nature, and may remain in their existing condition " with the guns which they possessed when the treaty came into force, and with supplies of ammunition which are not to exceed 1,500 rounds for small calibre and 500 rounds for large calibre guns. No new fortifications of any kind, and no increase in the existing armament, shall be made.

Such are the restrictions which the Allied experts and their Governments thought it worth while to impose upon the German navy by the Treaty of Versailles.

Washington Naval Convention

The Washington Conference was summoned in 1921 to end the stupendous race in new naval construction which had then

---

[1] Arts. 189 and 192, Para. 4; cf. chap. ix., *supra*.   [2] Art. 195.
[3] Part III. of Treaty of Versailles, Section XIII., Art. 115.

begun between powers who a few years before had been fighting side by side against a common foe. Some idea was given in Chapter II. of the appalling burden which that race imposed on the peoples of the states concerned. The convention which the Conference drew up is important not only because it stopped that race, but also because it is the only important naval treaty of a "voluntary" kind. The parties accepted its provisions not under compulsion, but exclusively because of their desire to safeguard the peace of the world and to mitigate the financial difficulties in which, as a consequence of the war, most of them were involved.

The Convention may fairly be said to have been " general " in the first meaning of the word, because its signatories included all the powers which in 1921 had substantial strength in the two classes of fighting ships with which it dealt; because it did not come into force until it was ratified by all of them;[1] and because, if any one of them denounced it, it forthwith ceased to bind the rest.[2] It was, of course, not " general " in the other meaning of the word, and, indeed, its whole nature, and the provisions which it included, were profoundly affected by the fact that it only dealt with two categories of ships. In considering whether any parts of it can serve as a model for a general treaty, this fact must be always borne in mind.

But the general point of most importance concerning the Washington Convention is this: that although the Conference had met under the ægis of a power which had refused to join the League of Nations, although its purpose in the eyes of the American Administration was at least in part to show that progress could be made in the peaceful ordering of international affairs without the machinery or the entanglements of the League, yet the first problem which had to be dealt with, before anything could be done about disarmament, was the old League problem of security in a different form. The stumbling-block which prevented progress, until it was removed, was the Anglo-Japanese Alliance. The point may best be put in the words of a distinguished commentator on the Conference and its work:

" As long as the Anglo-Japanese Alliance existed, Japan could rest assured that Singapore would never be a menace

---

[1] Art. 24.   [2] Art. 23.

to her. But as long as this Alliance existed, the United States could not be certain, looking at the question from the tactical standpoint, that the British and Japanese fleets would not be combined against her, making a ratio of 8 to 9. But if the Anglo-Japanese Alliance should be cancelled outright, as America wished, and an Anglo-American understanding established, it would be possible for the fleets of these two powers to combine against Japan, with Singapore as a base, and making a ratio of 10 to 3. The Japanese Delegation believed that such a preponderance would offset the disadvantage of distance under which the American and British fleets would have to operate. It also believed that the British base at Singapore, under these conditions, would serve as a joint base for both fleets, and that the advantage gained by Japan in the pledge of the United States not to construct bases of her own would thus be overcome. Consequently, if the United States should insist on cancelling the Anglo-Japanese Alliance, Japan would insist that some agreement be created which would assure her that the British and American fleets would not combine. These considerations led to the negotiation of the Four-Power Treaty."[1]

And again, Mr. Buell says that when the Anglo-Japanese Alliance had been removed there was

"no longer any possibility that the British and the Japanese fleets will serve as a unit against us (*i.e.*, the U.S.A.). As we have seen, this possibility was an obstacle which prevented the adoption of any plan for the limitation of armaments until it was removed."[2]

The Four-Power Treaty was a loose arrangement compared to the Security Pacts which are required in Europe. But it was none the less, in a true sense of the words, a " security " plan and one which by removing fears achieved its end.

Such is the general nature and importance of the Washington Convention. Its detailed clauses may now be discussed,

[1] Pp. 170-1, *Washington Conference*, by Raymond Leslie Buell.
[2] *Ibid.*

except those general provisions which are relevant, not only to naval armament, but to disarmament as a whole, and which, therefore, may more usefully be examined at a later stage.

1. *Limitation of Ships.*—The main purpose of the Convention is to limit the strength of the signatory powers in two principal categories of fighting units: battleships and aircraft-carriers.[1]

The method by which this limitation is effected is the fixing of the maximum tonnage in each of these two classes of ships which the signatories may respectively possess. No attempt is made to set up a standard unit in each class; the strength of the signatory parties is measured and compared by adding together the tonnage of various units of different sizes, and in the same way the agreed ratio between them is applied. But the mere acceptance of a maximum total tonnage was not thought to be enough; Part I. of Chapter II. of the Convention consists of tables setting out in detail the name and the tonnage of every vessel which the parties may retain. Thus, once an agreement had been made, no freedom of selection among their units was left to the naval staffs. This system of detailed restriction is important.

A necessary consequence of this primary limitation and of the agreement about what ships should be retained was a mutual undertaking to abandon the construction programmes which the various powers had announced, and for which some of them had obtained parliamentary votes and sanction. A further consequence was an agreement that all ships, whether built or building, not included in the schedules of permitted units, should be destroyed. It is plain that any reduction of naval strength must mean the ruthless destruction of fighting units on which great sums of public money have quite recently been spent. This no doubt explains why an operation which, without any risk to national safety, prevents great economic waste should be popularly called a " sacrifice."

2. *The Restriction of Weapons.*—The Washington Convention did not go so far as the Treaty of Versailles in restricting the kinds of weapon to be used in naval war. But it did something of real value in limiting the size of future ships and the calibre

[1] Arts. 4 and 7.

of the guns with which any ship of war may be equipped. Thus it provides:

(i.) That for the future no capital ship may be laid down which exceeds 35,000 tons displacement.[1]

(ii.) That no capital ship shall carry a gun with a calibre exceeding 16 inches.[2]

(iii.) That no aircraft-carrier shall be laid down which exceeds in displacement 27,000 tons, subject to the exception that any constructing power may build two aircraft-carriers of not more than 33,000 tons each, if it does not thereby exceed the total tonnage in aircraft-carriers which it is allowed.[3]

(iv.) That no aircraft-carrier may have a gun of more than 8-inch calibre; if an aircraft-carrier has any gun of over 6 inches, then by a complicated arrangement the total number of its guns exceeding 5 inches is limited to 10.

In addition to these provisions, the Convention went outside the two categories of ships, with which it was chiefly meant to deal, and included other important restrictions on the means of naval war. Thus:

(v.) No ship of any kind which exceeds 10,000 tons displacement shall be built or used, other than the capital ships and aircraft-carriers allowed for replacement by the treaty. This, of course, does not apply to merchant ships, which are not built as men-of-war nor taken under Government control in time of peace, but which may be employed on auxiliary fleet duties or as transports.

(vi.) No ship other than capital ships and aircraft-carriers may carry a gun of more than 8-inch calibre.

(vii.) An attempt was also made to abolish the submarine as a means of naval war. Had this attempt succeeded it would have been by far the most important part of the restriction of weapons which the Convention carried out.

But in spite of the failure over submarines, what was done is by no means worthy of contempt. It has no doubt prevented

[1] Art. 5   [2] Art. 6.   [3] Art. 9.

a dangerous competition in the size of fighting units and in the offensive armament with which they are equipped. It has happened, indeed, that the limitation of vessels other than capital ships and aircraft-carriers to a maximum size of 10,000 tons has had the unforeseen and unfortunate effect of making 10,000 tons the *minimum* standard for the cruisers which naval staffs have since constructed. It has thus added to the cost of cruiser programmes, and has rendered older cruisers obsolete. But the blame for this result does not lie with the authors of the Convention, whose only purpose, successfully achieved, was to prevent other, more dangerous, forms of competition.

3. *Armament Limitation.*—Beyond the restrictions just mentioned on the size of the weapons, there are few limitations in the Convention on the armament with which fighting ships may be equipped.

(i.) There is, of course, the limitation already mentioned on the number of guns allowed on aircraft-carriers.

(ii.) There is a provision that the retained ships listed in the schedules may not be reconstructed, nor their armour or their guns increased, beyond an additional 3,000 tons displacement allowed for every vessel for anti-aircraft and submarine defence. A special exception to this rule is made for the French and Italian navies, which may, if they desire, increase the calibre of their guns to sixteen inches, to equal those already possessed by the other signatory powers.[1]

(iii.) Apart from this, and apart from the general limitation on tonnage displacement, which, of course, automatically limits the armament with which a ship can be equipped, there is no attempt in the Convention to restrict the guns, torpedo tubes, or other weapons with which any unit may be equipped.

(iv.) Nor is there any attempt to limit the ammunition with which ships are furnished. This, of course, is right, for even if the parties had desired on this point—as no doubt they did not—to adopt the rigid system of Versailles, they could not have done so; since their Convention dealt

[1] Part 3, Section 1 D.

with a part only of their navies the observance of an ammunition agreement would have been impossible to control.

4. *Reserve Ships.*—There are, however, provisions as rigid as those of the Treaty of Versailles to prevent the keeping of additional reserve ships of the classes dealt with. Thus:

(i.) Ships which under the Convention are to be destroyed may not, on any ground whatever, be reconverted to warlike use.[1] An exception is made which allows the conversion of certain of them into aircraft-carriers. The purpose of this exception, of course, was merely to prevent needless expenditure upon new aircraft-carriers,[2] which under the Convention the signatories were allowed to have.

(ii.) Merchant ships may not be prepared in time of peace " for the installation of warlike armaments for the purpose of converting such ships into vessels of war "—*i.e.*, the signatories may not prepare a great reserve of armed merchant ships to act as auxiliary scouts or cruisers. The only preparation allowed in merchantmen is the stiffening of decks required for the mounting of the six-inch guns they need for anti-submarine defence.[3]

(iii.) It is further provided—and the clause is noteworthy —that if a signatory power should, for whatever reason, be engaged in war, it may not take into its own use any war-ship *of whatever kind* which is being built within its juris-diction for a foreign power. This no doubt is a necessary consequence of the principle of an agreed and mutual reduction, but it is none the less a most important change in the practice of the past. The result of these various clauses—to achieve it is the purpose of every disarmament agreement—is that the relative strength in ships of the signatory parties will be, in time of war, exactly what it is in time of peace. The Washington Convention leaves undone nothing that is useful to this end.

5. *The Destruction of Ships.*—Next, there are elaborate clauses laying down how " scrapped " ships shall be rendered

---

[1] Art. 13.   [2] Art. 13.   [3] Art. 14.

permanently unfit for further warlike use. There were, of course, no similar clauses in the Treaty of Versailles because the German ships were handed over for disposal to the Allies.

The Washington Convention allows two stages in destruction. First, within six months of the date on which a ship is due to be scrapped, the parties must have removed all its guns, armour, conning-towers, turrets, hydraulic or electric mountings, fire-control instruments, ammunition and mines, torpedoes and tubes, wireless telegraphy, and all landing and flying-off platforms and other aviation accessories. The ship, in short, must have been made quite useless for any warlike purpose. Second, within eighteen months from the same date " final scrapping " must have been effected in one of three specified ways. A vessel may be permanently sunk; or it may be " broken up," and all its machinery, boilers, and armour of every kind removed; or lastly, it may be put to target use.

For the ships to be scrapped when the Convention first came into force, the periods began to run from the moment of its ratification by all the powers. For ships to be scrapped, when in 1932 " replacement " first begins, the periods start on the date of completion of successor ships.[1]

6. *Replacement.*—The rules for the replacement of ships in a treaty of naval disarmament are, of course, of capital importance. Since the life of a fighting ship is brief, rigid replacement clauses may secure reductions at a later date for which no immediate agreement can be obtained. For this reason the replacement clauses of the Washington Convention deserve particular attention. They provide as follows:

> (i.) The life of capital ships and aircraft-carriers is laid down as twenty years—the period allowed for armoured vessels in the Treaty of Versailles.
> (ii.) In principle, therefore, ships retained may be replaced as and when they reach the age of twenty years. Accordingly the keels of new ships, for the construction of which three years are allowed, may be laid down seventeen years after the launching of the units which they are to substitute.

[1] Chap. ii., part 2.

(iii.) Moreover, the Convention lays down in a detailed schedule the exact dates at which each unit shall be replaced and on which its replacing ship may be begun, but it allows the parties, if they so desire, to alter the order in which their ships are scrapped. It would obviously not matter to any other power if, for reasons of an administrative or sentimental nature, a naval staff decided to retain an older and to scrap a younger ship.

(iv.) There follows a most important clause, which provides that no replacement building shall be begun for a period of ten years from the date when the Convention was drawn up, that is to say, until 1931, keels laid down in that year maturing, of course, for actual replacement of existing units in 1934. There would thus be no actual scrapping until 1934 of existing ships which the parties are permitted to retain.

This is the famous " Naval Holiday "—in itself of great importance, and capable of being used, if the parties so agreed, to even better purpose. For obviously at any moment up to 1931 the parties could quite easily agree to prolong the " Holiday " and to postpone the date at which replacement might begin.

(v.) It should be added that some small exceptions are made in the replacement clauses in favour of Italy and France, these two powers being allowed to scrap certain ships before they reach the statutory age of twenty years.

This favourable treatment was allowed on the ground that France and Italy, owing to their need for economic reconstruction—the point must be noted for future reference—had not been able since the war to keep their " proper place " in naval preparation.

(vi.) The dates of replacement in the schedules are arranged to allow the powers to keep their total tonnage in capital ships at the following figures :

U.S.A. and Great Britain	525,000
Japan	315,000
France and Italy	175,000

The agreed ratio between them will thus be permanently maintained.

Moreover, if the Naval Holiday were prolonged beyond ten years, or if the scheduled scrapping were carried out, as, of course, it might be, without replacement, thus bringing a general and equal reduction in the strength of all the powers, the agreed ratio of strength between them would still remain intact, and no new negotiation on the point would be required. This system of replacement by detailed schedules has, therefore, the immense advantage that it renders future agreement for increased reduction as simple as it well can be.

(vii.) Two exceptions to these general rules were made: First, while the other countries undertook to build for the future capital ships of 35,000 tons displacement, and, therefore, had their replacement units entered in the schedules under letters A, B, C, and D, etc., with the actual figure of 35,000 tons against each letter,[1] Italy, by special declaration, kept the right to build smaller units, if she desired to do so, within, of course, her total tonnage limit of 175,000 tons. Some experts think, on general grounds of naval policy, that it was Italy who chose the wiser part.[2]

Second, as in the Treaty of Versailles, if a ship is lost by accident, it may be replaced at once, the regular replacement programme being advanced to that extent. This provision, of course, is obviously required, if the agreed ratio of strength between the parties is to be maintained.

7. *Naval Personnel.*—The Washington Convention has no provisions for the limitation of naval personnel. Obviously there could be none in a Convention which dealt with part only of the navies of the signatory states.

8. *Arms Traffic.*—The provisions of the Convention about the traffic in arms, however, are particularly strong, as, of course, they must be to give the parties confidence that the Convention ratio will be in fact maintained. Thus:

(i.) No ships may be constructed, either in Government arsenals or by private firms, within the jurisdiction of the

---

[1] Cf. Tables in Appendix IV.   [2] Note to chap. ii., part 3, section 2.

parties, for any foreign navy, which exceed, either in tonnage or in armament, the ships which the parties themselves are allowed by the Convention to maintain.[1]

(ii.) If any fighting ship *of any kind* is built within the jurisdiction of a party for any power which is not a signatory to the Convention, the other parties must be immediately informed and furnished with full details of its construction. Thus, full publicity is secured for international traffic in ships of war between the signatories and the outside world.[2]

(iii.) Next, as has been already said, if any signatory is engaged in war, it may on no account whatsoever take into its own service any ships which have been or are being built within its jurisdiction—even by a Government arsenal—for foreign powers. This, again, is vital to the effective maintenance of the ratio, and it has also an important bearing on the problems of private manufacture of, and trade in, arms.[3]

(iv.) Last, every party gives a sweeping undertaking not to dispose in any way whatever, either by gift, sale, or any other " mode of transfer," *of any vessel of war of any category or description*, in such a way that that vessel may come into the service of a foreign power.[4] To those who remember the practice of the past, this may seem to be a drastic and surprising ordinance of self-denial; but it is, in fact, no more than commonsense. It is, moreover, a clause that is essential to prevent the gift of ships to non-signatory powers, with a secret undertaking that these powers would give them back to their previous owners if war should ever happen to break out. It shows once more the great importance of the problem of the traffic in arms in any treaty of general disarmament.

9. *Mutual Control.*—There is only the simplest of provisions in the Washington Convention for " mutual control." It consists in a general undertaking among the parties to exchange

---

[1] Art. 15—*i.e.*, 35,000 tons for capital ships, 27,000 for aircraft-carriers, 10,000 tons for other ships, etc., as above.

[2] Art. 16.   [3] Art. 17.   [4] Art. 18.

full information about the ships which they decide to scrap, about the units by which those ships shall be replaced, about the dates of Government authorization for these changes, and so on.[1]

It is so plainly impossible to keep secret anything to do with the building or destruction of great vessels like capital ships or aircraft-carriers that the mere exchange of information is no doubt all that was required for the purposes of the Washington Convention. Nothing so simple will be adequate for a general treaty, not even for its naval clauses, if they contain the additional restrictions which may be needed when the whole fleets of all the naval powers are limited and reduced.

10. *Fortifications and Naval Bases.*—It has been already said that fortifications and naval bases play in naval warfare a part quite different from that which fortifications can play in operations on dry land, because they may enormously increase the attacking strength of a given naval force.[2] In the Washington Convention they are dealt with by Article 19, and the negotiation which led to the adoption of this Article was one of the most important parts of the whole work of the conference.

By Article 19, the three signatories principally concerned— the United States, the British Empire, and Japan—agreed that they would maintain in all their respective territories and possessions within a specified area of the Pacific Ocean " the *status quo* at the time of the present treaty with regard to fortifications and naval bases." The specified area was intended to include all the islands or mainland ports from which an aggressive attack could be made upon Japan. It is so drawn as to leave the United States and Great Britain legally free to improve, if they desire to do so, the naval bases which they respectively maintain at Hawaii and Singapore. On the

[1] Chap. ii., part 3, section 1 B.
[2] Cf. Ballard, *The Influence of the Sea on the Political History of Japan*, p. 291: " For any attack on Japan as matters now stand the enemy must be in possession of a fleet about three times as powerful as that of the defence, because no other country has a fully equipped modern naval base and arsenal in the Eastern Pacific capable of docking two or three of the biggest ships simultaneously; or of removing guns 100 tons in weight; or of manufacturing wholesale supplies of heavy calibre ammunition; or, lastly, of storing the millions of tons of oil fuel required by a twentieth-century fleet in war."

13

other hand, it includes the Aleutian Islands near the Alaskan coast, which, though close to United States territory, were also, the Japanese delegation thought, sufficiently close to Japan to constitute a danger should they be made a naval base.

Article 19 contains three points:

(i.) *No new fortifications or naval bases* shall be established in the specified territories.

(ii.) No measures shall be taken to increase their existing facilities for the *repair and maintenance* of naval forces.

(iii.) No increase shall be made in their *coast defences*.

The Article adds, of course, that the parties may make such repair and replacement of worn-out weapons and equipment as is customary in time of peace.

These provisions are of special interest, because their general application will almost certainly be required in the treaty which is to limit all the navies of the world.

11. *Technical Aspects of the Washington Treaty.*—It is perhaps worth noting that in technical form the Washington Convention is as simple and straightforward as it well could be. The strength of the signatory powers is measured and compared by their total permitted tonnage in each of the classes of ship with which it deals. To make this a valid test, to prevent its being upset by new units, which would so outclass existing ships as to destroy the agreed balance of real strength, it was necessary also to place a limit upon the size of replacement vessels, and upon the calibre of the guns which they may have. These two parts of the Convention thus go together.

As for the ratio of strength which was adopted, the whole negotiation on this vital point was founded on the simple formula referred to—5 : 5 : 3 : 1·75 : 1·75. This agreed proportion —the point is of importance—was based roughly on the actual *status quo* of 1921. It was not exactly applied in the tonnage of existing ships to be retained in the different countries when the Convention first came into force. Great Britain, for example, was allowed to keep 580,000 tons, U.S.A., 500,000, Japan, 300,000. But this apparent superiority of Great Britain was agreed to because a great number of her permitted ships were older, smaller, and less powerfully armed than the units retained by the United States and by Japan, while in replacement tonnage, in which there will be no such difference between the parties in the size of ships, the ratio 5 : 5 : 3 : etc., has, of course, been rigidly applied.

It must be noted that in many ways throughout the Washington Convention the actual conditions of the *status quo* of 1921 have been retained. The maximum size of the capital ships and guns to be permitted for the future corresponds to the largest ships and guns which then existed.[1] The same is true of the limit fixed for aircraft-carriers. The agreed ratio of strength which was adopted was deliberately founded, as has been said, upon the relative strength of the parties at the moment when the Convention was drawn up. Again, in respect of fortifications and naval bases, it was upon the maintenance of the *status quo* that agreement was at long last secured.

It is not too much to say, therefore, that the maintenance of the *status quo* is a principle which runs right through the Washington Convention. It was a principle which in its application seemed right and natural both to the delegates who drafted the Convention and to the nations for whom they spoke. It was, of course, in connection with the ratio that it was of most—indeed of decisive—importance. The acceptance of that ratio by Great Britain in 1921 involved a fundamental change in her traditional policy of the two-power standard. It may well be said that the British public was reconciled to the stereotyping of that change by an international treaty only because the new arrangement made was founded on the basis of existing fact. The point must be remembered when the general problem of the ratio is discussed.

---

[1] In fact, the British Navy possessed one unit—the *Hood*—of 41,200 tons, which was much larger than the average size to be permitted for the future. It was, however, the only ship of its kind in any navy.

CHAPTER XI

THE PRINCIPLES OF A GENERAL AGREEMENT UPON NAVAL DISARMAMENT

FOR the reasons discussed in the last chapter, naval disarmament presents a problem which is essentially much simpler than disarmament on land or in the air. There should be no difficulty whatever in making a general agreement for the reduction and limitation of all the navies of the world; it is merely a matter of Government goodwill. Agreement, of course, might be prevented by trouble over land or air. It has been said that the three branches of military preparation constitute a single problem; and failure in either of the others might mean failure or partial failure in naval disarmament as well. But at least it is clear that, so far as the naval negotiations themselves are concerned, there should be no risk of failure, unless indeed it should be caused by the abstention of Russia from the Conference.[1]

Naval, land, and air disarmament should all be dealt with not only at the same general conference, but actually in a single general treaty which that conference must prepare. But there must, of course, be a separate agreement about navies, an agreement which, owing to its wholly different nature, will need separate preparation and negotiation from the start. But when it has been thus prepared by the naval section of the general conference, it ought to be made part of a single comprehensive instrument. This is right in theory, for naval forces have an obvious bearing on questions of military and aerial strength; and it has also the advantage that, if this were done, the naval agreement would be signed, not only by those powers which now have navies, but also by others which, in the future, might be able to build them up. This principle of general acceptance, proposed, it must be noted, by the Rome Conference of naval experts in its draft of an extended Wash-

[1] Compare above, chap. v.

196

ington Convention,[1] could no doubt be most easily secured as a sort of self-denying ordinance embodied in the general treaty which all the powers who attend the conference will sign.

The naval agreement will, no doubt, be different in form from the land agreement, and much more like the model which the work of Washington provides. That is natural and right. It may or may not limit naval man-power—that point will be considered later; but however it may be decided, man-power will not be the *basis* of naval limitation, as it must be of disarmament on land. Nor will budgetary appropriation play much part, as in the limitation of land forces it very likely will. The basis of the naval agreement will be the limitation of ships. That is the essential factor where fleets are concerned, and all the other clauses which may be devised are simply more or less desirable decorations.

As to the scale of the reduction which may be hoped for, no attempt to prophesy could be worth while. It might be great, if the Governments were serious about the League of Nations and the security which the Covenant might provide. In no other kind of defensive or offensive action would the joint co-operation of different states against aggression be so easy or effective. No aggressor could stand up for long against the united pressure of the other navies of the world, and, indeed, no fleet would be likely to attempt it. Even without a single naval action, the aggressor would suffer immense losses in his merchant shipping throughout the world, and, if he were susceptible to blockade, his people would suffer hardships of every kind. Here, then, is a case where " pooled " security may give immense returns in safety and in saving, and where, if they have confidence in their joint plans of action, the Governments may much reduce the price of the individual " insurance " which they pay.

Moreover, the present moment, even from the point of view of naval staffs, is a good one at which to reduce the cost of navies. Some eminent naval experts hold that all new construction at the present time is purest waste. Aircraft, they say, are rendering, or have already rendered, wholly obsolete the great fighting ships in which naval nations to-day place

---

[1] Cf. chap. vii., *supra.*

their trust.[1] The experimental use of aircraft against battleships has not yet gone far, but there have already been remarkable results. The United States Air Force, for example,
dropped bombs a year or two ago upon a battleship which had
been made over to them for the purpose. They used bombs
containing 2,000 pounds of high-explosive—barely half the size
which even then they could have used. They made no direct
hit upon their target, but with one bomb which fell beside it,
they created so tremendous an explosion in the sea that the
whole ship turned turtle and went down. Again, experiments
have successfully been begun in the use of wireless-steered
torpedoes launched from aircraft flying low. And yet another
method of aerial attack is now predicted: the direct bombardment of ships at sea by big-calibre guns from aeroplanes of a
size much greater than any yet in use.[2]

It must be added that the radius of aircraft action is continually increasing: that whereas it was estimated in 1918 at
not more than 200 miles from their base, it is now at least 350;
and that quite certainly it will soon be 500 miles or more. Thus
a great part of the sea (including the approaches to the British
Isles) can now be dominated by aircraft from the shore. If
present developments continue, therefore, the dangers which
will threaten navies in future warfare will be very great.

For another special reason, Great Britain at this moment
would do well to reduce the burden of her naval forces. Since the
destruction of the German fleet, there has been no foreign navy
which could menace the seat of government of the British
Empire, as the Germans used to do. But in the meantime
other dangers to its safety have appeared. The fact that
Great Britain is an island has ceased to be a source of strength,
as once it was. The British people are now open to direct

[1] Cf., *e.g.*, the late Lord Fisher: " Flying dominates future war both
by land and sea. . . . At sea the only way to avoid the air is to get
under the water." General Mitchell, when Assistant Chief of the
U.S. Air Service: " With our present air facilities properly developed,
we can sink any enemy vessel, armoured or unarmoured, that comes
within 200 miles of our coast." Quoted by Buell, *Washington Conference*, pp. 235-6.

[2] *Strategy and Tactics of Air Fighting*, by Major Oliver Stewart,
M.C., A.F.C., Appendix on " Air Fighting in the Future."

attack both against the great centres of their population and against the ocean trade-routes upon which for their vital food supplies they now depend. These reasons make it much to be desired that we should now reduce the great burden that we bear for what may prove to be quite obsolete machinery of self-defence, in order—if for nothing else—that we may at least conserve our strength, in case new efforts should be needed, for a new and more profitable start.

Yet it must be remembered that there will be strong forces against the scrapping of existing ships. Not only the power of service and national traditions, but the very cost of modern ships, make both Governments and peoples reluctant to send them incontinently to the bottom of the ocean on which they so majestically float. It is unlikely, therefore, that there will be agreement for any big reductions in the naval forces which now exist. Such reductions ought, of course, to be demanded, but, if they are refused, that will not be ground for undue pessimism. The *essential* object at the present time is not reduction; it is to prevent an increase in the number and the armament of ships. If that can once be done, reductions can later on be made by the methods described in Chapter X. For this reason a general naval treaty which did no more than stabilize the existing *status quo* might be worth while, provided its replacement clauses were severe. Such a treaty would not, indeed, do much to help us through the present economic and financial crisis, but if nothing better could be got, it would give at least the hope of great reductions later on, when the security systems of the League of Nations have produced the general confidence that is required.

Detailed suggestions may now perhaps be made about the provisions of a general naval treaty. In this discussion it must never be forgotten that in naval much more than in other armaments there are two sorts of powers—the great naval nations and the rest. Both should be dealt with in a single treaty, difficult though that may be. But it must be expected that the great difference in strength between the Great Powers and the rest will much affect the form both of the general naval clauses and of the schedules which are attached.

1. *Permitted Ships.*—(i.) First, it is plain that the ships of every kind which each signatory is permitted to retain must be limited, as in the Washington Convention, on a basis of their total tonnage, the agreed ratio of strength between the parties being applied in the total of the tonnage allowed to each.

(ii.) But how shall the tonnage of different sorts of ships be reckoned ? The point is far from easy. There are three possible ways, any one of which at first sight might seem to do.

First, the total tonnage of all classes of vessels, from capital ships to torpedo boats, might be added together, each country being allowed a total tonnage corresponding to its ratio co-efficient, and being free to distribute this tonnage among the different classes as it might think right.

Second, tonnage might be totalled up in each separate class of ship, the amount allocated to each party in each class varying strictly with the ratio; in other words, among the parties to the Washington Convention (who have already an agreed ratio from which to start) the proportion of 5: 5: 3, etc., would be applied, not only to capital ships and aircraft carriers, but to cruisers, light cruisers, destroyers, torpedo boats, submarines, etc. A variant of this second plan—it is a variant in form only —was actually proposed at Washington by Mr. Hughes, the American Secretary of State: " that the capital ship tonnage should be used as a measurement of strength for navies and a proportionate allowance of auxiliary combatant craft pre-scribed,"[1] a fixed complement of " auxiliary combatant craft " being prescribed for each capital ship in a scheduled list of permitted units of each class.

Third, Mr. Hughes' plan might be adopted, but with the difference that the fixed complement of " auxiliary combatant craft " should consist not of a prescribed list of permitted units, but of a certain total tonnage of minor craft, *i.e.*, of ships of less than 10,000 tons and with guns not larger than 8 inch, each party being free within the tonnage limit to develop those minor classes which it thinks most useful.

Of these three courses, the first almost certainly will not do.

[1] Buell, *Washington Conference*, p. 152.

To allow complete liberty of action within a total tonnage limitation would give great elasticity to the disarmament system, but it might also destroy the confidence upon which that system ought to rest. Some Government, by taking certain risks and putting its whole tonnage into units of great power, might secure a naval supremacy against its neighbours, and thus upset the balance upon which the ratio was based. For this reason, limitation by the total tonnage of all classes of vessels taken together seems, as a system, to be too loose.

But there are difficulties of the contrary description in the two other plans proposed. Either the second or the third might suit the great naval powers and, although their present practice varies about minor craft, they might nevertheless be willing to accept either the more rigid or the more elastic plan. But neither would meet the case of small powers which may have few capital ships, or even none at all, and which deliberately prefer to multiply their small defensive units, rather than to purchase at great expense even one of the great fighting monsters of to-day. For them, plainly, the capital ship cannot be the basis of the scheme, and therefore neither the second nor the third of these plans will apply.

Even for the great naval powers the second plan will hardly fit the facts. As has been said, even they possess at present very different strength in different classes of auxiliary ships. France, for example, has developed submarines much more than other countries. Great Britain heavily outnumbers her rivals in destroyers. Even for the great naval powers, therefore, the application of a rigid ratio to the tonnage allowed in each separate class of ship might not be easy, and for all the rest it plainly will not do. It may be concluded that it is not possible generally to apply a fixed ratio in each different class of ship.

(iii.) All these three plans being unworkable in practice, therefore, it seems to be inevitable that the application of the ratio in the schedules of the treaty must be made, not by the rigid application of any principle, but empirically—that is to say, by negotiation. The negotiation should be based, no doubt, on certain principles the utility of which is shown by the experience of Washington and Versailles. These principles appear to be as follows:

(*a*) There must be a primary agreement as to the total tonnage in the largest categories of ships (*i.e.*, in capital ships and aircraft-carriers) to be retained by all the states which now possess them. Among the powers which have a great number of such ships, and where naval strength thus principally consists in large fighting units, there must be in the largest classes an exact application in permitted tonnage of the basic ratio of strength agreed between them. In other words, for the great naval powers, the exact model of the Washington Convention must be adopted, so far, at least, as capital ships and aircraft-carriers are concerned.

(*b*) In order to maintain the balance of relative strength established in the largest classes by this primary agreement, there must be limits set on the size and armament of all fighting units, both of the largest classes and of minor auxiliary craft as well.

(*c*) The total tonnage allowed to each power in the smaller classes of auxiliary craft must be laid down. Among the great naval powers there must again be an exact application of their agreed ratio of strength, the ratio perhaps being applied, however, to total tonnage in all the minor classes taken together, and not to the tonnage in each individual class. The additional elasticity so allowed might remove complications and difficulties which otherwise it might be hard to overcome.

(*d*) Among the smaller powers, the ratio cannot be separately applied, as it must be for the great powers, to larger and smaller categories. On the contrary, for them whatever capital ships they may happen to possess must be taken together with their minor auxiliary craft, and the ratio applied in terms of their total tonnage of all kinds. This applies to all the smaller powers—that is to say, to all the powers with navies, excepting only Russia, which are not signatory to the Washington Convention.

(*e*) In spite of what was said in paragraph (*c*) above, it may be necessary for the great naval powers to accept the application of an agreed ratio of strength in certain other classes besides capital ships and aircraft-carriers. Submarines, for example, are now so great a menace to other craft that, in the opinion of some experts, they are, as weapons of offence, almost on a footing with capital ships and aircraft-carriers. It might, therefore, be necessary to have a special schedule for submarines, laying down an exact ratio between the powers who possess great strength in them. For smaller powers, submarines, no doubt, could be counted together with their other ships as part of their total tonnage.

These remarks are made on the supposition that the submarine will not be abolished.

(*f*) In any case, whatever plan may be adopted, it is necessary to secure in a general naval treaty no less a measure of exactitude than was in fact secured in the Washington Convention. To this end, every agreement in respect of every class of naval unit should be written down both in terms of limitations on replacement tonnage, and in terms of actual ships to be retained, set out by name, in accordance with the Washington model, in the schedules of the treaty.

The above principles may seem cumbrous and perhaps even unhelpful. But they may, in fact, be very easy to apply, since no doubt in practice the greater part of the general treaty will merely stabilize the existing *status quo*, with whatever mutual and proportionate reduction can by negotiation be obtained. It is difficult to hope that this reduction will be great enough to complicate the application of the principles discussed.

2. *Restriction of Weapons*.—It is plain that every effort should be made to secure all possible restrictions on the weapons to be used in war at sea.

(i.) Obviously, every nation would at once agree by the general treaty to accept at least the Washington limitations upon the size of capital ships, aircraft-carriers, and other minor craft, and upon the calibre of the guns which they may have. These maximum standards—35,000 tons displacement, and 16-inch guns for capital ships, etc.—are, in fact, so much above the general standards of all the nations not signatories to the Washington Convention that general agreement would be almost a matter of form.

(ii.) But just for that reason, such an agreement would do little good. Much more should be possible in limitation of the size of ships and guns—not, of course, of vessels that exist, but of the new units by which existing vessels, when they are obsolete, will be replaced. There seems to be no reason why the replacement vessels which will be built when the Naval Holiday is over should exceed, at the very most, say, 20,000 tons displacement, with an armament of 10-inch guns. There is in logic an unanswerable case for still greater reductions, and, indeed, for the general adoption of the limits imposed by the Treaty of Versailles on Germany:

For armoured ships	10,000 tons.
,, cruisers	6,000 ,,
,, destroyers	800 ,,
,, torpedo boats	200 ,,

Such limitations would give immense economies in cost and, if generally accepted, they could not possibly diminish the national security of any state.

(iii.) A determined effort should certainly be made to secure the abolition of the submarine. At the Washington Conference there was a vigorous debate between the British and continental experts as to whether the submarine is really a weapon of attack or of defence. However strong may be the British argument that it is in reality an offensive weapon, pure and simple, there is no doubt that many smaller nations regard it as a cheap and effective means of self-protection against the naval menace of more powerful states. And, in fact, the recent British agitation against the submarine met with a poor response. But the proposal might have a very different reception if it were part of a general scheme, including plans for joint security; and if, in addition, the British Government should offer to accept restrictions on the gun-power and the size of other ships, they might well by such concessions secure the abolition of the submarine by general consent. There is no doubt that, if this were done, it would not only remove some of the terrors of modern naval war, but it would also on purely naval grounds be an immense advantage to the British Admiralty. Its faithful observance would, of course, be easy to control.

(iv.) There is no other restriction upon the use of weapons in naval war which appears at present to be a matter of practical politics. There are others, such as the abolition of aircraft carriers or of torpedoes, which may on some grounds be desired, but for the adoption of which it is, in fact, difficult to hope.

3. *The Limitation of Armament.*—It is probably not possible to limit the number of guns carried by a warship otherwise than by limiting the tonnage of the ship itself. Nor, indeed, is it important to do so. The cost of additional guns and the extra ammunition which they involve is so small an item, compared to the whole cost of the ship itself, that it is not worth serious consideration.[1]

(ii.) The same remark applies to the limitation of the ammunition which fighting ships may have. It may be desirable to impose a limitation on ammunition, but it is plainly far less important to do so than it is on land. Naval armaments, while they may secure victory in a lengthy war, while they may bring great pressure upon an aggressor during Period A, can, by their nature, rarely if ever be used by an aggressor to force a victory in Period A. Thus the amount of ammunition which an aggressor's navy has in Period A matters far less than the amount which his army may possess.

Indeed, there are only two strong arguments for an attempt to limit naval ammunition. The first is that of economy; no opening for financial saving, however small it may appear, should be neglected. The second depends on whether or not army ammunition is limited by the general treaty. For if it is, then plainly naval ammunition must be limited too. Otherwise an intending aggressor might build up great stocks of so-called "naval" ammunition and perhaps even of naval guns, which, when the chosen moment of attack arrived, he could turn over to

---

[1] This, of course, applies only to the *number*, not to the calibre of guns. Calibre must be limited because a larger gun can outrange a smaller, and thus an increase in calibre may upset the balance of fighting strength upon which the ratio has been based.

his military forces. If for this reason it were necessary to limit naval ammunition and gun replacement, it might perhaps be done by an agreement for a fixed annual budgetary appropriation for naval ammunition and the replacement and repair of naval guns, a fixed sum of money being permitted, say, for every 10,000 tons of fighting ships allowed. This system, if it were adopted, would probably be less difficult to control than the budgetary appropriations for land armament above discussed.

But such a limitation of naval ammunition is not essential to a disarmament scheme; its importance lies, as has been said, in its bearing on the limitation of arms and ammunition for land forces.

4. *Ships in Reserve.*—It is plainly necessary that the three Washington clauses which deal with reserves of warships should be included in a general treaty. They provide that there shall be no reconversion of ships which have been scrapped; that merchantmen shall not be prepared in time of peace except for simple self-defence against submarine attack; and that if war breaks out, no signatory power shall take over ships which have been built within its jurisdiction for another country.[1]

Without similar clauses in the general treaty there could be no confidence that its system would be effectively maintained.

5. *Replacement of Obsolete Ships.*—Replacement of obsolete units is of crucial importance in naval disarmament, because the rules adopted on the subject will determine the burden of new construction in future years, and the progressive reductions in naval budgets for which we can hope.

No doubt, so far as may be, the replacement schedules of the general treaty will follow the model of the Washington Convention. In technical form, they will follow it exactly for capital ships, for aircraft carriers, and indeed for submarines, or other minor classes too, if they are treated as categories for which an exact ratio strength for different countries is required. For other classes, in which the ratio is applied by total tonnage of different classes taken together, the schedules would, of course, show the total existing permitted tonnage in this way, leaving the signatory parties free to use their replacement

---

[1] Cf. p. 188, *supra*.

tonnage on units of any size or description they desired, provided only they did not exceed the maximum sizes which the treaty will lay down.

The following special objects should be secured by the replacement rules:

(i.) There should be as long a Naval Holiday as the Governments can be persuaded to accept, during which there should be no new construction of naval units of any class. The moral and psychological effect of such a holiday would be immense; it would permit the reconversion of armament industry to productive ends; it would give great and immediate economies in national taxation.

(ii.) As a consequence of the new agreement just proposed, the Governments which signed the Washington Convention should extend their present Naval Holiday in capital ships beyond the year 1931, and should accordingly postpone both their replacement programmes and the Revision Conference which, by that Convention, they have undertaken to attend in 1929.[1]

(iii.) The general treaty, like the Washington Convention, must make provision for a Revision Conference, and by Article 8 of the Covenant this Conference must meet within ten years from the date at which the general treaty is drawn up. Of course, the authors of the Covenant intended that the Revision Conference should consider, after ten years' experience of a disarmament scheme, what further reductions in national armament could be made. The authors of the Washington Convention appeared to have a slightly different idea in view. They desired a Conference because " in view of possible technical and scientific developments " they believed that " changes in the treaty may be necessary to meet such developments "; in other words, because great new inventions might have changed the whole character of naval war, and might have rendered obsolete the ships of war on which Governments now rely. For both reasons, but, of course, especially for the first, it is essential that a Revision Conference should meet within the ten years' interval which the Covenant lays down.

(iv.) This Revision Conference must, of course, meet before the end of the Naval Holiday, that is to say, before replacement

[1] Article 21.

construction has been actually begun. It is most important that, whatever programme of replacement may be adopted at the original Disarmament Conference, it should not be definitive, but should be subject to further reduction or confirmation at the Revision Conference when it meets. If the door were thus left wide open for further postponement of the replacement programme or for further reductions in its scale, it might well be that the experience of ten years' working of a disarmament scheme, and the confidence which, if it succeeds, this scheme will create, would render possible progress which, at the present time, it seems quite Utopian to hope for.

The question of the size and armament of replacement units should also be left open for final decision by the Revision Conference, which should be free to make still more drastic limitations even than those upon which the original Conference may agree.

The Revision Conference, in short, when it meets in ten years' time, should have a free hand to modify by reduction or postponement, by change of type or tonnage, the replacement programmes to which the Governments now agree, these programmes being regarded simply as maxima which they will in no case exceed. This would plainly be in accordance with the spirit, and indeed with the literal provisions, of Article 8 of the Covenant.[1]

6. *Naval Personnel.*—Next, is it necessary in a general treaty to limit the man-power of navies ? It has been argued that as a factor in naval strength, reserves of man-power are of small importance, and from the point of view of navies only they might well be neglected. But when all kinds of armed forces are to be reduced and limited by a single plan, other considerations enter in. What, for example, would be the effect upon the limitation of land forces, if Governments were free to raise and organize and train as many naval corps as they might wish ? Would not such liberty of action enable a disloyal state to build up large bodies of well-trained troops which, though nominally raised for naval service, could, in fact, be used to augment the strength of its land army ?

---

[1] Art. 8, Para. 3: " Such plans shall be subject to reconsideration and revision at least every ten years."

For this reason, which seemed decisive to the Allied experts at Versailles, it will probably be necessary in the general treaty to limit the man-power which signatory Governments may use for the service of their fleets. A generous allowance, which would amply cover all the possible demands of naval staffs, could, of course, be made. In form, the limitation could be simple. It could allow a fixed number of personnel for, say, every ten thousand tons of permitted shipping which each country may retain. This would again establish a relation between man-power and material, like that established by the land disarmament system of the peace treaties, the relation being founded on the " dominant factor " which, with navies, is not the man-power but the fighting ships.

7. *Reserves of Man-power.*—Again, and for the same purpose of rendering effective the limitation of land forces, restrictions may be required in the general treaty, upon the raising and organization of naval reserves. It would need consideration which of the Peace Treaty clauses would apply. In many countries there is conscription for the navy, and for such countries only clauses consistent with the conscription system could be used. Broadly speaking, these clauses would be the same as those described in Chapter IX as applicable to land reserves under a conscription system.

8. *Limitation of the Total Naval Budget.*—Again, whether it is necessary to limit the total naval budget allowed to different countries depends on whether total army budgets are limited or not. Freedom of naval expenditure would make little difference in the actual fighting strength of any country, once a limitation of tonnage had been made. But unless naval budgets are controlled, it will not be possible to secure observance of limitations on total army budgets, for excess expenditure on armies might be disguised as naval, and evidence of guilt might be impossible to obtain.

For this reason a limitation on total naval budgets may be required, and if so it might be made by establishing a fixed proportion between annual expenditure and total tonnage, a given sum being allowed per annum for each ten thousand tons. This limitation, if made, would be, of course, in addition to and not instead of, the limitation of the special appropriation for ammunition and guns, and would mean a sum of money varying in amount for each signatory power with its average naval expenditure per ton in previous years.[1]

As for the control of the observance of such a total budgetary appropriation, the arguments used in Chapter IX concerning army budgets apply again.

9. *Arms Traffic.*—For the reasons discussed in Chapter X above, there must be stringent provisions about the arms traffic in the general naval treaty. Unless transference of fighting ships from one country to another, and indeed their whole production, is rigidly controlled, there can be no confidence that the agreed treaty ratio of armed strength will be maintained.

The general subject of the traffic in and manufacture of arms will be discussed in a later chapter. It may here be said that the minimum required in a general naval treaty is the acceptance by all the signatory powers of the undertakings of the Washington Convention on the subject. In particular, two points are of importance: that every power shall engage never to dispose of any ship of war in such a way that it may pass over to the navy of another country; and that no power shall on any ground permit within its jurisdiction the building of any naval unit which exceeds either in tonnage or in calibre of guns the limits which the general treaty will lay down.

10. *Fortifications and Naval Bases.*—Plainly the general naval treaty must place some limitation on fortifications and naval bases. Broadly speaking, it will probably be enough, at any rate when the treaty is first made, to stabilize the existing *status quo* by providing that no new naval bases or fortifications shall be made, and that existing bases shall be kept, both in their docking, repair, and other facilities, and their defensive armament, in their present state. In other words, general acceptance should be obtained for the provisions applied to a specified area by Article 19 of the Washington Convention.

Many people in Great Britain will believe that this agreement should include the port of Singapore, and should thus prevent the building of a great new base in the Pacific. There can be no doubt that if, as part of a general plan, the British Govern-

---

[1] Cf. chap. ix., *supra.*

ment gave up their present project, it would be taken as proof of their sincere intention to disarm, and that in return for this concession they might themselves obtain other, and perhaps valuable, concessions from Japan.

11. *Neutralized Zones.*—Another important question is certain to arise in the negotiations for a general naval treaty: that of the neutralization of certain zones, and, in particular, of the Black Sea and the Baltic. The decision taken on this subject may have an important effect upon the reductions of naval strength which can be made. The point will be discussed in a later chapter.

12. *Undertakings by Non-Naval Powers.*—The following undertakings should be given by *all* the powers which sign a general disarmament treaty, whether they themselves have fleets or not. They should promise:

(i.) Not to acquire any warships not allowed them by the treaty, until, by consent of all the parties, its schedules have been changed.

(ii.) To help to uphold the treaty system by strict observance of its rules concerning the production and sale of fighting ships or other naval arms.

(iii.) To create no new naval base within their jurisdictions, and to lease or sell no part of their territories for that purpose.

SUMMARY

A brief summary of the suggestions put forward above may now be made.

It has been proposed:

1. That a naval agreement to be accepted by all the powers taking part in the Disarmament Conference, whether at present they have fleets or not, should be drawn up and signed as an integral part of the general Disarmament Treaty to be made.

2. That this agreement should include both a general limitation of the total tonnage allowed to every naval power, and a supplementary limitation of their tonnage in the most important classes of fighting ships.

3. That a prolonged Naval Holiday should be agreed to,

during which there should be no construction of new naval units of any kind.

4. That as stringent a restriction as possible should be placed upon the maximum displacement of the ships that may be built in future, and upon the maximum calibre of the guns which they may have.

5. That an attempt should be made to secure the total abolition of the submarine as an instrument of war.

6. That limitation by annual budgetary appropriation should perhaps be made of expenditure on ammunition and on gun replacement and repair, a fixed sum being allowed for each ten thousand tons of permitted shipping.

7. That the total naval budget of each signatory power should perhaps also be limited, on the basis of a fixed appropriation per ten thousand tons, not equal in amount for all parties, but varying in accordance with their past expenditure.

8. That the total man-power in the service of the navy should be limited by establishing a proportion between man-power and tonnage.

9. That whatever restrictions may be consistent with the conscription system should be applied for the limitation of naval reserves.

10. That a stringent control of the traffic in naval armaments should be set up.

11. That an agreement should be made to maintain the *status quo* in respect of naval bases and fortifications.

It will be proposed hereafter:

12. That the question of neutralizing certain areas of the open sea should be reconsidered in the light of recent changes in national policy and of changes in the conditions of modern war.

Any agreement as elaborate as this would, of course, impose restrictions upon the liberty of the signatory powers in many ways. For that reason it might be difficult to secure general agreement for its more complicated parts. But, on the other hand, it can be argued that the more elaborate its provisions, the more factors in naval strength which it controls, the more confidence will it inspire, and the simpler will it be to secure its effective and loyal execution.

CHAPTER XII

AERIAL DISARMAMENT

UP to the present time no treaties have dealt with the problem of the reduction and limitation of air forces. The Treaties of Peace simply forbid the four ex-enemy powers to possess naval or military aircraft of any kind. Such wholesale abolition of military and naval aircraft, while it shows the importance attached to the matter by the Allied experts at Versailles, has little else to teach that is of value for the present purpose.

As the limitation of aerial forces is probably the crux upon which the whole policy of disarmament will succeed or fail, it may be worth while to state at some length what the problem is.

1. Aircraft, in the stage of development which they have so far reached, are able to fulfil a number of different functions in the operations of war.

They serve as scouts for land forces; they are by far the most efficient scouts in the history of war. They report to the higher command movements of enemy troops, both large-scale strategical movements on the enemy's lines of communication, and small-scale tactical movements on the front. They report on the fortifications and entrenchments which he makes, and, by their photographs, provide the staff with detailed maps of his defensive system. They report on the disposition of his guns, and assist in their destruction by directing counter-battery fire.

Next, they take a direct part in land operations by machine-gunning infantry positions that are to be attacked, by bombing or machine-gunning enemy troops that are advancing or retreating either on roads or over open country. They likewise help large-scale infantry attacks by breaking the enemy's communications, and by bombing and machine-gunning the routes by which he brings up his supplies. In all these functions aircraft serve as auxiliaries to forces operating on the ground. *Mutatis mutandis,* they could now perform the same auxiliary functions for fleets engaged at sea.

But, third, air forces have now developed another and a totally new function of their own. They have become a super-artillery—a means of bombarding the centres from which the enemy organizes and supplies his fighting troops. This function, of great importance in modern war, can be performed with the greater precision and effect as every year brings new improvements in the aeroplanes which carry it out.

Fourth, aircraft have yet another function—that of clearing the sky of hostile aircraft. By so doing, they render it possible for their own aircraft to fulfil the other functions of scouting, of auxiliary attack and of large-scale bombardment, without interference from the enemy, and with only the negligible loss which his land artillery may be able to inflict.

2. In the machines developed by the Air Staffs of the great aerial powers for the different functions above described, there has been, up to the present time, a broad tendency to differentiation of type. For clearing the sky of enemy aircraft, for scouting, and for co-operation in infantry attack, an aeroplane is needed which is very fast, which can climb with great rapidity—the power to gain height quickly is the supreme tactical advantage in aerial combat—which can resist the tremendous strain upon its framework caused by rapid diving and manœuvring at a speed of hundreds of miles per hour, which can overtake an escaping aeroplane or outdistance its pursuers, as the case may be. For bombing, on the other hand, a machine is needed which can carry great weights for a long distance and at a high speed. The capacity to lift great weights is of no consequence to a fighter or a scout, but it is the essential quality in bombing aircraft.

In addition to this main differentiation, there would, no doubt, also be minor divergences between the types respectively best adapted for fighting, for observation, for artillery control, and so on. But these divergences would be relatively small, while the divergences between such types and the perfect bomber are already great and are becoming, with every year that passes, greater still.

It is therefore fair to say that there is a definite and increasing differentiation between the type of aeroplane now being built for bombing purposes, on the one hand, and those being built for the other functions which aeroplanes fulfil, on the other.

3. It is worth while to consider in more detail the characteristics of the two broad types distinguished.

First, the fighting aeroplane (if the phrase may for brevity be used to cover aeroplanes which fight, observe, and co-operate in an auxiliary capacity with forces on the ground) is becoming every year a more highly specialized machine. The only thing considered in its construction is its maximum possible " performance." Here is a description taken from a recent work on aerial warfare:

> " The fighting aeroplane of the future will be a very small all-steel monoplane, mounting a 1,000 h.p. gas turbine engine, and possibly incorporating some form of jet propulsion. It will be capable of 400 miles per hour on the level, and will have a terminal velocity in the dive of nearly 800 miles per hour. In other words, it will be able to travel faster than sound.
>
> " It will climb to 20,000 feet in four minutes, and its service ' ceiling ' (which is the height at which the rate of climb falls below 100 feet per minute) will be 60,000 feet."[1]

These figures " are more likely to prove under-estimates than over-estimates."[1]

Machines for observation need not, perhaps, be capable of quite such high " performance " as the fighter thus described; but if they are much inferior in speed or in capacity to manœuvre, they will not be able to fulfil their proper functions, which, of course, must be carried out by day, when they are liable to attack by fighters of the kind described. There must therefore be, in all aeroplanes which have to operate by day, a strong tendency to specialize in high speed and a capacity for quick manœuvre; they must achieve in these respects a standard of performance which no bomber designed to lift large weights

[1] *The Strategy and Tactics of Air Fighting*, by Major Oliver Stewart, M.C., A.F.C., pp. 191-2.

could possibly produce. Hence the differentiation of type which has been mentioned.

The next important fact about the fighting aeroplane is this: that it is quality and not quantity, performance and not numbers, that will count. Here is another passage from the work just cited: " It is not appreciated sufficiently that quality is more important than quantity in the air. If a thousand well-armed aeroplanes of pre-war design were matched against one modern single-seater fighter, it is probable that the fighter would shoot down the thousand aeroplanes if its fuel and ammunition held out long enough. Anyhow, the 1,000 would be perfectly incapable of offensive action against the one, if the one wished to avoid their attack."[1] It follows from this that bombing machines alone will never make a country strong in air power against an enemy who is strong in fighting aircraft. Neither the bombers nor their pilots could compete for a moment with the fighters; they would be shot down in dozens. Thus bombers will not be able to perform their duties when they are subject to attack by enemy fighters, unless they are heavily protected by fighters of their own.

There is, however, one limitation of great importance upon the capacity of the fighter. It cannot work at night. Some new devices, indeed, have been invented which, over a certain restricted area (*e.g.*, a city), might enable defending fighters to inflict some loss upon a raiding force. The best of these devices consists in the creation, by immense reflectors, of a zone of light across the sky. The defending aircraft fly high above this zone, and see the enemy raiders pass across it like moving shadows far beneath. Then they dive down and endeavour to destroy them. But even this device will probably do little to improve the performance of the fighting aeroplane by night. It is, indeed, inherent in the nature of air fighting, which must be done at a tremendous speed, and which depends upon fast manœuvre over great distances, that it should only be possible when the pilot can see the enemy he is endeavouring to attack. Until an artificial substitute for the sun has been invented, there will be no probability that aerial fighting can be carried on at night.

[1] *The Strategy and Tactics of Air Fighting*, by Major Oliver Stewart, M.C., A.F.C., p. 187.

As a result of this, bombing aeroplanes can work at night virtually without interference from the enemy's forces. If the enemy is lucky, he may, either by his defensive aircraft or by anti-aircraft guns, inflict upon a raiding force the loss of a few aeroplanes in every hundred; but for all military purposes the proportion will be negligibly small. This assertion is not only founded on the experience of the war, but upon the unanimous opinion of every air expert at the present time.[1]

4. So much for the qualities and the limitations of the fighter. The bombing aeroplane is a completely different weapon. It is the new form of artillery, and an immensely more effective form—except, indeed, upon a small target and at the shortest range—than any which projects explosives through a rifled tube. For all long-range work and for all large targets, the bomber is by far the most effective gun that has ever been conceived. Thus:

(i.) It is much cheaper than a big gun, and it has a longer life.

(ii.) It has an incomparably greater range than any gun can have. At the present time the average radius of action of the bomber is somewhere between 200 and 250 miles from its base. This radius is increasing every year, and it is no doubt a safe prediction to say that within ten years from now it will

[1] The following words were written in 1922 by Brig.-Gen. P. R. C. Groves, Director of Air Operations for the British forces in 1918: " It may be argued that it will be possible to protect the great cities by means of anti-aircraft defences. The following considerations will show that that view is fallacious. In 1918 the London anti-aircraft defences consisted of 11 specially trained night-flying squadrons of aeroplanes, 180 guns on the ground, in addition to a number of guns mounted upon motor vehicles, 10 balloon aprons, and a large number of searchlights. The number of aircraft was nearly 300, and the total number of men employed some 30,000—*i.e.*, the equivalent of two divisions of infantry. In addition, there were a number of specially prepared night landing grounds, extensive telephone installations, and a large headquarters staff to co-ordinate and direct the whole defensive organization. Great as was the scale of these defences, London was bombed, although the largest number of aeroplanes in any single raid was only 36. Obviously, it would be impossible to maintain defences on the above scale for every city and other nerve centres in a state; but even if it were possible, such defence would be useless against aerial attack delivered by thousands or even by hundreds of aircraft." L.N. Document C.T.A. 210, 1923.

be at least 500 miles.   This lengthening of radius is an important fact.

(iii.) At the present time, it is of quite equal accuracy with gunfire at long range, and its accuracy is increasing every year.

(iv.) It can carry bombs of far greater calibre and destructive power than any shell that can be thrown by a gun.   The shell of a 16-inch gun is in great part composed of steel, and the quantity of high-explosive is, therefore, relatively small.   An aerial bomb needs only a light steel casing, and thus the proportion of explosive is much greater.   Not only so, but bombs have already been used which are much greater in actual weight, and therefore infinitely greater in destructive power, than any shell could be, while there is literally no limit to probable expansion in this respect.   An aeroplane may quite soon be produced which can carry 20 or 30 tons of high-explosive.

For these reasons the bombing aeroplane would be a deadly weapon if it attacked a city or any other target of considerable size.   And in addition there is another probable improvement which would make aircraft very accurate against even quite small targets of particular importance: the large gun mounted on the aeroplane.   The author above quoted considers it as certain that within a short time there will be an aerial big gun, which can be used in low altitude attacks, and which will be extremely accurate against ships, arsenals, munition dumps, government offices, army commands, and so on.[1]

But even without such " air-artillery," bombing aircraft are in every way a great improvement on the ground-artillery of the past.   They can, of course, be used at night, when defending fighters are not able to attack, and when ground-defences will produce only the wholly inadequate effect which General Groves describes.[2]   They would bombard the nerve centres of the enemy's population, communication, and supply, and would open their assaults by the use of incendiary bombs. There are now improved forms of incendiary bombs which start

[1] Major Oliver Stewart, *loc. cit.*

[2] It is necessary to add that anti-aircraft guns and range-finding have been improved since General Groves wrote the words which are quoted. Against this, however, must be set the prospect of silent engines, which Colonel Mitchell of the U.S. Air Force predicted in the course of his recent court-martial at Washington.

fires against which water, in whatever quantity, has no effect. A large number of such bombs, dropped in different parts of a city at night and with a favourable wind, would cause a conflagration which no fire brigade could possibly put out, and which would compel the whole population to evacuate their homes. When the population had thus been driven out of doors, and the attacking aeroplanes had been provided with an illumination which would enable them to find the targets they were most anxious to destroy, they would then proceed to drop their high-explosives, and after their high-explosives, great quantities of poison-gas. The new gases, which have a great " spread," and which are fatal if they reach any part of the human body, would no doubt cause a stupendous mortality among the population of the place attacked, quite apart from the other effects of the bombardment.

Thus bombing aircraft have made gas a vitally important weapon of offence, and in so doing have altered the whole nature of future war.[1] In a still broader sense they may have changed it by altering the function of bombardment. Hitherto, bombardment has been the preparation for the decisive blow of an assaulting force. Hereafter, aerial bombardment may itself become the decisive blow which brings a victory.

5. It must be added that aircraft are, of all possible weapons, those which most favour a surprise attack. They can be mobilized with great rapidity. Their attacks require less staff direction, less movement from their bases, less of all the visible signs of preparation, than any other method of offence. This applies to bombing aeroplanes no less than to fighters.

6. The assumption, moreover, which is made above, that in any future war aircraft will be used against large cities, is a just and inevitable assumption. There is no intelligible theory of modern war by which such use can be condemned, once fighting has been permitted to begin. The only thing that could prevent it would be so close a balance in aerial strength between the

---

[1] Cf., *e.g.*, Major Lefebure, a high authority, speaking as long ago as 1921: " Aircraft were the most effective instruments for a gas attack. . . . It would be practical to put out of action by an aerial gas attack half a million persons in London " (*Problems of Peace and War*, Grotius Society, p. 166. Cf. also chap. xiv., *infra*).

opposing sides, that each would fear that it might suffer most if it first attacked the cities of the other. But even if this happened for a time, even if at the outbreak of hostilities neither side attempted to obtain an initial, perhaps a decisive, advantage, some moment in the conflict would arrive when one or other of them, believing that it had a momentary supremacy in the air, a more effective poison-gas, or some other hope of victory, would seek to strike a mortal blow by air bombardment.

7. And, as was said above, there is no possible defence against air bombardment carried out by night. In daylight, if there is a balance of strength in " fighters," the risks taken by raiding bombers may be great. But at night-time they are slight. The only means of defence is counter-attack upon the enemy's air-force bases and his towns.

It is true, indeed, that if the fighters of one side gained complete supremacy, they could then by daylight bombing expeditions wipe out all the aerodromes and depôts upon which the enemy's air-force could be based. In that way, no doubt, defence can be made against aerial attack. But then, if such supremacy were gained, the war would be already over.

8. It has been said above that recent years have brought a marked differentiation between the types of aircraft which have been roughly classed together as " fighters " and " bombers." The same differentiation has, of course, occurred between fighters and commercial aircraft. The power to climb with great rapidity, to bear the strain of sudden manœuvring in the middle of a dive, are not qualities that have commercial value.

On the other hand, there is no such differentiation between aircraft designed for bombing and for commerce. The qualities principally required in commercial aircraft are (1) speed, (2) carrying capacity, (3) radius of action. These are precisely the qualities which a bomber needs. Thus, while commercial aircraft will be valueless as fighters, while, like bombers, they will be unable to resist fighters who attack in daylight, they will, for night-bombing purposes, be of the greatest use.

The importance of the fact is increased by the consideration that, for bombing, it is the quantity of aircraft, not the quality, which counts; numbers, not performance. If an aeroplane can carry bombs fast enough to reach its target and to get back to its base, or at least to its own lines, during the hours of darkness, it will serve as an efficient bomber.

It is true that commercial aircraft might need some small adjustments to adapt them for bombardment work, but they are changes which need only take an hour. Commercial pilots and air personnel (mechanics, etc.) can similarly be used at once and without special training (though not of course without organization and command) for bombing a large target like a city.

9. There is, moreover, an essential and inevitable connection between the existence of commercial aviation and potential war-power in the air. For commercial aviation implies an aircraft industry which, in its turn, means the power both to keep a host of aircraft in the air, and rapidly to expand the production of machines. The importance of aircraft industry is shown by the simple fact that, at the end of the Great War, a single factory in the United States contracted to produce one hundred aeroplanes a day.[1] The connection between commercial aviation and potential air-power needs no further proof.

10. Commercial aviation is very rapidly becoming an economically profitable proposition. Until recently it was mostly maintained by Government subsidy. That is no longer universally true. It is estimated that in 1924 about 6,000 pilots and 1,400 planes were engaged in commercial aviation in the U.S.A., and that in that year they flew about 2,000,000 miles for commercial purposes.[2] The passengers carried commercially in Germany increased from 4,500 in 1924 to 45,000 in 1925.[3] Such figures show prospect of immense expansions at an early date.

The essential facts of the situation, then, are these: that aerial bombardment will, in all human probability, be the principal offensive weapon of any future war; that defensive fighting aircraft cannot remove the danger of such attack, unless complete and total air supremacy be obtained—a

[1] Recorded by the Aircraft Committee of the Washington Conference, 1921 (vide Cmd. 1627, 1922, p. 33).
[2] *Atlas of World's Airways*, Field, p. 75.
[3] *The Times*, February 26, 1926.

prospect, even for the strongest nation, improbable in the extreme; that the main factor in the efficacy of air bombardment is the number of aeroplanes employed; that commercial aircraft will be equally effective with military aircraft for the purpose; that the scale of commercial aviation will enormously increase when it becomes, as no doubt it will, an economically profitable proposition; and that there is, for all purposes of aerial warfare, an essential and inevitable connection between the possession of commercial aviation and potential war-power in the air.

This, therefore, is the problem which aerial armaments present: can anything be done to reduce and limit the aircraft which constitute so grave a menace to civilization? It is a problem which affects disarmament both on land and sea, and which in itself evokes the most terrifying prospect which mankind has ever had to face.

It may be said at once that something *must* be done about aircraft, something that will remove or that at least will mitigate their menace to mankind, or else all hope of real disarmament is gone. In theory, it is possible to limit armies without restricting air forces at all. But it is at least doubtful whether general agreement could be secured for such a course. It is no less doubtful whether, if it could, such agreement would be better than none at all. For it would leave open the most dangerous path to armament competition, a path along which some powers have started— England and France among them, as the parliamentary debates of recent years can show. Whatever else it did, therefore, such an agreement would leave unfulfilled the most important purpose of a disarmament treaty. And in the present temper of the Governments it might well be feared that whatever economies they made on other forces, they would devote to the expansion of their war-power in the air. Thus such a partial treaty might actually do more harm than good by precipitating changes in competitive preparation which otherwise, under the influence of staffs of land-trained soldiers, might be long delayed.

Something, therefore, must be done if it is humanly possible to do it. And the decisions which are required must be taken with a full sense of the grave—it is hardly too much to say the desperate—dangers that are involved. It may be, indeed, appropriate to preface the detailed examination of the various possible methods of air disarmament by some words spoken in October, 1925, by Sir Samuel Hoare, Secretary of State for Air, one among the many striking warnings which he has given. Speaking of the risk of air attack on London, Sir Samuel said that London " was of all the great capitals of the world the most vulnerable to air attack, owing to its geographical situation. The attacks launched against London during the war, judged by the standards of to-day, and still more by the standards of the future, were on an altogether insignificant scale. The Government proposed . . . to press on with the policy of peace. They wanted to make the possibility he had hinted at remote and to lose no opportunity of reducing the great burden of armaments expenditure. As Secretary for Air, the more he saw of the possibilities of air warfare in the future, the *more anxious he was to take every legitimate opportunity of making impossible developments which, if left to themselves, might destroy civilization.*"[1] The responsible head of a Service Department could hardly have used more emphatic, not to say alarmist, language.

What, then, are the possible methods by which a diminution of the dangers of air warfare can be sought in a disarmament treaty ? They may be considered one by one.

1. *The Total Abolition of Aviation.*—It has been seriously proposed to take the unprecedented step of making an international agreement for the total abolition of aviation. No such abandonment of a great scientific achievement has ever been proposed before. But since the suggestion has been made it must be examined.

[1] *The Times*, October 20, 1925; cf. also his words in another speech: " It is much more probable that the critical battles of the future will be fought over our great cities, and the chief sufferers will be the civilians—men, women, and children. . . . In the late war some 300 tons of bombs only were dropped upon this country. Air forces to-day could drop the same weight in the first twenty-four hours of war, and could continue this scale of attack indefinitely. I need not dilate upon this terrible and repulsive picture."—*The Times*, October 17, 1925.

There are two questions which must be asked and answered. First, if agreement could be got, would it be desirable to abolish aviation ? Second, if it is desirable, can agreement be secured ?

To the first of these questions the answers which are made will vary with the varying appreciation of the risks of war. Two expert and authoritative opinions have been given. The first is in the report made to the Washington Conference by its Aircraft Committee. They considered the plan of total abolition and rejected it because they held that " any addition to the transport and communication facilities of the world should operate to improve the distribution of resources and likewise to lessen the causes of misunderstanding between peoples and thus lessen the causes of warfare."[1]

Air-Chief Marshal Sir Hugh Trenchard, the present Chief of the Imperial Air Staff, speaking before the Cambridge University Aeronautical Society, expressed a different view. " I do not want you to think that I look upon air as a blessing altogether," he said. " It may be more of a blessing for this Empire than for any other country in the world, but I feel that all the good it will do in civil life cannot balance the harm that may be done in war by it, and *if I had the casting vote, I would say abolish the air*. I feel that it is an infinitely more harmful weapon of war than any other."[2]

There is thus no clear answer to be gained from these two expert, but conflicting, opinions as to whether it is desirable to abolish aviation. Nor is it worth while to canvass the question in more detail, for, in fact, it is quite certain that no proposal to abolish aviation would be agreed to by the Government of any considerable power. If, by a miracle, international agreement were secured, then the whole problem with which this chapter deals would disappear. But if, as may be assumed, the proposal is not even seriously considered, let alone adopted, some other policy must be sought which will fit the facts above described.

2. *The Abolition of Military and Naval Aviation.*—There is a second possible course less sweeping in its scope: the general

[1] Cmd. 1627, 1922, p. 25.
[2] *Daily News*, October 25, 1925.

adoption of the Peace Treaty system. Under this system civil aviation would be allowed, but military and naval aviation of every kind would be abolished.

Few will doubt that if agreement could be secured for such a plan, it would be desirable on every ground to carry it out. Indeed, on grounds of reason and of public welfare, there seems to be no single argument on the other side. National security should be the only purpose of all armament, and military aircraft must always and obviously create insecurity for all concerned.

But, again, whatever it might be desirable to do, there is little hope that Governments, in fact, will seriously consider the total abolition of military and naval aircraft. Some policy, therefore, which aims not at abolition, but at reduction and limitation, must be found.

3. *The Limitation of the Numbers and the Size of Commercial Aircraft.*—It may help to clarify the issues if at the outset two other questions of general policy are asked and answered, in principle at least. Is it desirable to limit the number and the size (not, it should be noted, the *type*) of commercial aircraft ? And second, if it is desirable, is it at all likely to be done ?

Again the answer to the first question will vary with the varying appreciation of the risk. The Washington Committee on Aircraft answered as before, that it was *not* desirable to limit in any way freedom of development in commercial aviation, since such freedom in their opinion was essential to the progress of human knowledge and welfare. Sir Hugh Trenchard, and many ordinary mortals who think with him, would answer that it would be desirable to make such a limitation, if it could be done. But, again, it is the second question which decides, and again there can be no doubt about the answer: no limitation of the numbers or the size of commercial aircraft will in fact be agreed to, and it is on this assumption, therefore, that the policy to be adopted must be framed.

4. *Limitation of Military Aircraft.*—In view of this and in view of the fact that the dominating weapon of future warfare will in all likelihood be aerial bombardment carried out at least in part by commercial aircraft, is it desirable and is it possible

to limit *military* aircraft in any way ? And if so, how can it be done ?[1]

To the first question there is this time no doubt about the answer that will be generally made. On every ground it is emphatically to be desired that military aircraft should be limited, if it can be done. The following reasons, though some only of many that apply, are conclusive.

First, as has above been argued, if military aircraft are not dealt with, it is doubtful whether any disarmament treaty can be made; and if it is made, whether it will do more good than harm.

Second, it is important on economic grounds to limit the financial burden which air forces now involve. This burden is still relatively light, as the cost per unit is less than the cost of corresponding units of land or naval forces. But the great expansion of air forces which has begun and which, if no limitation is agreed to, will go on, will add very seriously to the burden they impose.

Third, the indefinite expansion of aerial forces would almost certainly involve, as a direct result, the militarization of aviation as a whole. It might thus hamper and divert the normal technical development of commercial aircraft, for every measure would be taken which would render commercial aviation readily available for war.[2]

Fourth, the existence of a large cadre of military aircraft would render a given number of commercial aircraft far more effective as an offensive weapon by facilitating in many ways their organization and command when they were mobilized. It would thus increase the temptation to potential aggressors to make surprise attacks.

Fifth, rival competition in air force preparation will, in view of the menace it involves to civilian populations, create even

---

[1] It should be noted that in the following discussion the phrase " military aircraft " is used to include aircraft used for both military and naval purposes.

[2] " Carrying surface can be increased by the standardization and interchangeability of wings and other methods, and it is not impossible to conceive of civil and commercial aircraft being designed with a view to ultimate war requirements."—Report of Washington Committee, *loc. cit.*, p. 27.

more suspicion and distrust, and an even greater sense of insecurity, than the armament competitions of the past. It will thus increase directly the risk of war.

The objects of an air force limitation should be two: first, the limitation of the actual battle-strength in " fighters " of the different states; second, the limitation of the total air force cadre which is available for policing, organizing and commanding whatever aircraft of all kinds a nation could mobilize for purposes of war. How can these two objects be secured?

There would be two distinct elements in a perfect treaty: the limitation of the *type* of aircraft and the limitation of their *numbers*.

The Limitation of Military Type.—As for the limitation of type, it would be obviously desirable to effect it if there were any way in which it could be done. The opinion of Major Stewart may be recalled, that one fighter of the present day might be able to defeat a thousand pre-war 'planes. If this be even approximately true, the fighting strength of any air force for aerial combat must depend upon the type of aircraft which it uses, upon their horse-power, their speed, their power to climb, to dive and to manœuvre.

Is there any way in which the type of aircraft can be controlled? Two methods were considered by the Washington Committee: by limitation of horse-power and by limitation of lift-tonnage. Obviously for fighting purposes horse-power is more effective than the capacity to lift great weights. But limitation by either means would be difficult to devise and still more difficult to control in application. " Measurements of horse-power, supporting surface, fuel capacity and weight will be necessary if security against evasion is to be ensured. . . . But taking rules as drafted and even assuming continuous inspection of a most stringent character, it appears that there are still loopholes for evasion. No rules can prevent aircraft being designed in peace to permit of the ready instalment of larger tanks in war; engines can be made interchangeable, enabling one of higher power to be installed, etc. . . ."[1] Again, on the limitation of horse-power the Committee says: " This

[1] *Ibid.*, p. 27.

can only be based on the cubic capacity of the engines; there will be no guarantee that a nation has not discovered a secret which will enable greater horse-power to be got out of a limited capacity, nor is it reasonable to expect any nation to disclose such a secret." Besides these technical reasons the Committee also urged that an attempt to control the observance of such a system would, if it were effective, " entail such detailed inspection by a foreign Commission as to be intolerable to any nation."[1]

These reasons are of such force that it is necessary to agree that any limitation of the type of aircraft will be technically and practically very difficult, if not impossible, to carry out. It may be taken as virtually certain, therefore, that even if theoretically it were possible to impose restrictions on the type of aircraft, no such restrictions would, in fact, be made.

This fact must be regretted, but it is not fatal to an agreement for the limitation of air forces. It is at least probable that a rough balance in type of individual military machines will be maintained by the different powers which have pretensions to aerial strength. It would be against all previous experience in the development of weapons if this were not so. And if the total numbers of military aircraft are rigidly restricted, the risks involved in the free development of type will be, if not extinguished, at least much reduced.

The Limitation of Air Forces.—How then can the numbers of military aircraft and the total strength of the air force cadre be limited ?

Five possible plans were discussed and rejected by the Washington Committee. The matter is so important that their arguments require examination. Their five plans were as follows:

> " (i.) The limitation of the *number* of military aircraft.
> (ii.) The limitation of the amount of *horse-power* for military aircraft.
> (iii.) The limitation of *lift-tonnage* for military aircraft.
> (iv.) The limitation of *personnel* for military aircraft.
> (v.) The limitation of military aircraft *budgets.*"[2]

[1] Cmd. 1627, 1922, p. 32.   [2] *Ibid.*, p. 31.

Two of these plans, limitation by horse-power and by lift-tonnage, have been already mentioned in discussing the limitation of the type of individual machines. It is plain that since they are unworkable for the purpose of controlling the power and efficiency of individual machines, they will be still more unworkable for limiting the total power or capacity of a number of machines taken together. And this, in fact, is the argument by which the Washington Committee reject the plans of limiting total military aircraft by allotting to each country either a fixed amount of permitted horse-power or a fixed maximum lift-tonnage. If their argument is accepted, as no doubt it will be, in respect of limitation of type, it must also be accepted in respect of total air force strength.

These two methods of limitation, by horse-power or by lift-tonnage, may thus be ruled out of the debate.

Limitation by Number of Aircraft.—There comes next the plan of limitation by " number of military aircraft "—*i.e.*, limitation " on a numerical basis." This again they reject on two different grounds.

They urge, first, the argument used by Major Stewart, that in fighting aircraft it is the type that matters, and from it they conclude that it would be of little use for different countries simply to agree to limit the total numbers of their machines. To secure equality of result, their agreement would have to include a limitation of the numbers of machines permitted in each type; that would involve the definition, and, of course, the limitation of the types themselves. And since they have already rejected such limitation of type as too difficult to carry out, they conclude that no agreement concerning total numbers can be of use.

Second, they argue that even if type *could* be limited, the problem of restricting the numbers of aircraft to fixed totals would in itself be highly complex, and that again evasion might be impossible to prevent. Any agreement concerning numbers would have to limit not only the total machines actually in use, but also machines kept in reserve, engines in reserve, and the replacement of machines which by the passage of time become obsolete, or which by accident or otherwise are damaged or destroyed. The Committee point out the great difficulty of making any such agreement in an age when aircraft become obsolete in a few months, when peace wastage is relatively high, and when war wastage may be more than 200 per cent *per month*.

For these reasons the limitation of aircraft on a numerical basis would be difficult to arrange, and still more difficult to control.

Indeed, of all the three plans so far considered, it must be admitted that, even if the arguments of the Washington Report about international inspection are rejected as out of date, the plans themselves are hardly of a nature to inspire confidence in the signatories to a disarmament agreement that the undertakings they would involve would be observed. It may, therefore, be assumed that none of them in fact will be adopted.

Limitation of Air Force Personnel.—The next method of limitation proposed by the Washington Committee is that of personnel. Again the Committee reject it, and their argument is this:

" The fourth method of limitation, whether of the total of organized personnel for war aircraft, or only of pilots in the permanent military establishments, fails by reason of the difference in organization between different states. A nation which has a separate air service has to include in its organized personnel those employed in recruiting, supply, transport, administrative headquarters, etc. In the case of nations whose air forces are contained in their naval and military forces, supply, etc., personnel are included in naval and military establishments; a fair comparison cannot therefore be made. Moreover, the difference in terms of service, long or short, voluntary service or conscription, must introduce incalculable factors which directly affect the efficiency of organized air forces and the size and efficiency of the ' reserve.' "[1]

This argument, like that on the limitation of aircraft budgets, which is considered later, was, of course, used by the Washington Committee, not of a proposal to limit all the armaments of all

[1] Cmd. 1627, p. 32, Para 33.

the nations of the world, but of a proposal to limit air forces only, and to do so at a time when, as the Committee no doubt rightly held, the Governments had no serious intention of making any general change in the organization of their military machines. It does not, therefore, apply to the present situation, and, indeed, as soon as general disarmament is seriously considered with a firm intention to secure results, it becomes wholly inconclusive. For whatever the present practices of states may be, whatever their present organization, there is no possible reason why they should not change them, if they have any real intention to disarm. It would obviously be quite simple for an international committee of air and military experts to draw up common rules to define what services should be included in the air force proper, and on the basis of these rules the air-effectives allowed to every state could be laid down in application of whatever general ratio might be agreed.

It is true that compulsory short-term service causes here the same complications that it causes in the limitation of land forces. Perhaps, indeed, the complications are even greater, because short-term service in an air force might much increase the number of qualified pilots upon whom the efficacy of the whole force evidently depends. But, broadly speaking, the same arguments apply to air as to land reserves. The difficulties are a necessary result of the conscription system. They do not make the limitation of air forces impossible, any more than they make the limitation of armies impossible. They do make it desirable to keep the standing forces as small as may be and to reduce the period of training which the air-effectives may receive to the shortest possible period that can be agreed.

Again, as with land forces, there is no real danger that the total strength of air-effectives, if thus limited by treaty, would in practice be secretly exceeded. The control of the agreement would, of course, be made much simpler by the similar limitation of total armed effectives of all kinds, which it is urged above is the essential element of land disarmament and a desirable element in disarmament at sea.

There is, moreover, another sub-limitation of personnel that might be made. It is that of the total number of pilots.

Attached to the Report of the Washington Committee there is the following note:

> "The Italian representative believes and desires to place on record that one way in which it would be possible to limit the air power of a nation would be by placing a limit upon the number of pilots in the permanent military establishment.—RICCARDO MOIZO, *Colonel, R.I.A.*"[1]

Aeroplanes cannot be flown without highly trained pilots; they are almost as much the " dominant factor " in air strength as fighting ships are in strength at sea. A rigid limitation of military pilots will therefore limit the effective fighting strength of the air force of a country, and the more specialized military machines become, the more developed is the technique of aerial fighting, the greater will be the effect produced by such limitation of military pilots, and the fewer will be the reserves that can be mobilized to swell their ranks, if hostilities should begin.

There is another advantage in limiting not only total air personnel, but also the number of pilots: that it would prevent inequalities resulting if any Government discovered means of reducing below the normal average the number of *ground* personnel required, thus releasing a greater proportion of their total personnel to serve as pilots. The proportion of ground personnel required is, in fact, already going down. In the British Air Force it was in 1921 as high as seventy men for every aeroplane; to-day it is considerably less. If mechanical improvements and superior staff work should still further reduce the number, the limitation of air force personnel might thus fail of its effect unless there were also this supplementary limitation on the proportion of permitted pilots that is allowed. There would appear to be no sound objection to such a double limitation, which would, no doubt, achieve an effective limitation of air strength both in time of peace and, if war broke out, also in Period A.

Limitation of Air Force Budgets.—There remains the fifth plan suggested by the Washington Committee, the limitation

---

[1] *Loc. cit.,* p. 37.

of military aircraft budgets. Their argument for its rejection is as follows:

" The fifth method of limitation, limitation by means of limiting the budget and thereby controlling the amount of money that may be expended annually for aviation, seems simple in theory, but it is difficult of application. The various methods of distributing budgets for material under different subheads make it impracticable to determine or compare the actual sums expended exclusively for aircraft, and the question is at present further complicated by the factor of the relative purchasing power of the currency of various nations."[1]

Again, it is plain that this argument does not apply when a treaty of general disarmament is being considered with serious intention to achieve results. For obviously an international committee of experts in military budgets could easily work out a system of common rules of air-force accountancy, and a model budget which every nation could apply. It could also obviously prepare a workable scheme for air-force budgetary appropriations by agreeing on a fixed sum of money to be allowed for every hundred or for every thousand permitted air effectives. These appropriations might cover either the total cost of the air force or the separate cost of aircraft and their armament and ammunition; or, preferably, there might be two separate appropriations to cover both. *Mutatis mutandis*, the arguments used above about observance, and control of budgetary limitations for the army, again apply.[2] It is true, no doubt, that small-scale evasions might occur, that excess aeroplanes in small numbers might be kept, that the armament and ammunition depots of a disloyal state might without detection somewhat exceed the maximum it was allowed. But such evasions would be relatively slight, and, broadly speaking, the agreed limitation would be effectively achieved.

The arguments of the Washington Committee are, therefore, not conclusive against these two plans of limitation. On the contrary, both plans can be applied, and if they are applied

[1] *Ibid.*, p. 33, Para. 34.   [2] Cf. chap. ix., *supra*.

in the ways proposed above, they will secure a real and effective limitation of the air forces which different states maintain. Plainly, if anything is done, it would be better to apply, not one of them alone, but both together. This would secure the limitation of personnel on a numerical basis and of material through a budgetary appropriation, and thus a system analogous to that proposed above for land forces would result.

It may be that agreement could not be secured for such a rigid scheme. If so, the same system could be applied in a more elastic way. The permitted air personnel might be merged together with the effectives permitted for the army, and the budgetary appropriation for aircraft and armament with the total budgetary appropriation allowed for the whole land armament of each given state. This plan would leave each country full liberty to develop its military aviation up to the limits of the total personnel and budgetary appropriations which it was allowed for its whole land and aerial forces. But, of course, developments of aviation would be made at the expense of other arms, and since no state is likely either entirely to give up or even greatly to reduce its army, an effective limitation of air forces might be thus secured.

This scheme, no doubt, would involve greater risks of inequality among the contracting powers than the more rigid scheme above proposed, but it might in practice work. Risks of some sort are inevitable, if the Governments desire to retain full freedom to develop air power as they may think fit. Here, indeed, the Governments must choose. Do they desire a system that will give them great liberty of action, complete freedom to choose between different weapons and methods of defence ? Or do they desire a more rigid system which will more strictly control the grave menace of air preparation, and which will give them greater confidence that rival states will not be able in some way to outstrip them in the competition for military power of some special kind ?

It will be observed that this plan of merging air personnel and budgets in the totals allowed for land and air together would avoid the necessity of fixing a separate ratio in air-strength between the different countries. This would no doubt be an advantage, if it were sound on other grounds. Whether it would be sound will be considered when the problem of the ratio in general is discussed.

5. *Civil Aviation.*—There are some other special points to be considered.

The Washington Committee gave the designation " Civil Aviation " to aircraft used by a state for other than military purposes, that is to say, for posts, police work, coast defence, etc. It seems plain that if military aircraft are limited, " civil " aircraft must be included in the total which each country is allowed. For civil aircraft stand on the same footing as " auxiliary " land forces. They are under complete state control; they are in full-time service; they can therefore be used at any moment exactly as the Government may dictate. Not only so, but in present conditions it is almost certain that a Government which had a large number of such civil aircraft would, in fact, give their personnel at least a partial training for air force work.

It is true that this plan might somewhat restrict the use of aircraft for ordinary civil purposes. If so, this is part of the price which must be paid to secure an effective limitation of military aircraft.

It may, perhaps, be held that the price would be particularly heavy for Great Britain, because the different Governments of the Empire may be able to make great use of state-owned aircraft for maintaining imperial communications, for policing remote and turbulent colonies, and so on. But, of course, if the British Government desired to increase their civil aviation for extra-European, *bona fide*, non-military ends, special allowance above the normal ratio might well be allowed by other states.

It may be added that aircraft for coast defence should obviously be included in the total military aircraft which are allowed.

6. *Lighter-than-Air Craft.*—There remains the question of aircraft that are lighter than air, in other words, of airships.

For various technical reasons, which need not be reproduced here, the Washington Conference came to the conclusion that lighter-than-air craft could be limited both in size and in number, and that the observance of such limitations could be easily controlled.

The importance of lighter-than-air craft in air operations is at present very small. But it is expected that, when they are technically improved, they will fulfil important functions by rendering air units even more mobile than they already are. Thus, in the speech which has been quoted, Sir Hugh Trenchard said: " So long as you have these facilities and arrangements (*i.e.*, aerodromes, etc.), the actual unit becomes very mobile and will be a thousand times still more mobile when the great aircraft carriers of the future—airships—come into being." Lighter-than-air craft may therefore play a great part in the organization of aerial forces, and may have an important bearing upon the utility of aircraft as a means of carrying out international undertakings of mutual guarantee.[1]

But in spite of this it seems unnecessary to make any special supplementary arrangements in a disarmament treaty for their limitation. It could, of course, quite easily be done, as the Washington Committee have explained, if the Governments desired to do it. But the simplest plan, and one that would, no doubt, be quite effective, is to include the personnel and the budgetary appropriation required for lighter-than-air craft in the total personnel and budgetary appropriations allowed for the total air force of each state.

7. *The Remaining Problem: The Control of Commercial Aviation.*—What will be the real effect of the measures of limitation suggested in the paragraphs above ? At the best they can achieve in part only the purposes for which an air disarmament agreement is desired. Even if the Governments adopted the more rigid of the two alternative systems just

---

[1] The following details concerning new dirigibles for the American Navy were recently issued by Admiral Moffat, Chief of the U.S. Naval Air Service: " They will have a capacity of 6 million cubic feet; each ship will be armed with 30 heavy machine-guns and one 1-pounder automatic cannon. These weapons will be provided with 9,700 rounds of ammunition, and bombs will also be carried. They will be filled with helium and could fly at a speed of 50 knots for 2,000 miles, with a military load of 43 tons. Each dirigible could, if necessary, carry 6 fighting aeroplanes, for 5,000 sea miles, at a speed of 50 knots."— *Daily News*, March 11, 1926.

described, even if under this system the air forces allowed to each state were rigidly cut down to the most modest scale, the resulting arrangements would still have serious defects. What these defects would be is shown by the facts discussed above.

(i.) Since there will, in all likelihood, be no agreement for any limitation of military type, there must remain a certain risk of air supremacy, of the invention of some superior device for the mastery of the air, by a single country or a group of countries. This risk will be much lessened if the military air forces that are allowed are very small, and if the specialization of fighting type continues in the future, as no doubt it will. But, none the less, we must bear in mind the risk of air supremacy and of the temptations which it might present to disloyal Governments that contemplate aggression.

(ii.) The coefficient of expansion for air forces if mobilization occurs will no doubt be great. For every state with any considerable amount of military air force will endeavour so to organize its commercial aviation that it can use it for aerial bombardment, which it was said may well be the decisive weapon of attack in any future war. Commercial aviation lends itself readily to organization for bombing work.

(iii.) And it must be repeated that as commercial aviation becomes in the future an economically profitable proposition, reserves of both commercial aircraft and commercial pilots will much increase. This is an inevitable result of the improvement in aviation which is destined to occur; the only way to reduce the " air potential " of a nation is to reduce its commercial air production in time of peace. This, it was argued above, the Governments will in no case agree to do.

(iv.) The reduction and limitation of military aviation will, as the Washington Committee pointed out, serve to increase the relative importance of commercial aircraft in any subsequent air operations there may be.[1] This, of course, is true; but as it will result not from any increase in the offensive power of

[1] " The Committee also desires to lay stress on the fact that even if such a limitation was practicable (*i.e.*, of military aircraft), it would not prevent the use of air power in war, but would only operate to give greater comparative importance to the other element of air power, which cannot be limited for the reasons given in the Report."—Cmd. 1627, 1925, p. 36.

commercial aircraft, but merely from the decrease of the total air power that each state will have, it is not a consideration that need cause much alarm.

What, then, in view of this situation, should be done? What should be the policy of the Governments in general, and the policy of Great Britain in particular, towards this menacing and inevitable problem? There is no obvious and coherent principle of action, but the following scattered suggestions may be made.

(i.) First, no purpose can be served by any attempt at international agreement not to use commercial aircraft for purposes of war. If war actually broke out, no Government and no people would have the slightest confidence that any such agreement would be observed. It would, therefore, not only be valueless in itself, but would tend to reduce confidence all round in the agreements by which disarmament is brought about.

(ii.) If aviation is to develop, as no doubt it will, the only certain way to avoid intense and devastating aerial warfare is to avoid war itself. We thus return, as a result of detailed consideration of the vital factor of aircraft, to the central propositions that an essential part of a policy of disarmament is a supplementary policy for preventing war, and that, if Governments are seriously minded in the matter, they must take every measure in their power to strengthen the available machinery for the purpose.

(iii.) Military aviation should plainly be cut down to the narrowest limits for which agreement can be secured. If it is true, as the Washington Committee said, that this would increase the comparative importance of commercial aircraft, it is also true that it will *decrease* the proportion of total aircraft which can be used for offensive action in the early stages of a war. For a great reduction of air forces will make the organization and command of commercial reserves far more difficult, and will thus make the numbers used far smaller and their work much less effective than if the military air cadre were unrestricted.

Above all, it is the interest of Great Britain to secure reduction of military air forces to the narrowest limits. The greatest danger to the British fleet and, above all, to its command of European waters, lies in the military and naval aircraft which foreign states are building. By land the menace is no less; the certainty of air attack upon our cities has wiped out the immunity which the country, as an island, has hitherto enjoyed. Above all other Governments, therefore, the British Government has everything to gain by the mutual restriction of air forces. This, indeed, without any doubt, should be the cardinal principle of the policy it adopts.

(iv.) Next, can nothing more be done about commercial aviation ?

The difficulties are great, for as was said above, the production of aircraft for commercial use cannot in all probability be controlled, either as to numbers of machines or their individual size.

But the question of the *type* of machines is different from that of size or number. If the present differentiation between the fighting and commercial types of aircraft should continue, as all experts now believe it will, it might be possible to secure agreement among Governments that they will not divert the development of commercial aircraft from the most efficient economic type, in order to adapt them better to military ends.

It is, to say the least, most probable that no perversion of commercial type will happen, except under the stimulus of Government subsidy. An agreement might therefore usefully be inserted in the disarmament treaty, that the signatories in making subsidies to commercial aviation will attach no condition about the type of machine that is constructed, and that they will make no attempt of this or any other kind to encourage the construction of types suitable for war. If such an agreement were to prevent commercial aircraft from being made available for use as fighters, this would be a result the importance of which needs no explanation.

It might be possible to add, as an additional agreement, that all subsidies to commercial aircraft should be taken from the budgetary appropriation allowed to each state for its air force. The effect of this would be that subsidies given to commercial aircraft would *pro tanto* reduce the air force. This would at least discourage attempts by disloyal Governments to prepare commercial aviation for aggressive use.

(v.) A parallel proposal which is worth discussion is that of an international agreement not to give military training, either voluntarily or compulsorily, to commercial personnel. Such an agreement, if once accepted, would be comparatively easy to control, because most commercial air services are international; and if it were observed, it would be of value: it would help in some measure to prevent what has been called the militarization of aviation; and it would reduce the expansion coefficient and the general offensive strength of an air force, if it were mobilized for war.

(vi.) But if all these measures were adopted, if everything were done that can be done without abolition of aviation, commercial aircraft would still remain available for offensive military action of a peculiarly devastating kind. Its very existence thus remains a grave menace to the world. It would, indeed, be certain, if the old pre-war system of international relations still continued, that sooner or later aircraft competition would lead to war, first perhaps on a small scale, then on the largest scale and with terrible results. Even with the new international system of the League of Nations, even with all the measures above proposed, the danger would not be altogether removed.

There appears to be only one other means by which it can be reduced: the systematic organization of joint international defence against sudden aggression by air attack. It has been pointed out above that the only defence—if such it can be called—against large-scale air bombardment lies in counter-bombardment against the enemy state. This fact suggests that, to prevent aggression, it may be necessary to restrain a potential aggressor by the certainty of counter-attack more formidable than any air attack which he himself can launch.

This would, of course, involve, if it were to be effective, he organization of a system of mutual guarantee under which the air forces of the signatory powers would be pledged to joint defence of any state which was aggressively attacked. If such a system were once established, and if there were general confidence that the whole or part of the air forces of the signatory states would join in action against an aggressor, whoever he might be, there can be little doubt that this would prove so formidable a prospect that no aggression would, in fact, occur. For if military aircraft were limited as above proposed, no potential aggressor could hope to establish air supremacy soon enough to prevent counter-attack against himself by night bombardment, and this fact would have a great restraining power.

It is true that at the present time there would be certain limitations on the practical effect of such a system of mutual air defence. These limitations result from the present inequality of the air forces of different nations, and from the limited radius of aircraft action.

But inequalities of air-strength are being to some extent reduced, and it may be hoped that they will be reduced much more by the disarmament treaty, when it is made. And as for the radius of aircraft action, the difficulty is being rapidly made less by the technical improvements which every year now brings. It is true, as has been said, that the average radius of all military aircraft taken together is at present little more than 200 to 250 miles from their base. But it is also true that the largest bombing machines can now fly ten hours at an average speed of 95 miles per hour, and that with this capacity air experts calculate their operations radius at 330 miles. It is also true that the average radius of aircraft is, as again was said above, increasing and increasing fast, and that it is almost certain that within ten years it will be at least 500 miles—an increase which will obviously much improve the efficiency of aircraft in implementing obligations of mutual guarantee.[1]

It is also true, as air experts admit, that military aircraft could be used for joint international action with considerable rapidity and without the detailed preparation of plans in advance. The technical difficulties of co-ordinating the action

[1] Cf. Report by Committee of Imperial Defence, written in July, 1923: "Though certain types of aeroplanes have a radius of action up to 500 to 600 miles, and others up to 300 to 400 miles, neither the British nor any other service is yet equipped with aeroplanes whose normal effective radius of action exceeds about 200 miles. . . . But it must be remembered that the types of aeroplanes now in service use *continue steadily to be replaced by machines of greater power and wider radius of action.*"—Cmd. 2029, 1924.

of different air forces are scarcely greater than those of co-ordinating different naval forces; indeed, the principles of naval warfare to some extent apply. The division of rôle between different contingents would be simple, for any given contingent could be allotted by wireless certain cities or areas to bomb, and could obviously carry out its task and report on the results without elaborate preparation in advance. Similarly, the concentration of different contingents at a decisive point could easily be arranged by telegram without elaborate preparation in advance.

Again, air forces can easily operate at a distance from their home country, and could do so with very small delay, for the transport of aircraft from one base to another is relatively easy. Thus:

(*a*) The air units would fly their own fleets and personnel to their new base.

(*b*) Their repair equipment and their general establishment could follow either by rail, by road (this, if possible, would be very rapid), or as Sir Hugh Trenchard forecasts, by airship.

(*c*) The state attacked could itself supply them in their new base with all their essential requirements, since they are requirements which, it must be always remembered, do not need to be standardized to any national pattern—*e.g.*, petrol, oil, food, bombs, etc. Any state expecting to be aggressively attacked would no doubt, if it relied on a system of mutual guarantee, prepare, as part of its normal staff arrangements, skeleton bases and depôts for the use of foreign air units which might lend their help.

(vii.) Aircraft, then, are well adapted—far better adapted than land forces—for implementing an agreement of mutual guarantee, which, it has been argued, may be the only means of effectively removing the danger inherent in the existence of unlimited numbers of commercial aircraft. The scheme, which since Locarno should not appear Utopian, however it might have appeared when the Washington Conference met in 1921, would have other advantages which must not be forgotten:

(*a*) If states were specially pledged to provide, for the purposes of mutual support, a large proportion of their air force, that would, in a considerable measure, remove the temptation to increase the amount of their permitted military resources which they devote to aircraft. This, of course, would be of particular importance if the more elastic of the two suggested systems of air limitation were adopted.

(*b*) By removing the temptation to utilize commercial aircraft for large-scale surprise attacks, it would increase the effect of the measures proposed above for preventing the militarization of commercial aviation.

(*c*) At the same time it would leave absolute freedom to commercial aviation to develop in whatever direction may prove to be economically most advantageous.

SUMMARY OF CONCLUSIONS

The conclusions arrived at in this chapter may now be summarized as follows:

1. Whether it is desirable or not to do so, it is almost certainly not possible to limit the numbers or the size of commercial aircraft.

2. An agreement should, however, be made not to grant Government subsidies to commercial aircraft on conditions that would encourage the perversion of their type from economic to military efficiency.

3. An agreement should also be made not to give to the personnel of commercial aviation any compulsory or voluntary military training.

4. It is probably not possible effectively to limit the type of military aircraft.

5. It is, however, both desirable and possible to limit the air forces which states maintain as part of their system of national defence. It is further desirable to reduce these forces to the lowest possible level for which agreement can be secured.

In particular, it is of paramount interest to Great Britain that this should be done.

6. Military air forces may be dealt with:

(i.) By the limitation of the total air force personnel.

(ii.) By restricting the number of permitted pilots to a fixed proportion of the permitted air force personnel.

(iii.) By the limitation of the budgetary appropriation permitted every year for aircraft construction, armament, and ammunition.

(iv.) Perhaps also by the limitation of the total budget allowed for the whole air force costs.

7. A more elastic, but less satisfactory, variant of this plan would be to include the total air force personnel and aircraft budgetary appropriation in the total number of effectives and armament appropriation allowed for the land forces of the different states. Such a limitation, while giving the Governments greater latitude of action, would for that reason be less satisfactory; but if it were accepted, it might prove a practicable plan.

8. To meet the danger of surprise aggression, inherent in the existence of unlimited numbers of commercial aircraft, there should be set up a system of mutual guarantee, depending largely on aircraft for its effect. It is desirable to this end that as large a proportion as possible of the military air forces of different states should be pledged by treaty to co-operation in mutual defence. This question of mutual aerial guarantee may be of vast importance since, as some experts hold, all other measures of disarmament, however necessary and useful they may be, may yet within a short time prove to be irrelevant to the gravest dangers which may threaten in the future the peace and security of the world.

CHAPTER XIII

PROBLEM OF THE RATIO

THE factors of military, naval, and air strength which it is desirable to limit, and the methods by which their limitation may be attempted, have both now been discussed. There remains the problem of the strength, calculated in these various factors in combination, to be allowed to each of the parties to a disarmament treaty—that is to say, the problem of how the Disarmament Conference shall settle the relative position to be established among the nations which take part in its deliberations.

This has been called the problem of the ratio. The phrase is convenient, and will be adhered to. But, lest it be misleading, it must be explained that the establishment of a ratio does not necessarily involve the drawing up of a complete table of national coefficients like that of Lord Esher's scheme. This, it has been shown, was done at the Washington Conference, where the relative strength of the different participating powers was determined by agreements, after a complex negotiation, on a simple arithmetical proportion of $5 : 5 : 3 : 1\cdot75 : 1\cdot75$. And probably in a general Disarmament Conference it will be more convenient, as it was at Washington, to prepare a similar table of coefficients, and to work on the basis which it provides. But, of course, that is not essential. Cumbrous though it would be, it is quite possible, as was said above, for the Conference to work without a formal unit of measurement, and to negotiate from start to finish in terms of the total personnel and armament which each country will retain. Whether or not there is a table of coefficients is thus a matter more of form than of substance. The question might conceivably have a real importance, because of the psychological effect produced by " coefficients." Lord Esher's simple table aroused so much Government resentment that it no doubt did much to cause the rejection of his scheme. But probably his table, translated into terms of total effectives and armament, would have had the same results. For what the Governments objected to in 1922 was not so much the form of Lord Esher's table as the fact of any concrete proposition of any kind.

The advantage of the establishment of a ratio in the form of a simple list of coefficients is that it might simplify—as, indeed, was proved at Washington—negotiations that must in any case be difficult in the extreme. It will therefore be assumed, for the purpose of this chapter, that such a list will be prepared.

But, whatever form it may be given, the real problem of the ratio is the same. And it is, of course, the crux of the disarmament problem. If the Peace Treaty system were to be generally adopted as it stands, the ratio would remain the only question with which the Conference would have to deal.[1] Even if a new and more elastic form of treaty is invented, it may still be the most important question to be faced. And it must be faced, not only by the Disarmament Conference itself, but by the Preparatory Committee and the Council of the League as well: for no " plans " which did not include proposals for the ratio would be complete.

It is the crux of the disarmament problem, because it involves the inherent and fundamental political difficulty of that problem, a difficulty which cannot be removed, and without a solution of which nothing can be done. This difficulty results from the natural fact that the members of international society are widely different in size, in geographical situation, in historical development, and in other ways, and that for these and other reasons they are able to support, and feel themselves to need, very different quantities of the means of self-defence. They cannot, therefore, all be given an equal military strength; even if that were possible as a system, none of them would want it to be applied.

Since, therefore, different states must have differing scales of armament, two questions arise which must be answered: On what *principle* can the strength of each state be settled relatively to that of all the rest ? And by what *method* can agreement on the subject be achieved ?

[1] Except, of course, the important problems dealt with in chap. xiv. below.

The second of these two questions may be taken first, and one of the conclusions of this chapter may be anticipated. Agreement on the ratio will only be reached by means of a long and difficult diplomatic negotiation. No mere formula, however simple or however intricate, can solve the questions which must inevitably arise. The Conference of Washington furnishes an illustration, if such be needed, of this truth. Its ratio 5:5:3 was as simple as any ratio could be, and, moreover, it was based on the principle of the maintenance of the *status quo*. Yet its adoption involved prolonged and difficult negotiation, not only about the basic principle of the *status quo*, but also about its practical application in terms of ships. For weeks the Conference hung in doubt, while the delegations debated whether this ship or that should be retained or scrapped, whether compensation should be allowed in this or in the other way,[1] before agreement was finally achieved.

Without doubt there must be a similar negotiation by Government representatives either at the general Disarmament Conference or before the Conference itself takes place. Without doubt this negotiation will be much more complicated than that of Washington, which only affected five powers and two categories of naval ships. In each kind of armament— land, sea, and air—the question of the ratio will arise; its solution will need far more careful study in advance than that given to the Washington proposals; and agreement at the Conference itself may take far longer to achieve.

But if this must be the method, cannot its application be made simpler by some formula or principle on which the necessary negotiation can be based? Is there not some logical starting point, such as the size of the population, or, as at Washington, the maintenance of the existing *status quo*, by reference to which the military strength allowed to different states could be provisionally laid down, subject, of course, to modification on various grounds, if in the negotiations that should seem to be required?

[1] Vide Buell, *Washington Conference*, pp. 155-60, concerning the negotiations about the Japanese retention of the *Mutsu*, the British retention of two battleships of the Hood class, the scrapping of four ships of the King George V class, etc.

Such a principle or formula, if it could be found, would for the following reasons be extremely useful:

First, it would obviously simplify the negotiation in itself. If there were some logical and generally accepted point of departure from which changes were only admitted when on one ground or another they could be shown to be required, that would obviously facilitate the task of those who must agree.

Second, the representatives of different states will more easily be able to accept without protest the coefficients or quotas of military strength which they are respectively allowed, if these coefficients or quotas can be justified on some ground of principle which has been generally applied. They may need all the arguments which they can find when they seek the endorsement of their disarmament treaty by their Parliaments at home, and a general principle for the ratio might enable them to defend concessions they had made to rivals, which otherwise they might find it difficult to explain.

Third, the same argument applies, with no less force, to the national psychology of the peoples upon whom both statesmen and Parliaments depend. If its allotted strength can be justified on some general principle, a nation will be less likely to consider that it has been treated with injustice, or that its interests have been foolishly betrayed.

For these reasons it is desirable to find some principle or formula on which the ratio negotiations can be based, and it is the duty of the Preparatory Committee and of the Council of the League to make proposals on the point.

There has already been some discussion of the subject, and a number of different principles have been tentatively proposed. Before their respective merits are discussed, it may be well to clear the ground by a brief consideration of the purposes for which, in the general estimation, national armed forces are now maintained. These purposes are plainly relevant to the question of the ratio; for the reasons for which states desire to have armed forces may well give guidance as to the quantities they ought to have.

Broadly speaking, there are three essentially divergent views which lead, of course, to different results.

The first, for the most part unconsciously, but none the less firmly, held, is that the purpose of armed forces is to neutralize the grave natural dangers of international life in a savage and disordered world; that armaments in themselves give security from the aggression which will inevitably overwhelm any state that is without them, and that the more armaments a country possesses the greater its security will be, whatever the level of the armaments which other neighbouring countries may keep up. This is a view which the whole of history disproves, for if the development of the world has shown one thing more clearly than another, it is that the possession of great armaments does not by itself protect nations from overwhelming military disaster. If examples are required, Napoleonic France and Imperial Germany provide them. But it is none the less a view which, although it has been denounced by historians and by statesmen, is still, in spite of their warning and of the teaching of events, very widely held. A striking statement of it may be taken from the press. The able correspondent of *The Times* in Berlin, in discussing the attitude of German opinion towards a League Disarmament Conference, writes as follows:

> " The German theory may be stated to envisage two possible courses—either the other nations must disarm to the same degree as Germany, or Germany must be allowed to readjust her armaments to an extent consistent with her own defence, having regard to the armaments of the other nations. There can be no doubt that the majority of the German people would prefer the latter course, the country having little faith in the power of the Locarno treaties to guarantee its frontiers, or to afford it the opportunity of revising them."[1]

If this doctrine were logically applied, the only principle upon which a negotiation on the ratio could be based would be that of allowing every country to strive for the maximum armament which the other parties could be induced to allow it to retain.

The second view of the purpose of armaments is not unlike

[1] *The Times*, January 9, 1926.

the first, except that it is inspired by other motives besides that of fear. It is that armaments serve not only to make a nation safe, but also to promote its wealth, prestige, and power. If it were accepted, the only logical reason for disarmament would be to save expense, to gain material well-being of some kinds by giving up the other kinds of both material and moral well-being which armaments secure. And, if it were accepted, the only method upon which the ratio negotiation could be conducted would once more be that of allowing every power to strive by bargaining to retain as much armament as the other contracting parties would allow. For a Government which takes this view must regard every reduction in its military strength as a " sacrifice " to be jealously avoided, and to be made only if other rival states will give up more. The doctrine logically would lead, indeed, to some such principle as that of the military *potentiel* which will be discussed below, for it would give a quasi-moral right to every state to have a strength proportionate to the absolute maximum which it could develop, if it extended its military forces to their greatest possible extent.

The third, or League of Nations view of armaments, is that their purpose is to keep the peace, to repress national and international crime, to maintain order within the state at home, and security against attack upon its frontiers from abroad. This is the only view that can be publicly accepted without grave inconsistency by any Member of the League. If it were logically applied, it would lead to a very different result from the two others. The Covenant has made security a matter of " pooled " and common interest, to be achieved for Members of the League by their joint action. If they had confidence in this new system, and if they genuinely accepted the League of Nations view of armaments, it would be no more than common sense for each of them to seek to pay as little as it could towards the international police. Their attitude to armament would then become that of citizens towards taxation for the upkeep of the police; they would regard it as a sacrifice to public welfare. Large states, like rich men, having greater material interests to be protected, would pay greater taxes for their protection than their poorer neighbours. But all states, large and small alike, would seek to make the smallest contribution that the organs of public authority would allow.

Which, in fact, of these divergent views do Governments and peoples hold ? It is difficult to say. Certainly in disarmament discussions the first two frequently appear. Any reduction under a disarmament treaty—for example, the scrapping of British vessels under the Washington Convention—is not only referred to in the public press, but is actually regarded by general opinion as a " sacrifice " only to be made with deep regret. But it is also true that many Governments have now begun to regard the Covenant of the League of Nations as the basis of their foreign policy. The old conceptions that armaments are a source of privilege and power, that they give prestige and wealth which cannot be obtained by other means, that expansion of territory by force is in itself to be desired— these conceptions are still far from dead, but they are weakening, while the sense of the solidarity of international interests, though incomplete, is growing. It is beginning to be true that the prestige of a nation is due not to its military strength, but to the standards of its culture and its civilization, and to the political ability and force of those who represent it in international affairs.

It can, indeed, be fairly said that opinion is moving at least reasonably fast towards these League conceptions. And its movement has certainly been helped by the League discussions on disarmament since 1921. For these discussions have always started from propositions consistent with the fundamental nature of the League. Thus, in 1921, the Temporary Mixed Commission prepared a questionnaire about the factors which the Governments might wish to be considered when the scale of their armed forces was laid down. Their own summary of this proposal was as follows:

" Each of the Governments should be asked to furnish a statement of considerations it may wish to urge in regard to the requirements of the national security, its international obligations, its geographical situation, and its special circumstances. The Governments should be specially requested to indicate separately the police and military forces which they consider necessary for the preservation of domestic order."

The maintenance of order at home, the prevention of aggression from abroad, the preservation of peace by joint international action—these alone were the purposes of armament which, from the beginning, the Temporary Mixed Commission recognized as just.

The point is by no means academic, for the Second Assembly endorsed the proposals of the Temporary Mixed Commission, their questionnaire was sent out, a great number of Governments sent replies, and it has been on the basis of the questionnaire and these replies that discussion of the subject ever since has been carried on. No one who has followed these discussions can doubt that they have done much to form opinion, and that as a result the new conception of armaments and their purpose has gained ground, while the so-called imperialist conceptions are beginning to weaken, though not to disappear.

But the change is so far from complete that it is useless to seek in these general considerations a practical principle for the ratio which, by reason of the general philosophy they accept, will carry weight with politicians and with peoples. In other words, there is no principle drawn from the conceptions which have been discussed which will at the present time impose itself as just, for opinion is still midway between doctrines which are not only divergent, but radically opposed.

This conclusion does not mean, as this chapter may serve to show, that these general considerations throw no light on the basis of the settlement which it may be advisable to adopt.

In recent years the following principles for the ratio have been proposed. They probably include among them all that deserve consideration, though no doubt other principles, or combinations of principles, could be devised.

1. Size of population.
2. The *barême* of the International Budget of the League.
3. The military *potentiel* of each state—*i.e.*, the maximum military strength which it could develop in a prolonged war,

if it threw into the struggle its whole resources of every kind.

4. The prevention of hegemony, or of the power of any one state successfully to take aggressive action.

5. The maintenance of the *status quo* of relative military strength at the present time.

6. A return to the *status quo ante bellum*—*i.e.*, to the relative military strength of the year 1913.

7. A return to the *status quo* of 1900—*i.e.*, to the relative military strength of different countries before the crisis of competitive preparation had reached its height.

In addition to the above principles, there are other factors which, it has been sometimes urged, must be considered when the ratio is discussed. They are factors obviously in themselves not important enough, nor of a nature, to serve as a basic principle for determination of the ratio as a whole, but which, it may be held with show of reason, are relevant. Mention of the following factors of this kind may be found scattered throughout the recent report of the Council Committee,[1] the Preamble of the Central American Treaty of Disarmament, and other reports and documents upon the subject:

1. The geographical situation of the various countries.

2. The length and nature of their maritime communications.

3. The density and character of their railways.

4. The vulnerability of the frontiers and of the important vital centres near the frontiers.

5. The special position of countries which, in modern history, have often been the victim of aggression.

6. The special position of countries with professional armies.

7. The specal position of agricultural countries without large industrial resources.

8. The degree of security which in the event of aggression a state could receive under the provisions of the Covenant, or of separate engagements contracted towards that state.

[1] L.N. Document, C.P.D., December 1, 1925.

All these are factors which obviously may be relevant to the relative military strength which countries should be allowed.

It is necessary now to consider more in detail the principles proposed, and to examine which, if any, of them might serve as a basis for the ratio.   The other factors mentioned must also be discussed, in order to determine how and in what measure they should be taken into account.   The principles may be taken first and one by one.

1. *Population.*—The most obvious of the proposals made is that the ratio of military strength should be based upon the population of the different states, either the gross population, as revealed by the national census on a given date, or the annual " class " of recruits liable in conscription countries each year to begin their service, being taken as the guiding figure.

This proposal is defended by a double argument which varies with varying conceptions of the purposes for which armed forces are maintained.

Its first form is this: that man-power is the foundation of all military strength; that, therefore, a nation of a given size can, if it cares to do so, build up as strong an army as any other nation of a similar size; that, therefore, it has the moral right to be allowed a military strength exactly proportionate to the greatest force which, if it so desired, it could produce.

Its second form is different.   Every individual, it is said, has an equal, or an approximately equal, interest in the peace, not only of his nation, but of the world at large; therefore it is just that all men should make an equal sacrifice both to maintain internal order, and to repress international crime; and sacrifice can be distributed most equally by making the ratio between the different nations vary exactly with the respective populations which they have.

Neither of these arguments is logically convincing.

Whatever view of the purpose served by armaments be held, some other of the remaining principles proposed will be more consistent with it than the principle of population.

2. *Barême of the League of Nations' Budget.*—If the principle of equality of sacrifice for national and international peace by every citizen of every nation is accepted as right and just, then

the ratio of armament ought to vary with the *barême* of the international budget of the League. For the sacrifice imposed by armaments consists of the real wealth which a people must give up in the form of taxation for national defence; and the giving up of a fixed amount of real wealth means far more hardship to a poor and backward people than to one which is rich and highly organized. This difference in real burden caused by an equal sacrifice of wealth would not be allowed for by the principle of population, but it is allowed for by the *barême* of the budget of the League. That *barême* is the result of most elaborate efforts, made over several years by an international committee of experts, to adjust the burden of League taxation to the real taxable strength of the various nations of which the League consists. The principle of the *barême* would, therefore, in theory be logical and just, if it were universally agreed that the sole purpose served by armaments is, by joint and individual action, to preserve national and international peace.

But in practice the adoption of this principle would be open to objection. To begin with, current public opinion is such that the principle of equal sacrifice would emphatically not carry general conviction that it was just. Further, the taxable strength of different countries varies so greatly that it would give immense inequalities of military strength—inequalities more considerable than those given by any of the other principles proposed, and of such a kind that they might lead to serious hegemonies in different quarters of the world. It would, for example, give to the British Commonwealth of Nations a proportion of the armament of the world (in fact, more than a quarter of it) which other countries might be most unwilling to allow, and which the British nations do not wish to have.

For these reasons the adoption of the budget *barême* principle would seem unnatural at the present time. But it is possible that in the future general opinion and the nature of international relations may so change, that it will seem the obvious principle to adopt.

3. *The Military Potentiel.*—The principle of the *potentiel* is, in philosophic doctrine, the exact opposite of the principle of the *barême* of the budget of the League. It is the logical

result of the view that armaments serve to promote the wealth, prestige, and power of nations, and that, therefore, each nation should strive to maintain the maximum forces for which it can afford to pay.

The national *potentiel* of any given nation is the military name for the maximum armed forces which that nation can maintain upon the field of battle for a period of time by devoting to the purpose the whole of its national resources of every kind. But how could it be determined what the *potentiel* of different countries really is with sufficient accuracy to make it the basis for the ratio of their future strength? The belligerents in the late war might point to the forces which they then maintained; but even for them the experience of the late war would not now be quite decisive, and no doubt the experts of all countries would demand a new discussion of the principles on which the calculation of their respective national *potentiels* should be based. What lines could these discussions follow? By what methods could the *potentiel* be determined if it were not based upon the experience of the past?

Two methods have been proposed. The first is in the nature of a mathematical fantasy. It is suggested that a list should be made of every conceivable factor which affects the military strength of nations—that is to say, their man-power, their existing armament, their industry of various kinds, their raw materials capable of use in war, their geographical situation, the length and nature of their communications system, and so on. An estimate should then be made of the relative importance of these various factors to military strength, and to each should be given a fixed percentage value. Thus, for example, man-power might be given 40 per cent, armament 30 per cent, industry 15 per cent, raw materials 5 per cent, and so on. It should then be reckoned what is the maximum amount of each quantitative factor—man-power, armament, raw material, etc., which each nation could possibly develop. To that nation which had most of any given factor, a full percentage should be given—for example, 40 per cent to the nation with the greatest man-power, and a corresponding percentage to each other nation, according to its relative strength in men. Similarly, for the non-quantitative factors, such as strategical geography, communication systems, and the rest, the relative advantages of each nation should be calculated by impartial experts. Again, a full percentage should be given to the nation with the most favourable position, and a lower percentage to other nations, according to their respective strength or weakness in each factor. The percentages for the different factors having been thus determined for each nation, they should be added together, and the results will give the fighting strength which in theory each nation would be able, by its maximum effort, to produce.

According to this *potentiel* doctrine, each nation will have a moral right to have under a disarmament scheme a strength proportionate to that which its maximum effort would allow. The ratio would therefore reflect the exact results of the mathematical process which has been described.

This method of determining the *potentiel* seems fantastic when it is written down in plain words. It deserves explanation only because serious attempts have, in fact, been made to seek a basis for a ratio in this way.[1]

The second and more practical method proposed for the determination of the *potentiel* of different states is to give the task to an impartial body of military experts. Working on data provided by the general staff of each individual state, allowing for the man-power required for the maintenance of national industry, for the protection of communications, for the defence of exposed or difficult strategical positions, and, of course, above all, for the replacement of wastage due to losses of effectives in the field, these experts could calculate the greatest total force in armed effectives which each nation could keep in the field in a lengthy war. When they had done this, they would then have found the relative hope of victory which each nation would have against any other with which it might be involved in war, and the ratio, founded upon the *potentiel* thus discovered, would translate this hope into the concrete schedules of the Disarmament Treaty.

But by whatever method the *potentiel* may be determined, the adoption of a ratio based upon it is open to the same objections. It must be admitted that it is a logical deduction

[1] Cf. Proceedings of T.M.C., 1921, 1922.

from one view of the purpose of armaments, which is very
widely held, and that, for that reason, to many ordinary men,
and not merely to military experts, it would seem " the least
artificial " of any of the principles now being discussed.

But it is in direct conflict with the new conceptions upon
which the machinery and the obligations of the League of
Nations have been built. If it be accepted, the rational basis
of a disarmament policy will disappear. Not only so, but in
the practical discussions which have taken place, the spokes-
men of many states have dissented from it. At the Moscow
Conference, for example, the Polish representative, speaking
for his country and for the other border states, insisted that
they should be allowed an extra quota of peace-time strength
to compensate them for the fact that they had but little national
industry with which they could, if war broke out, provide
their troops with arms and ammunition.[1] This was a plain
attempt to *invert* the principle of the *potentiel*, and to insist
that, if a nation is weak in certain factors, it must for that
reason be allowed more and not less standing forces. The
same view was expressed with force by the Italian delegate,
General De Marinis, in the Council Committee which met in
December, 1925:

> " Un pays dont l'industrie est peu developpée devrait
> être autorisé d'avance, faute de pouvoir recourir a cette
> transformation des usines de production et faute de
> matières premières pour les alimenter, à posseder en
> temps de paix un matériel proportionnellement plus con-
> sidérable."[2]

General De Marinis was supported in this view by M. Boncour, the delegate of France, and the same opinion could be
found in many other speeches made at various times in League
debates.

It may therefore be concluded that, whatever would have
been true a few years ago before general conceptions about
armaments had begun to change, the *potentiel* principle would
not to-day receive sufficiently general acceptance to make

[1] L.N. Document C.T.A., 205, 1923, p. 6.
[2] L.N. Document C.P.D., 1, p. 30.

it a possible basis to adopt. But, of course, it must be added that certain factors allowed for in the *potentiel* calculations —for example, economic strength—will have to be taken into account when the ratio is made.

4. *The Prevention of Hegemony.*—The next principle, if such it can be called, can be best stated by reproducing Point 6 of a draft questionnaire presented to the Council Committee by M. Paul Boncour in December, 1925:

> " Examen du principe d'après lequel aucune Puissance ne devrait pouvoir entretenir des armements susceptibles, si elle se rendait coupable d'une agression, de lui permettre de disposer de forces supérieures à celles que l'Etat victime de l'agression et la Société des Nations pourraient réunir pour les lui opposer, soit en vertu de l'article 16 du Pacte soit par l'application des accords régionaux prévus par l'article 21 du Pacte."[1]

In other words, the ratio shall be so arranged that no state shall be left with a military hegemony which would enable it to break the " peace of nations " with hopes of being able to resist the joint forces which under a League security plan will be brought against it. There is no doubt that this object, which is entirely consistent with the purpose of the League, should be borne in mind; but it is hardly of a nature to serve as a general basic principle by means of which the strength of every state could be laid down. It would not provide for the detailed graduation of strength upon which Governments, whether rationally or not, are likely to insist.

It should therefore be counted, not as a basic principle, but as one of the other considerations by reference to which the results of such a principle must be checked, and, if necessary, altered.

5. *The Status Quo.*—The next principle suggested is that of the *status quo*. The theoretical case for the adoption of the *status quo* is twofold.

First it is said that, of all possible principles, it is the least artificial, because it is based upon the effort which, at the time when the disarmament treaty comes into force, each nation

[1] L.N. Document C.P.D., I, p. 41.

will be making for its own defence, and because it will allocate to each nation the relative position as against other states which as a matter of national policy it has thought it right independently to build up.

Second, it is said that, by the adoption of the principle of the *status quo*, allowance will be made for important factors to which otherwise it will be difficult to give a proper weight. Up to the present time each general staff, in determining the forces which their country needs, have taken into account its international position, its general or special obligations to other countries, the strength and weakness of its strategical geography, the other special circumstances which may affect their case. They have thus allowed for factors to which it is not possible to assign an exact or measured weight. They have made a guess as to what strength their country needed, and then they have modified their guess according to its capacity to pay. To adopt the ratio of the *status quo*, therefore, will, it is said, save a lot of trouble in allowing for these imponderable factors, which must be taken into account, but to which no measured import-ance can be assigned.

One other practical argument is used in favour of the principle of the *status quo :* that it reflects, beyond all others, public opinion in its present transitional stage about armaments and their purpose.

As was said above, two variants of this principle of the *status quo* have also been proposed. The first is that the ratio should be based not on the relative positions of different nations in 1927 (or whenever the disarmament treaty is actually drawn up), but on their relative positions in 1913, before the Great War began. The other is that, instead of the year 1927 or 1913, the year 1900 should be taken; that is to say, before the great crisis of competitive military preparation had properly begun. The discussion of the merits of these variants may for the moment be deferred.

Such being the different general principles proposed, there must be considered next the other factors by which the applica-tion of the chosen principles must be checked.

1. *Geographical Position and Vulnerability of Frontiers.*—It is plain that on the basis of this factor alone no ratio could be constructed; but equally no ratio would carry conviction which did not make allowance for the geographical weaknesses or advantage of states. It is also plain that in making allowance for a weak frontier a greater and not a less amount of strength must be allowed. Any other arrangement would, in the present state of opinion, seem both unjust and artificial.

It may be noted that this is an inversion of the *potentiel* principle.

2. *Industrial and Other Economic Resources.*—It will probably be held that allowance must be made for the possession or non-possession of national industries, or of other economic resources, of value to a state engaged in war; but it is not plain in what way this will be made to count. Should states without industry be allotted more effectives, as General De Marinis argued in the speech which has been quoted, or will such inversion of the *potentiel* principle in this case seem " artificial " ?

No firm answer can be made, but, as was said above, discussion up to now would seem to point again to the inversion of the *potentiel* principle, and the allowance of compensating strength to countries which are weak in this respect. As international stability and the prevention of aggression become more and more the aim of policy, so will this view seem increasingly right.

3. *Transit Systems.*—The same remarks apply. To some it will seem unnatural that a state which is weak in transport should on that account be allowed additional strength, but that it should be is again plainly consistent with the conceptions which are now gaining ground.

4. *The Position of Agricultural States without Industry.*—What was said under No. 2 above again applies.

5. *The Position of States with Professional Long-Service Armies.*—There are so few of these states that their special position can no doubt be dealt with by negotiation. No formula can be devised for measuring the superior fighting value of professional as against conscript armies, and their advantage in this respect must be offset by their weakness in reserves. Probably on the balance a certain extra quota of effectives will

be allowed to professional armies, and in any case little difficulty is in practice likely to arise.

6. *Special Dangers to which, for Historical Reasons, Certain States are Exposed.*—It will certainly be held, and, indeed, it has, up to the present time, been universally admitted, that it is right and necessary to allow in the ratio for the greater risks of war to which, by reason of their geographical position or of their history, some states are now exposed. Again, it is not possible to make any formula by which the factor of " war risk " can be automatically applied. It will be necessary, however, to give to it in negotiation its proper value. No doubt it will be made the basis of exaggerated claims by certain states to which security is the first of national problems.

7. *Security under the Covenant or by Special Pacts.*—It is suggested in the report of the Council Committee that in determining the ratio allowance must be made for the security afforded to different states by the existence of the Covenant, and by the mutual undertakings of groups of states under such defensive treaties as the Locarno Pacts. No doubt, again, it is right and in accordance with the principles of the League that such elements of security should be taken into account. But it is probably impossible to find a rigid mathematical system of reducing the effectives allowed to one state in exact proportion to the assistance promised to it by another, though the Report also suggests that this might be done. The value of security so given must be allowed for " empirically," as the Spanish member said—that is to say, not by any automatic process, but in the general negotiation that will be required.

An attempt may now be made to draw from the above discussion a conclusion concerning the way in which the ratio of the Disarmament Treaty may be fixed.

It must first be repeated that whichever principle is adopted, it will not be used irrevocably to settle the ratio by an exact and rigid application of the results to which it leads. On the contrary, it will be no more than the basis of a prolonged and probably a difficult negotiation i n the course of which it will, no doubt, be modified by some or all of the other factors which have been discussed.

This being so, less importance attaches to the principle adopted, less effort need be made to find a perfect philosophical basis, less time and trouble need be spent in securing the views of the Governments upon the point. Attention may be concentrated on finding the principle which will best serve the practical purposes above described; which will most facilitate, that is to say, the actual disarmament negotiation, which will best enable statesmen to justify to their respective Parliaments the concessions they have made, which will most readily convince those Parliaments and their peoples that general justice has been done.

And there can be little doubt that for these purposes one of the variants of the principle of the *status quo* would be the best. There is no need to repeat the general arguments in their favour which have been given above. The most important of them on every ground is that the principle of the *status quo* will carry conviction to the popular mind, because it is based on the actual effort which the different peoples in the past have thought it worth their while to make.

But it is known that some Governments hold that the armament situation at the present time is quite abnormal. They urge that while some states have been over-arming ever since the war, others, for economy, have deliberately built up less armament than they feel themselves entitled to demand. From this it is concluded that the present ratio of strength is quite " unnatural," by which, no doubt, is meant that it differs from the ratio which the *potentiel* principle would give. And if to this extent the principle of the *potentiel* really carries weight, then no doubt the ratio of 1913 has this advantage, that it would reflect the efforts made by the various peoples at a moment when they expected that their armaments would soon be used. To many it will for this reason seem more " natural " than any other principle that can be found.

On general grounds of doctrine, the case for the ratio of 1900, before the European crisis of armament competition had begun, is stronger than the case for that of 1913. But none the less it may be doubted if in practice it would now carry the same measure of conviction to statesmen, Parliaments, and peoples.

Probably, then, it will be most convenient to base the ratio on the pre-war *status quo*. The results which that principle would give must, of course, be checked by the other factors mentioned—factors of geographical advantage, special " war-risk," transit facilities, and so on—if it can be shown that they have not been allowed for in the basic principle itself.

How can this be done ? Plainly, there are no formulas or rules more exact than the general considerations above put forward. It is contrary to common sense to try to translate geographical advantage into percentage values. Such factors must be allowed for empirically—that is to say, by negotiation.

It may be added that it will, of course, be the duty of the Preparatory Committee and of the Council of the League not only to propose a general principle upon which the ratio should be based, but also to indicate the various other factors which must be taken into account, and the relative importance which, in general terms, they should be allowed. On the basis of their proposals on these points, the actual negotiation of the ratio would be carried on.

Perhaps at this juncture something further may be said about the nature and the method of the negotiation needed.

If any variant of the principle of the *status quo* is adopted, three questions will arise in its application.

The first concerns the determination of what the *status quo* in the selected basic year really was. There will have to be mutual verification and agreement by the Governments concerned of their respective strengths in the selected year in each of the various factors to be limited; for land forces, for example, agreement as to what the relative strength of each country was in 1913 in effectives, militia, and armament; for naval forces, agreement as to the total tonnage which each power possessed, and the real value which that tonnage, according to its age, armament, etc., should be allowed. Calculations, of course, will also have to be made concerning the strength to be allowed to states which did not exist in 1913, but this should cause no difficulty. The agreement on these points will give a provisional ratio from which subsequent negotiations can start. So far, of course, the Preparatory Committee and the Council ought plainly, with the full statistics in their possession, to be able to make concrete proposals.

Second, certain changes must be made in the provisional ratio so arrived at, on account of the various factors mentioned above—for example, geography (especially that of the new states) and the fact that some of the states have "under-armed" in the last few years.[1] Again, if they wish, the Preparatory Committee and the Council can make proposals and establish a corrected ratio in their plans. This, of course, would be a more difficult task than the first, because it would be at least in part political in nature.

Thirdly, there would remain the translation of the corrected ratio into terms of the actual armaments which states retain— *i.e.*, for land forces, into terms of the number of men of each category allowed to each state and of the amount of its permitted armament measured either in money or otherwise; for naval forces, into terms of the total tonnage of each state, of the categories of ships of which this total tonnage may be composed, or even perhaps of the actual ships which different countries keep. Once more, if they desired to do so, the Preparatory Committee and the Council could plainly make proposals for this concrete application.

If they did so they would almost certainly make it easier for the Governments to reach a subsequent agreement, for any proposal put forward with the authority of the Council would not only serve as a useful basis, but would also carry great weight.

But even if this were done, there would still be needed the vitally important stage of direct dealing between the Governments concerned. This direct inter-governmental dealing might either be confined wholly to the Conference itself, or it might be begun before the full Conference actually met. It is plain—for it follows from the proposition that disarmament, to be successful, must be general—that the ultimate ratio to be established between the various participating countries must be in one sense a single whole, since it must cover all the countries with whose armament the treaty deals. But in another sense this single ratio will be a combination of different

[1] Only, of course, if 1927 is taken as the basic year.

parts. While the military strength of any country may indirectly affect the strength of almost any other country, it affects much more vitally and directly the strength of its immediate neighbours. Thus it might facilitate the final negotiations of the Conference as a whole to secure in advance a series of regional agreements about the ratio to be established among groups of neighbour states. To this end the Council might summon a series of preliminary Conferences, to which groups of powers—for example, the Balkan or the Scandinavian states—would send their experts. These experts, meeting in Geneva under impartial chairmen provided by the Council, assisted either by the expert services of the Preparatory Committee or by a special commission of that Committee, might then negotiate, on the basis of the principles laid down in the Council's plan, a provisional ratio to be set up among themselves and its provisional translation into terms of the armed forces which each should be allowed. Every group, of course, would be divided into sub-committees on naval, land, and aerial forces. If these negotiations led to satisfactory results in the application of the principles adopted, that would clearly simplify the task of the Disarmament Conference proper. For, acting on the results which these group Conferences achieved, the Council could correlate their different plans, and so prepare its final comprehensive proposition for the Conference. It could, of course, in its discretion, suggest greater reductions than the group Conferences proposed; or if it found, as it well might, that the plans of different groups were in mutual conflict, it could suggest whatever compensating changes it might think necessary. From the final scheme which thus emerged the Disarmament Conference proper could begin.

In another sense as well, of course, the final ratio must be a combination of different parts. As has just been indicated, there must be established a separate ratio between different countries in land, naval, and air forces—perhaps separately arranged, but forming together a single whole.

This fact gives rise to what is perhaps the decisive advantage of adopting as the basis of the ratio one of the variants of the principle of the *status quo*, and preferably that of 1913. The advantage is this: that it would largely, if not altogether, obviate the difficulty, the insuperable difficulty, of measuring the relative value and importance to nations of their naval, military, and air armaments. This difficulty would inevitably arise if any of the other principles discussed above were to be adopted. Suppose, for example, the ratio were based on the *barème* of the League of Nations budget: on this basis Great Britain would have, say, the coefficient 11, France the co-efficient 8, Italy the coefficient 6, and so on. It would then have to be agreed how much of the total strength, represented by the figure 12, should be reckoned up against Great Britain in respect of the fleet she will retain, and how much will be left over for her army and air force; the same, of course, will have to be done for France (beginning, no doubt, with her army), and for every other country. By whatever means this sort of calculation were attempted, it would virtually amount to a measurement in terms of mathematics of the relative value of the different arms—an operation which simply is not common sense. The only alternative would be empirical negotiation, without, be it noted, any real basic principle at all.

But the greater part of this difficulty is altogether avoided if the principle of the *status quo*—*e.g.*, in 1913—is adopted. It is true, of course, as has been said above, that the strength allowed to any nation in one given arm must have a great effect upon its permitted strength in other arms—hence the need for " generality " in the second sense. But this can be allowed for by a negotiation, which will be simple, if the starting point is the principle of the *status quo ;* because, of course, in determining their strength in each arm in the past the general staffs have themselves made their own decisions about the imponderable factors which make desirable for their respective countries the development of one arm or another; presumably they were, broadly speaking, content with the position in each arm which they previously held; presumably, therefore, if this position is continued in the future, subject to minor modifications of the kind discussed, neither they nor their Parliaments or peoples can have cause for complaint. On the contrary, indeed, the arrangement is almost certain to seem more just than any other, both to service and to popular opinion, while if it is adopted the fantastic mathematics above referred to will in no way be required. Thus it may be concluded that in the parallel negotiations that will be needed for the settlement of the ratio in each separate arm, the practice of the past furnishes, if it can be satisfactorily applied, both the most practically convenient and, in the empirical sense of the word, the most equitable basis for the relative future strength of different states.

This would seem so far to be decisive concerning naval and military forces, in which the practice of the past is very easy to apply. But the same is not true of air forces, and here, therefore, the ratio may present a new and complicated problem. It would not arise, of course, if air forces were amalgamated with land armies on the looser plan suggested in Chapter XII above; for then there would be a single ratio, based on the *status quo* of the selected year, for land and air forces together.[1]

But if, as may be hoped, air forces are limited by a separate and more rigid plan, then the new problem will arise. For then there must be a separate ratio for the air, or at least a separate negotiation and arrangement on the subject. And for this arrangement the principle of the *status quo* does not greatly help. The practice of 1913, for example, gives no guidance, for in 1913 there were no air forces, or virtually none; nor does the present *status quo* in air-strength, for reasons which will shortly be discussed. Some new principle is, therefore, needed. But what can this new principle be? It is difficult to find an answer that will carry conviction; so difficult that the Washington Conference Aircraft Committee pronounced this question of the ratio to be an " almost insuperable " obstacle to any arrangement for the reduction and limitation of aerial forces. Their remarks on the subject are so important that they must be reproduced.

" When the details of such an agreement are considered, it will be found a matter of great difficulty to find a reasonable basis on which the allotment of relative strength can be made. For example:

    (i.) " The *status quo* cannot serve as a starting point, since the state of development of air services differs widely

[1] Cf. pp. 234-5, *supra*.

in the case of the various powers (see Appendices), and in no case can these services be considered as complete.

(ii.) The size of a nation's navy and army will influence the basis, in so far as aircraft are essential auxiliaries to those services.

(iii.) National policy will differ as between nations; some nations, for example, will wish to have large air forces for coast defence, where others prefer to trust to older methods. Development on the lines of the substitution of air forces for other forms of force are likely to be considerable.

(iv.) The potentialities of air forces in policing and garrisoning semi-civilized or uncivilized countries are as yet only partially realized. The number of aircraft required for such duties will vary with the size and nature of the territories to be patrolled, and with the value placed on their services by different nations.

(v.) The geographical position and peculiarities of a state, the situation and strength of its possible enemies, and the nature of a possible attack must influence the number of aircraft it will desire to maintain.

(vi.) Different terms of service for personnel will influence the effectiveness of air services and the size of the reserve.

(vii.) The state of development or possibilities for civil aeronautics will have, as has been shown above, a direct bearing on the number of military aircraft which it may be desirable for a state to maintain."

What is the exact meaning and the real importance of the various arguments thus adduced by the Washington Committee in support of their contention that the difficulty of finding a sound basis for an air ratio is an " almost insuperable " obstacle to air disarmament ? They may be taken one by one, omitting for the moment the second point.

(i.) First, they say that the *status quo* of 1921 could not serve " as a starting point " because the services then maintained by different states could " in no sense . . . be considered as complete." What is the real meaning of this sentence ? If the air forces of France, then and now the strongest in the world, are not " complete," when will they be so ? The language used, indeed, is open to misunderstanding, and on the face of it it would seem to show that the Washington experts had in their minds the conception that every ratio of military strength ought to be based upon the real *potentiel* of the states concerned. Such a conception, it has been argued above, cannot be admitted, and that being so, the only valid meaning which can be given to the Committee's words is this: that there now exists no balance of strength among the different air forces of the world which would, if it were perpetuated by a disarmament agreement, carry conviction to the public mind that it was just.

If this be true, then whatever the Washington experts may have meant, their conclusion may on grounds of expedience be accepted, that the present *status quo* cannot furnish us with the principle we need.

(ii.) Their third argument may be taken next. They urge that, if the normal course of events is not disturbed, " development on the lines of the substitution of air forces for other forms of force is likely to be considerable."

In this contention they are obviously right, unless, indeed, as is at present for the most part happening, air forces are not substituted for, but are added to, existing fleets and armies. But surely it is one of the important objects of disarmament to prevent the great growth of military air forces, whether that growth be by way of substitution or addition. The reason, proved to demonstration by the facts set out in Chapter XII above, is that aircraft are to-day so much the most dangerous of all the means of war. This argument of the Washington Committee, therefore, is perhaps the strongest argument that can be used for an immediate limitation of air forces.

It may be quite consistently admitted that a general belief exists that, if the normal course of things were not disturbed, a redistribution of air-power might occur. This general belief may no doubt complicate the problem of finding a principle for the air ratio which will carry conviction to the public mind.

(iii.) It was argued in Chapter XII above that the fourth difficulty raised by the Washington Committee—that the potentialities of air forces for policing undeveloped countries are still unknown—can be dealt with by negotiation. Considerable latitude on the point might, without great disadvantage, be left in the supplementary agreement to be made about colonial forces.

(iv.) Their fifth point—the varying character of strategical geography, and the varying risk of air attack—is in reality to a great extent the same as their third point, which has been discussed. So far as this is not so, it merely restates some factors which, it has been argued, must be taken into account in making any ratio of military strength. No doubt they must be given their proper weight in making a new and separate air ratio, if such should be required. But it must be noted that the most important of them, the air-strength of the possible enemies of any given state whose coefficient is to be determined, touches the very root of all discussion about disarmament. It is the strength of possible enemy states which creates the problem of security. To make no attempt to limit aerial forces—which is what the Washington Committee virtually propose—until a balance of " natural " (*i.e.*, surely of " potential ") strength has in course of time been achieved, is simply to wait for new and great dangers to national security to grow up.

The argument cannot, therefore, be admitted as valid for the purpose for which it was used.

(v.) The two remaining arguments of the Washington Committee, concerning the difference in service systems in different countries and the development of civil aeronautics, have been dealt with in Chapter XII above, and it is unnecessary to repeat again what was there said.

So far, then, the contentions of the Washington Committee do not seem, to say the least, self-evidently right, while the conclusion which they drew from them seems, if this may be said without disrespect, contrary to common sense. For, they conclude, as has been said, that " the problem of finding a suitable ratio between the air forces of the various powers is thus at the present time almost insuperable."

But who can doubt that if the Governments want aerial

disarmament, as they say they do, this insuperable difficulty can be very easily removed? Of course, much depends on what is meant by the word " suitable." The Washington Committee seem to imply by the phrases which they use that no ratio could be suitable till every nation's aerial forces are what they call " complete "—that is to say, presumably until they have been so developed as to correspond to their respective air potentials. If this is what they meant, then with all deference it must be said that it is a fantastic proposition. It is equivalent to saying that one must wait for a foreseen disaster to occur before a way to avert it can be found. It is, indeed, quite evident that if the Governments and their peoples mean serious business, some working and acceptable basis for an air ratio can easily be found.

A suggestion may, perhaps, be made which, in default of something better, might be accepted. It is founded partly on the general conclusions of Chapter XII above about the functions of an air force in time of war, and partly on the second of the Washington Committee's points—viz., that " the size of a nation's army and navy will influence the basis, in so far as aircraft are essential auxiliaries to those services."

In Chapter XII it was argued that, if no disarmament treaty is adopted, and if wars of the old kind continue to break out, aircraft will inevitably be used for the bombardment of large cities. This, indeed, will probably become their first and most important function, their use as auxiliaries to land and naval forces being quite subordinate.

But it will surely not be disputed that their first function, aerial bombardment, however inevitable it may be if conditions are not radically changed, is still abhorrent to the instincts and conceptions of the vast majority of the human race. That, on the other hand, and equally obviously, is *not* true of the use of aircraft in their other functions as auxiliaries to land and naval forces; on the contrary, as the result of the experience of the late war, such use now seems to the generality of men not only inevitable, but also right.

If this be true, why should not public opinion be reflected in the ratio arrangements that are made? An intelligible and convenient principle could be found in the following propositions:

(i.) Aerial bombardment is repugnant to the general conscience of mankind; therefore let this function of aircraft be altogether excluded in considering the ratio.

(ii.) In consequence of this it should be assumed that if coercive measures under Article 16 were ever required against an aggressor state, aerial bombardment will be avoided unless the aggressor himself begins.

(iii.) For purposes of the ratio, therefore, only those functions of aircraft should be considered in which they act as auxiliaries to land and naval forces—functions which are now commonly regarded as legitimate.

(iv.) If this be done, it is reasonable to establish a fixed relation between the air forces to be allowed to states and the military and naval forces which they are allowed. In other words, a certain strength of air force proportionate to its permitted army, and a further strength proportionate to its permitted navy, should be allowed to every country, the fixed proportions to armies and navies being the same for all the signatory states.

If this principle were accepted, its practical application would be simple. A certain fixed amount of air strength, measured in air effectives and air budgetary appropriation, would be allowed for every thousand men permitted to each army, and for every thousand tons displacement of each fleet. In fixing this amount it would be desirable for all the reasons discussed in Chapter XII, and particularly from the British point of view, to keep the proportion of air to land and naval forces at the lowest point for which agreement could be secured.[1]

If this plan were adopted, the air ratio would become a mere result of the land and naval ratios, that is to say, if the principle here advocated were to be accepted, of the military and naval *status quo* in 1913. Such a solution, it may fairly be claimed, would violate the sentiments of no one; it might well carry general conviction that it was reasonable and just:

[1] Cf. pp. 197-199, 238-9, *supra*.

it is therefore in accord with the practical principles from which this chapter started; while in its application it would in fact allow a relative strength to the three Great Powers now engaged in aerial competition—Great Britain, France, and Italy—which could be accepted with dignity by them all.

Finally, it may be said that if the proposed solution seems too artificial—as no doubt the Washington Committee, for example, would have thought it—and if, for that reason, it is rejected, then some other more acceptable principle *must* be found instead. For the alternative is a policy of suicidal drift. And if the Governments are content to drift simply because a theoretical or political difficulty of this kind should happen to arise, it will merely mean that they are not in earnest. If that be so, of course, disarmament will remain a distant dream.

CHAPTER XIV

CHEMICAL WARFARE

MAJOR VICTOR LEFEBURE has been quoted in Chapter IV above as saying that chemical warfare is " the most important problem in the future reconstruction of the world."[1]

Whether he exaggerates or not, it is at least certain that no plan of disarmament can be wholly satisfactory which leaves the weapon of poison-gas untouched. This would be true even of a plan which secured a large reduction in all other armaments. It is therefore necessary to examine the part which chemical warfare, if it were uncontrolled, might play in future war, and the measures which can be taken to control it.

THE PLACE OF CHEMICAL WARFARE IN FUTURE MILITARY OPERATIONS

There is no doubt that the general staffs of all military powers now regard the use of gas as a normal part of warlike operations, and make their plans on this assumption. It is certain, in fact, that, unless the disarmament treaty can prevent it, gas will be used in many different ways.

Major Lefebure has explained in detail the probable methods of its application in war on land, and it may be worth while to reproduce some of his conclusions:

(i.) He thinks it certain that gases will be discovered which will be highly lethal, very persistent, easily camouflaged by other so-called " stink " gases, the contact of which on any part of the body would be fatal, against which, therefore, the protective devices of oiled suits, chemical pastes, etc.—in themselves a grave handicap to troops compelled to use them—will in the long run be ineffective. Mustard gas, he says, has many of these qualities, and the new gas, Lewisite, has them all. Such gases could be used to make great areas on a battlefield

---

[1] *The Riddle of the Rhine*, chap. x., p. 232.

impassable, or passable only at such a cost in casualties that no staff would pay the price. Mustard gas was thus used in the late war by the Germans, and British troops on some occasions could only cross it by " bleaching " roads through the infected zone—a device only possible on a minor scale, because it is impracticable to manufacture sufficient quantities of " bleach." These gases will thus create a new type of tactical and strategic obstacle which may be decisively important for defence against infantry assault, for isolating a zone to be attacked, for covering an open flank, and so on.

(ii.) The use of gas might perhaps be countered by the tank, if the tank becomes not only a weapon of direct attack, but also a means for the large scale transport of troops. But for this to be possible, of course, the tank designers must first solve the problem of protecting tanks against the use of gas. In discussing Colonel Fuller's views of the future of tank warfare,[1] Major Lefebure remarks:

> " With the increase in depth of infected zones, through the increasingly lethal nature of the persistent compound, the tank will be compelled to rely on filtration methods of protection, instead of the use of compressed oxygen in a gas-tight compartment. Once committed to the use of oxygen, the only safe procedure will be to close up the tanks, and employ the oxygen while there is any suspicion of the presence of gas, and, under these conditions, oxygen transport would become a factor militating against the prime purpose of the tank—the transport of troops and arms. It is safe to forecast a tense struggle between chemical weapons and protective tank devices in the event of future wars."[2]

Major Lefebure's forecasts would, no doubt, be accepted by all competent experts, and it may therefore be taken as agreed that if in future war occurs, and if gas is left uncontrolled, its use will be a vitally important factor in land operations.

(iii.) Next, as was urged above, gas will be of great importance in aircraft attacks against the nerve centres of enemy strength,

[1] Cf. *Tanks in the Great War*, by Colonel Fuller.
[2] *The Riddle of the Rhine*, p. 230.

that is to say, against the industrial cities which produce munitions for the front, against the seat of government, and against the larger towns, upon the morale of which the resistance of the enemy state will obviously depend.

There is no need to elaborate the point, which again is generally agreed by all competent experts. The following quotations may be useful illustrations:

Major Lefebure:

> " Aircraft are the most effective instruments for a gas attack. . . . It would be practicable to put out of action by an aerial gas attack half a million persons in London. This would mean that the whole of London would be demoralized."[1]

These words were written as long ago as 1921.

General P. R. C. Groves, Director of Air Operations for the British Air Force on all fronts in 1918:

> " The gas bomb is probably by far the most effective weapon for use from aircraft. . . . This form of attack upon great cities, such as London or Paris, might entail the loss of millions of lives in the course of a few hours. The gas bombs employed would contain gas in liquid form, the liquid would be released on impact and expand to many hundred times its volume. The gas clouds so formed would be heavier than air and would thus flow into the cellars and tubes in which the population had taken refuge. As the bombardment continued, the gas would thicken up until it flowed through the streets of the city in rivers. All gas experts are agreed that it would be impossible to devise means to protect the civil population from this form of attack."[2]

Brigadier-General Mitchell, of the United States Army, before the House of Representatives Committee of Appropriations:

> " A few planes could visit New York as the central point of a territory 100 miles square, every eight days, and drop

[1] "Chemical Warfare—Possibilities of its Control": *Problems of Peace and War*. Grotius Society Transactions, vol. vii., p. 166.
[2] L.N. Document C.T.A., 210, 1923.

enough gas to keep the entire area inundated. . . . Two hundred tons of phosgene gas could be laid every eight days, and would be enough to kill every inhabitant."[1]

General Bradner, Chief of Research of the Chemical Warfare Service of the American Army, at a Congressional Hearing:

" One plane, carrying 2 tons of the liquid (a certain gas-generating compound), could cover an area of 100 feet wide and seven miles long, and could deposit enough material to kill every man in that area by action on his skin. It would be entirely possible for this country to manufacture over a thousand tons a day of it, provided the necessary plant had been built. If Germany had had 4,000 tons of this material and three or four hundred planes equipped in this way for its distribution, the entire First American Army would have been annihilated in ten to twelve hours."[1]

General Fries and Major West of the United States Army:

" We naturally think of dropping gas in bombs when we speak of the use of gas by the Air Service. The gas will be so used in bombs of perhaps 1,000 lbs. or even a ton in weight, at least 50 per cent of which will be gas. . . . Mustard gas, which is a third again as heavy as water, may be sprinkled through a small opening, such as a bung-hole, in a tank that simply lets liquid flow out. The speed of the aeroplane will atomise it. In this way gas can be sprinkled over whole areas. . . . Lewisite will be used. . . . The burns from a quantity equal to three drops will usually cause death. The material can be made up by hundreds and even thousands of tons per month."[2]

(iv.) It must also be remembered that in chemical warfare there lies the risk that some country will find a gas against which there is no defence and which will therefore be an irresistible and decisive weapon. The point has been mentioned in Chapter IV above. It is, to say the least, a point of great importance, and when so experienced an authority as Major

---

[1] Cited by Irwin, *The Next War*, pp. 46, 47.
[2] *Chemical Warfare*, p. 380.

Lefebure thinks it quite possible that an irresistible compound may be discovered, there is no need to argue that the danger is real.

Major Lefebure gives illustrations of what he thinks the irresistible compound may be like, but there is perhaps no purpose to be served by their reproduction.[1]

There is no need to illustrate any further the potential importance of chemical warfare in future operations. Enough has been said, perhaps, to show that no disarmament treaty which neglects it can be wholly satisfactory to the signatory powers.

METHODS OF CONTROL: THE GENEVA AND WASHINGTON CONVENTIONS

It is also plain that a simple agreement not to use poison-gas in time of war, on the lines of the Geneva and Washington Conventions above referred to,[2] cannot by itself be enough. Unless effective measures are also taken to prevent its preparation, no Government will have confidence that the undertakings given will be faithfully observed. And without such confidence each Government will be obliged itself to prepare for the possible disloyalty of rival states, just as, in fact, at the present time, in spite of their signature of the Washington and Geneva Conventions, all important military powers are now engaged in elaborate chemical preparation. But once preparation of any kind begins, there will exist the danger of a secret development of the chemical weapon on a scale which might make a sudden, decisive attack quite possible.[3] This risk might drive some state, which thought that it was menaced, itself to seek security by a sudden " defensive " attack; in this or some other way the chemical weapon would certainly be used in the event of future war, if the Governments had continued their present preparation until its outbreak. If this should happen, agreements such as the Washington and Geneva Conventions would be either a cloak for intense competitive preparation or else—still worse—a trap for loyal

---

[1] Cf., *e.g.*, *The Riddle of the Rhine*, pp. 214 *seqq.*
[2] Cf. pp. 45-46, *supra.*   [3] Cf. *infra.*

states. It may therefore be concluded that such treaties, including the Washington and Geneva Conventions themselves, are useless for the purpose they are intended to achieve.

LIMITATION OF CHEMICAL PREPARATION

Nor can any proposal to limit chemical preparation *in amount* serve any useful purpose, as it is above suggested that such limitation can for other weapons.

A rigid restriction of army chemical personnel and budgetary appropriation might, perhaps, to some extent diminish the risks of chemical preparation. But the danger would always remain that even a small staff of army chemists might discover the irresistible compound above discussed. And not only so; such a staff could not only do research for new compounds, it could also keep in working order the machinery and facilities required for large-scale production of compounds already known. The risk of such large-scale production of *known* gases is the greater since chemical factories are capable of immediate conversion. Thus Major Lefebure says:

> "The great ease and rapidity with which the German dye factories mobilized for poison-gas production, on a super-industrial scale, has already been demonstrated. It took 40 years and more to develop these factories, yet 40 days saw many of these plants producing huge tonnages of poison-gas, *and as many hours were sufficient for others.*"[1]

It must be added that preparation for such large-scale production of poison-gas can be made without the knowledge of the workers engaged in the chemical industry, since in many cases only the last stage in the preparation of a lethal compound is toxic. Thus, if a Government decided on aggression, it could, by taking into its confidence only the directors of its chemical industry, begin such large-scale production of poison-gas that it could have, when the chosen moment came, large stocks ready, or almost ready, for use in the attack. A small skeleton staff could maintain all the machinery required

[1] *The Riddle of the Rhine*, pp. 250-251.

for converting the industry and for making effective use in the field of the chemicals produced. There is thus scope, in this and other ways, for a dangerous combination of military and civilian resources and personnel which it might be impossible for any external investigator to detect.

For these reasons no limitation of *amount* (either of money or personnel) could be a satisfactory method of dealing with the problem of preparation for chemical war. It is necessary, if it can be done, not to limit such preparation in amount, but to prohibit it altogether, and to this end to embody in the disarmament treaty a detailed agreement laying down the measures which every Government will take to make the prohibition practically effective.[1]

THE PROHIBITION OF CHEMICAL PREPARATION

Of what nature can such measures be ?

It would be absurd for anyone without an expert knowledge, not only of the theory of organic chemistry, but of the chemical industry and of the practical problems of chemical warfare in the field, to hazard any suggestion, however tentative. And there are no experts with these qualifications who have yet ventured to make proposals on the subject, with the single and honourable exception of Major Lefebure; and he has done no more than put forward certain tentative ideas. The remainder of this chapter will be confined to a faithful summary, for the most part in his own words, of the various proposals which Major Lefebure has made.

To begin with, he offers two negative conclusions at which he has arrived.

The first is that there is no external factor of " normal armament " (*e.g.*, artillery, projectors, etc.) which is so essential to the exploitation of chemical warfare, that by its limitation the latter would be automatically checked. Chemical warfare, while it can be thoroughly exploited by normal armament, is also independent of it, since it can be used with deadly effect in other ways—for example, by commercial aircraft.[2]

[1] Cf. also *The Riddle of the Rhine*, pp. 244 *seqq.*
[2] *Problems of Peace and War.* Proceedings of Grotius Society, pp. 156-7.

His second negative conclusion is that "no single measure of control can with certainty check chemical warfare, and once the possibility of such control is entertained, it becomes a question of relying upon the cumulative effect of a series of partial disarmament measures."[1]

These two propositions Major Lefebure makes his starting-point, adding to them a third: which is that, owing to the high convertibility of the chemical industry, to the great similarity of many processes in the production of peaceful chemical substances to the processes required for poison-gas, and to the consequent secrecy with which either illicit research or illicit large-scale production can be carried on, the preparation of chemicals for warlike use must be, even in favourable conditions, extremely difficult to control.

But he also believes that the difficulty may be overcome by a series of "partial disarmament measures." What are these measures in the cumulative effect of which he has at least a tentative confidence?

They involve control over all the four stages through which "a new war agency" must pass in its life-history. These stages he defines as follows:

> "First invention or pure research; then two kinds of large-scale experiment; and finally actual bulk manufacture."[2]

For each of these stages Major Lefebure proposes certain specific measures of control. They may be taken in turn:

1. *Research.*—For this he suggests that there should be—

(i.) "An internationally accepted prohibition of chemical warfare, which implies some form of international organization."[3]

He presumes that under such conditions participation in poison-gas and similar research could be made unlawful, and that in consequence organized research by Governments would automatically cease. "One could never be certain," he admits, "that a limited amount of work was not being carried on surreptitiously, but its volume would be much smaller

---

[1] *Ibid.*, p. 153.　　[2] *Ibid.*, p. 160.　　[3] *Ibid.*, p. 161.

than the efforts, say, of a few hundred organic chemists in a large research establishment, such as those of the Rhine factories or of Edgwood Arsenal."[1]

(ii.) For the prevention of even such surreptitious research he believes that other means might be adopted. " Would it not be possible," he asks, " to invoke the aid of professional organizations ? Many of them are already in a position so to impose penalties or remove privileges that they have a serious hold on professional men;"[2] and he believes that if chemical warfare were internationally forbidden such associations might agree to help.

(iii.) He believes, indeed, that joint action among different professional organizations might be arranged. Thus: " Much might be done by linking up international scientific and technical organizations with . . . an association " (of nations); while " by a much freer exchange of scientific personnel and ideas the difficulties and objectionable features of mutual inspection might be overcome."[3]

(iv.) A danger, no doubt, would still exist, that " in some secret place or in the great industrial organizations work might be carried on which would escape detection. I suggest, however, that if penalties were sufficiently severe, such organizations would hesitate to prejudice thus their commercial future."[4]

As the result of these various measures Major Lefebure comes to a firm conclusion: " Given international prohibition of gas warfare and an intelligent central organization with certain powers, there is no reason, in my opinion, why research on poison-gas could not be very largely suppressed."[5]

2. *Large-Scale Military Tests.*—The next stage is that of large-scale military tests. " Almost without exception all the important recent chemical warfare developments were compelled to spend long periods in great experimental stations." In these stations " every aspect in the transition of research ideas to actual weapons " has to be given minute attention. Long experiments are required on the ballistics of gas shell, on the method of filling it, on the correct solvent and the correct quantities, on the correct cement for shell joints, on the nature

---

[1] *Ibid.*, p. 161.   [2] *Ibid.*, p. 161.   [3] *Ibid.*, pp. 161-2.
[4] *Ibid.*, p. 162.   [5] *Ibid.*, p. 162.

of the cloud burst, the breaking of the shell, the number of duds, etc. These experiments are carried on in great military testing grounds, such as Edgwood in America, Fontainebleau in France, Porton in England, and the Krupp grounds in Germany. " Can such organizations be concealed ?" asks Major Lefebure. " Practically the answer is, ' No.' The great Krupp station was 15 kilometres in length, with elaborate personnel and equipment and systems for signalling and transport; it could not be concealed. I suppose hardly any measures could so cripple serious development on the new agencies of war as the suppression of these vast experimental stations. Even if research went on in spite of restrictions, its results must in most cases pass through this relatively easily controlled stage in order to be of sufficiently proved value to be the chief card for a sudden attack on a large scale. A serious effort to follow the prohibition of chemical warfare by practical measures could not fail to lay hands on these vital field experimental stations."[1]

3. *Large-Scale Research Tests.*—The other type of large-scale experiment, experiment for manufacture, is the next stage in the preparation of warlike compounds. It would, Major Lefebure says, be " difficult to suppress," for the reason already mentioned, that the only toxic stage is often the last, while " the first four or five could quite well be claimed as preliminaries to some new or old commercial chemical. " I fear the only check could operate *through the personnel directing the tests or through very severe penalties,* for the actual operators need never know the purpose of manufacture."

4. *Large-Scale Production.*—The last stage is that of " actual bulk manufacture," which Major Lefebure believes to be the most important. He says, of course, that manufacture in Government chemical arsenals could obviously be stopped by an agreement in the disarmament treaty to abolish the arsenals. But the organic chemical industries of peaceful commerce, " the most perfect type of convertible industry," would remain. And he holds that something must be done to control them, " otherwise any other measures to suppress chemical warfare, on the lines suggested above, would be futile."[2]

On the other hand, it is extremely difficult to control the

[1] *Ibid.*, pp. 162-3.   [2] *Ibid.*, p. 163.

organic chemical industries. Their factories " are more silently converted into arsenals than any other type."[1] " In many of the processes the materials do not appear to the naked eye after the introduction into the first plant unit, being fed by gravity or pressure from one enclosed apparatus to another. It would be absolutely essential for any inspection to conduct chemical tests at the different stages."[2]

" In most cases an enemy with a strong organic chemical industry need not undertake manufacture during peace. He could rely on the potentialities of his chemical industry, which would enable him to commence production in his existing plant immediately on the outbreak of war."[3]

Faced with these difficulties, Major Lefebure proposes sweeping measures which at first glance may seem impossibly ambitious. He defends them by urging that the organic chemical industry is a " critical " industry, which " rational disarmament must harness." To this end he suggests:

(i.) " The first and crying need is to effect a redistribution of these organic chemical forces," in order that no one state should have the monopoly which would give it potentially predominant power.[4] Therefore the monopoly of Germany must be removed and no monopoly must ever be allowed to develop in any country.[5] This is the one solid chemical disarmament measure which can and must be brought about.[6]

(ii.) He suggests as an alternative—though, of course, it is not necessarily an alternative, for both measures might be taken—the establishment of an international control of the present monopoly by means, presumably, of an international directorate imposed upon the private enterprises by which the industry is now carried on.[7] This directorate would presumably be nominated by the League.

Major Lefebure's proposals for the control of bulk manufacture are thus: (i.) The distribution of the organic chemical industry among a number of different countries; (ii.) its control by an international directorate; (iii.) a close system of inter-

---

[1] *The Riddle of the Rhine*, p. 244.   [2] *Ibid.*, p. 247.
[3] *Ibid.*, p. 247.   [4] *Ibid.*, p. 257.
[5] *Problems of Peace and War*, p. 164.   [6] *Ibid.*   [7] *Ibid.*

national supervision and inspection under the authority of the League.

Major Lefebure is by no means confident that the " cumulative effect " of this " series of partial disarmament measures " would, in fact, be water-tight. He admits that certain risks of evasion would remain, and that they might involve a potential menace to signatory states which carried out his plans with loyalty. He adds that, although the risks exist, he is clear in his own mind " that the risks of unhampered and unlimited development of the new agencies of war are far greater than those which will accompany a really comprehensive and effectively operated attempt to control them."[1]

Conclusions.—A few observations on these proposals may be allowed.

(i.) First, it would seem to the layman that Major Lefebure's controls are more adapted to prevent the preparation of *new* gases than that of known gases, every detail in the production processes of which is already carefully recorded by the chemical staff of every army. For, in respect of such known gases, an intending aggressor need go through none of Major Lefebure's four stages of production except the last—bulk manufacture for field use. And to check production at this last stage, League directorates and controls would be quite useless, once an aggressor had definitely decided upon war. Thus, owing to the ready convertibility of chemical industries, a large supply of these known gases (including, no doubt, Lewisite) would, if the aggressor had enough commercial plant, be available for his use within a brief period of time.[2]

To this argument Major Lefebure would no doubt reply that his most important and, indeed, indispensable proposal is for the international redistribution of the chemical industries. But even if that too were carried out, his plans, as he admits, might still break down. It may be, indeed, as some people hold, that no plans will work until there is a resolute determina-

---

[1] *Ibid.*, p. 164.
[2] How brief does not appear in Major Lefebure's writings. Even poison-gas must be filled into shells or bombs, and filling is not a very rapid process, even if the shell-cases are ready.

tion among *all* Governments to work them. If this were so, we might be forced to the conclusion that the only way to avoid gas warfare lies in avoiding war itself.

On this hypothesis the proper policy which would follow from the facts put forward in this chapter would consist in, first, the immediate preparation of plans for general security—including in such plans, if it could be done, the distribution of chemical industry among different countries, which Major Lefebure suggests; second, the strengthening and improvement of the existing methods for the pacific settlement of international disputes; third, a rigid reduction and limitation of "normal armaments," since such armaments, if unlimited, are themselves a cause of war.

(ii.) But it is, of course, possible to carry pessimism even further, and to say not only that no plans of chemical disarmament will work, but that for this reason no disarmament of any kind can be successful. And it is, indeed, sometimes actually contended that the reduction of other armaments might, if chemical preparations were left free, only serve to create a new competition in chemical preparation, which might do more harm than all the good which such a partial disarmament might otherwise achieve. This, indeed, is the view taken by Major Lefebure himself; he holds that, without effective chemical disarmament, other forms of disarmament would be not only useless, but positively pernicious.

For this view, however, his case is not conclusive, and probably few people who have thought about the subject would accept it. A plan of general disarmament which neglected chemical warfare altogether might none the less, by greatly reducing the burden of armaments, produce a profound psychological effect on Governments and peoples; it would thus achieve both the moral and the material purposes of disarmament, and might therefore bring a real and stable peace. A treaty of this kind would, of course, in theory, for all the reasons discussed above, be incomplete; it might inspire so little confidence that it would be generally rejected; but if it were once accepted and put into force, it might in practice be a complete success.

(iii.) But such an incomplete treaty would, of course, be only a second best. It is essential also to deal with chemical preparation, if it is in any way possible to do so. And, happily, there is no need whatever, at least without much further expert investigation of the matter, to accept the conclusion that Major Lefebure's plans would not succeed, either in respect of new or of existing gases. While these plans are tentative, they are, by reason of his great practical experience, of high authority, and they deserve the fullest possible consideration.

For this purpose, it may be suggested, the Preparatory Committee of the League should institute an exhaustive enquiry into the whole subject by an international committee of experts who, like Major Lefebure himself, know both the chemical industry and the problems of chemical warfare in the field. This committee could work on the basis of Major Lefebure's proposals or of any others that may be put forward; they should be formally instructed to propose any measures of any kind which they may think required for effective control of the production of chemical substances for warlike use; they should be specifically invited to consider all forms of international action, whether by prohibition of Government chemical industry, by constant investigation of private enterprises, or by the imposition on individual firms or combines of foreign directors with expert knowledge, whose function it would be to report direct to the League upon the work of the firms in whose management they assist. The report of this Committee should be submitted to the Preparatory Committee and to the Council of the League, and should be simultaneously published to the world at large.

Finally, it may be suggested that whatever practical proposals this Committee may recommend should be unhesitatingly adopted by the Council of the League, however radical and however ambitious they may be. For again in this matter of chemical warfare, as in the problem of aircraft discussed above, there is involved a public interest of supreme importance. To promote this public interest, the necessary measures should be ruthlessly applied, whatever sacrifice of private liberty, whatever interference with the normal working of economic laws they may require. The problem is too grave for the Governments to risk failure for the sake of individual freedom, private

profit, or even national " sovereignty."   Against the claims of
freedom, against all national prejudice and hesitation, the
paramount and over-riding international interest of all nations
should prevail.   There may be doubt about the efficacy of the
means proposed to achieve the end in view; about the end
itself there can be none.

CHAPTER XV

THE RESTRICTION OF WEAPONS: DEMILITARIZED AND NEUTRALIZED ZONES

THE RESTRICTION OF WEAPONS

WHAT has been called in this book the Restriction of Weapons was an important, indeed, an essential part of the Peace Treaty system of disarmament imposed on Germany and her allies. It is not an essential part of the various suggestions made above for a more elastic limitation of the different factors of military strength. These suggestions would be practicable even if no restrictions of any kind were placed upon the types of weapon that might be used. But although it is not essential, it is, of course, desirable to restrict weapons as rigidly as possible in a general treaty, and to abolish some at least of the more costly and dangerous types of weapon and to limit the permitted size or power of others.

This is desirable for two reasons:

First, such restrictions will obviously make it easier to lay down in the disarmament treaty smaller standard budgetary appropriations for land armament and ammunition, for aerial construction, and for the maintenance of ships of war, than will be accepted if, when the scale of these appropriations comes to be determined, the contracting parties include in their calculations all the means of war which they at present use. Likewise, at a later stage, when proposals for further reductions of the standard appropriations are put forward, the possession of large and costly weapons might be made the reason or excuse for their rejection. At either moment such a result would be unfortunate, because, as has been said *ad nauseam* above, the smaller the standard appropriations that are agreed, the more completely will the disarmament treaty achieve its purposes.

Second, a drastic restriction of weapons would be an important earnest to the public opinion of the world that the Governments are moved by serious intentions in making their agreement to disarm. The abolition of tanks, the abolition of submarines, the reduction of capital ships from 35,000 tons to say 10,000—such measures would have a symbolic value even greater than that of the economy, both of treasure and of brain-power, which they would effect. They would strike the imagination of the peoples, and would thus help to mobilize behind the disarmament treaty the support of the countless but as yet inarticulate multitudes who to-day desire to demilitarize the world in which they live. It may be added that in so doing they would make easier the task of securing the effective observance of all the disarmament treaty undertakings of every sort.

A good deal has been said in previous chapters about the restriction of weapons of various kinds. Thus the abolition of submarines,[1] the limitation of the size of ships of war and of their armament,[2] the abolition of military aircraft and the limitation of their type,[3] and the abolition of chemical warfare of all kinds,[4] have been discussed. A few words may perhaps be added here about tanks and land artillery.

Tanks.—It is held by many experts that tanks, if they are not limited by treaty, may develop into great land dreadnoughts which can carry large crews and heavy armament over any country at almost the speed with which the dreadnought travels on the sea. Whether or not this be extravagant exaggeration, the present remarkable improvements in tank construction, and especially in their armament and speed, make it certain that much further progress is, as an engineering proposition, quite feasible.[5] It is also certain that in the view of every general staff the rôle of tanks in land operations is continually increasing in importance. It is therefore more than possible that the Governments, hypnotized by dreams of great tank armies, may indulge in a limitless competitive development of tank construction; and if they did so they might well imperil some at least of the other good results of a disarmament treaty.

[1] Vide p. 204, *supra.*   [2] Vide pp. 203-5, *supra.*
[3] Vide chap. xii, *supra.*   [4] Vide chap. xiv, *supra.*
[5] A tank has been built which carries three guns.—Mr. Arthur Ponsonby in the House of Commons, April 1, 1926.

Against this danger the abolition of the tank would be, of course, the most effective measure. And it may be added that an agreement for its abolition would be quite easy to control. Special costly types of machinery are needed to construct tanks; the training of their crews requires a special terrain and a large area of country; neither their construction, therefore, nor their training practice could be successfully concealed.

Perhaps it may be urged that their total abolition by the disarmament treaty is neither necessary nor even really desirable. The development of great fleets of tanks would be most expensive; if a rigid limitation were placed, as proposed above, on the sums of money allowed for armament construction, any considerable expansion would be automatically stopped. On the other hand, it may be argued that tanks may be of use in policing undeveloped countries, where ordered government still depends more on the force behind the law than on the goodwill of the governed. For this and other less convincing reasons, it is improbable that, in fact, the Governments will agree to abolish tanks, at least when the disarmament treaty is first made.

In this case it would still be possible to limit by treaty the size and armament of tanks. This could no doubt be done, as for warships, by limiting the maximum permitted tonnage of a tank. Some of the arguments in favour of the limitation of the type of fighting aircraft would here, *mutatis mutandis*, again apply. But again, as with aircraft, it must be doubted whether any limitation of type will be in fact accepted, and reliance must therefore be principally placed on the indirect limitation secured by restrictions on the budgetary appropriations allowed for land armament.

Land Artillery.—The same remarks apply for the most part also to the limitation of the calibre of guns.

Artillery under the pressure of international competition now increases every year in range and power; it is confidently predicted that there will shortly be a gun that can fire 100 miles. Every increase in range, calibre, or weight of shell, is no doubt to be regretted as a useless waste. It cannot possibly be held that a 16-inch gun is a more effective police weapon than an 8-inch gun; neither of them would, in fact, in any circumstances that can be conceived, ever be used for police work, either in civilized or even—owing to the difficulties of transport—in uncivilized countries. Therefore, from a social point of view, large-calibre artillery involves a total waste.

The prohibition of such artillery would again, and for the same reasons as with tanks, be relatively easy to control; but again a rigid budgetary limitation would suffice to prevent dangerous competition. The limitation of the calibre of guns, therefore—and once more it resembles the abolition or limitation of tanks—is chiefly of importance because of its possible effect on the scale of standard budgetary appropriation likely to be adopted in the disarmament treaty for land armament and ammunition. If a low scale of appropriation were agreed to, then a limitation of the calibre of guns would be no more than an attractive decoration to an effective working scheme.

DEMILITARIZED ZONES: ON LAND

The subject of neutralized or demilitarized areas or zones rightly falls within the scope of a discussion on disarmament; for demilitarized zones are not only one means of reducing armaments themselves, but may be, what is perhaps still more important, an effective means of removing the dangers which armaments involve.

The system of neutralization was considerably used during the nineteenth century, and, broadly speaking, it was a success. There were occasions—notably the German invasion of Belgium —when it broke down. That was, perhaps, inevitable when it was used, as it often was, not as part of a general system for stabilizing international relations, but as an isolated expedient for dealing with special problems, for which no other solution could be found. But against its rare failures there are some brilliant examples of its success. No doubt the most important is the demilitarization of the frontier between Canada and the U.S.A. by the Rush-Bagot Agreement of 1818, under which the naval armament of the parties on the American Lakes was restricted to a few police vessels. Not only has this agreement lasted until to-day, but by tacit consent of the two Governments its terms have been applied not only to the Great Lakes, but also to an immensely long land frontier across open country; and many eminent historians have expressed the view that, above all other causes, the demilitarization of this frontier has prevented war between Great Britain and the United States from breaking out even when adverse forces and acute disputes have placed a heavy strain upon their good relations. As a direct result, the idea of war between Canada and the U.S.A. is now inconceivable to anyone on either side. This ideal consummation would obviously not have happened if the two countries had been engaged in competitive military preparation on the frontier. The success of demilitarization in this case, therefore, has been quite complete.

Another wholly successful example is furnished by the neutral zone set up by Sweden and Norway along their mutual frontier, when their union was dissolved in 1905. This zone is "to possess the advantage of perpetual neutrality"; it may not be fortified in any way; no military operations shall be carried on in it; it has worked without any hitch of any kind; and neither party has ever suggested that it should be changed. Other examples could be cited did space permit.

It has sometimes been suggested that in modern conditions, with aircraft, motor transport, and so on, demilitarized zones have lost the usefulness they had. It is enough, perhaps, to answer that the Allied experts thought it worth their while to impose the Rhineland zone upon the Germans by the Treaty of Versailles and the Maritza zone on Greece and Turkey by the Treaty of Lausanne.

In the discussion of the Temporary Mixed Commission it was claimed that the establishment of demilitarized zones on certain frontiers might serve—

(i.) To assist in determining, under a general security scheme, which state had committed an act of aggression.

(ii.) To delay an aggressive attack, and thus to give more time for effective mutual assistance to be furnished by other signatories to the state attacked.

(iii.) To assist in preventing war by removing from immediate contact the forces of potentially hostile states.

It is surely obvious that all these claims are justified. If in violation of a security pact aggression should occur, the mere presence of the forces of one side or another in the demilitarized zone would enable the Council of the League to know with certainty which side had committed the first act of armed aggression. Likewise, a system which removes the point of concentration of the aggressor's forces to a considerable distance from their first objective must plainly give advantage to the defending states. Every battle of the late war showed that, in spite of the rapidity of modern transport, an advance of 40 to 50 kilometres placed an attacking force in a position of great difficulty, if not of danger, until it had moved up its bases of supply—a process which necessarily requires a certain time. Again, it is surely obvious that the separation of potentially hostile forces by a neutral zone must diminish the chances of a collision, and so reduce the risk of war. It is said that, even with such difficult Governments as those of Greece and Turkey, the Maritza zone above referred to has in this respect worked well.

It may be concluded, therefore, on grounds both of theory and of practice, that demilitarized zones may in some cases serve a very useful purpose as a supplement to a general treaty of disarmament.

Something may next be said about the detailed provisions that would be desirable in agreements to create such frontier zones. Judging by the experience of the past, Governments which wish by means of zones to achieve the three purposes discussed above would probably agree to the following arrangements:

(i.) A zone should be perhaps 15 to 30 miles across. The Maritza zone is 30 kilometres in depth on either side of the frontier, the Rhineland zone is 50 kilometres across, the Swedish-Norwegian zone 40 kilometres. The exact depth would have to vary with local geography.

(ii.) "All permanent fortifications, and field works actually in existence, shall be disarmed and dismantled by the power on whose territory they are situated."[1]

[1] Lausanne Convention respecting the Thracian Frontier (*i.e.*, Maritza zone).

(iii.) " No new fortification or work of this nature shall be constructed."[1]

(iv.) " No depôt of arms or of war material or any other offensive or defensive installation either of military, of naval, or of aeronautical character shall be organized."[2]

(v.) The conscription or military training of the population of the zone should be forbidden. (But this, while desirable, is clearly not essential.)

(vi.) No military camps or barracks should be stationed in the zone.

(vii.) No manufacture of arms and munitions of any sort should be carried out there.

(viii.) " No armed forces other than the special elements, such as Gendarmerie, Police, Customs Officers, and Frontier Guards, necessary for ensuring internal order and the supervision of the frontiers, shall be stationed or moved in the zones."[3]

The Lausanne Convention specifies the total number of men whom such elements may include—*i.e.*, 5,000—and lays down their armament, permitting only 4 Lewis guns per 100 men and no artillery of any kind.

(ix.) " Military or naval aircraft of any flag whatsoever are forbidden to fly over a demilitarized zone."[4]

(x.) Only such railway lines and sidings as are necessary for commercial traffic should be permitted in the zone, legitimate requirements in this respect being determined by impartial experts appointed by the Transport Committee of the League. (This, while desirable, might be difficult in practice to carry out.)

(xi.) For ensuring that the obligations of the Lausanne Convention are carried out, its fourth Article provides that any complaint of non-observance may be brought before the Council of the League. This, as a rule, should prove an effective safeguard.

But if it were desired to supplement it, there is no reason why the Council of the League should not appoint an impartial Commissioner or Commissioners who would

[1] Lausanne Convention respecting the Thracian Frontier.
[2] *Ibid.*   [3] *Ibid.*   [4] *Ibid.*

live in the zone, have full rights of inspection and enquiry, and be responsible to the Council of the League alone. Such League Officers—there are already precedents of a kind for their appointment—would not only secure faithful observance of a demilitarization treaty; under a security agreement they would also, by their mere presence, give the greatest possible guarantee against aggression, for their impartial report to the Council as to whose troops had first violated the forbidden zone would by itself be conclusive proof of guilt. If the Governments really want security against aggression from without, here is a simple way to get it.

It must be added, however, that the system of demilitarized zones cannot be universally applied. On mountain frontiers the advantage of a zone might be outweighed by the loss of strong defensive military positions. In areas which are densely populated, Governments may feel obliged to protect their inhabitants even against unresisted foreign attack. But, even so, it cannot be doubted that on many frontiers demilitarization would have an admirable effect, would permit a great reduction of existing armament, and would much diminish, if not definitely remove, as in Canada it has done, the danger of aggressive war.

Since, however, the plan is not of general application, it can hardly form part of the disarmament treaty. Proposals for zones might much affect negotiations about the ratio and the scale of armaments to be allowed; but agreements on the subject would have to be supplementary to the general treaty, as the Thracian Frontier Convention was supplementary to the Treaty of Lausanne.

NEUTRALIZATION AT SEA

The system of neutralization at sea may be briefly dealt with.

In the past, it has been applied in two ways: to international straits and canals; and, in one instance only, to the open sea.

The first kind of application is illustrated by the Convention of Constantinople of 1888 for the Neutralization of the Suez Canal. Under this Convention—

1. The Canal is to be open in time of peace, as well as war, to merchantmen and men-of-war of all nations.
2. The Canal can never be blockaded.
3. In time of war no act of hostility is allowed, either in the Canal itself, or within three sea miles from its ports.
4. Belligerent men-of-war may not stay in the Canal more than twenty-four hours, except in case of absolute necessity.
5. Men-of-war may not be stationed in the Canal.
6. No permanent fortifications are allowed in the Canal, etc.[1]

The second kind of application has occurred only in the neutralization of the Black Sea by the Treaty of Paris of 1856. Article XI of that Treaty is in the following terms:

" La Mer Noire est neutralisée; ouverts a la marine marchande de toutes les nations, ses eaux et ses ports sont solennellement et a perpetuité interdits au pavillon de guerre, soit des puissances riveraines, soit de toute autre puissance."

This neutralization, in fact, came to an end in 1871.

It is clear that, both for straits and open sea, the principle of neutralization would need to-day a different application to meet the changes made by the Covenant of the League. It would plainly be absurd to put an aggressor state, as these old treaties would do, on the same footing with the states which are co-operating for the League against it. And, in fact, the necessary changes have actually been made for the Dardanelles and Bosphorus by the Straits Convention adopted at the Conference of Lausanne, for it is laid down that " the present provision, which forms an integral part of those relating to the demilitarization and to the freedom of the Straits, does not pre-judice the rights and obligations of the High Contracting Parties under the Covenant of the League of Nations."[2] This pro-

---

[1] Cf. Oppenheim, *International Law*, vol. i., p. 250.   [2] Article 18.

vision, which clearly needs general application to all straits, safeguards the right of Members of the League to take any measure in the Straits and the bordering demilitarized zones which may be necessary to carry out the obligations of Article 16.

But straits are only of indirect importance to disarmament. The question of the open sea is different.

It was argued in Chapter V above that the participation of Russia in the naval clauses of a disarmament treaty is particularly important. At the Rome Naval " Conference " of 1924 the Russian Delegation demanded for their Government a capital ship tonnage of 490,000 tons, but offered, on certain conditions, to accept 280,000. The conditions were as follows:[1]

" (i.) That the Bosphorus and Dardanelles (Straits) are closed.

" (ii.) That vessels of war belonging to non-riparian States of the Baltic are forbidden access to the Baltic by the Sound and Belt.

" (iii.) That the Straits of Korea are demilitarized (disarmed)."[2]

This proposal was emphasized on several occasions during the debates of the Rome Conference by the Russian Delegate.[3] No attention need be given to the tonnage figures; what matters is the principle of great reduction in naval strength in return for the demilitarization of certain portions of the open sea.

It is known that strong parties in the Baltic countries support the Russian proposal to neutralize the Baltic Sea. But the British Government has always in the past opposed it, and at the Conference of Lausanne they equally opposed the neutralization of the Black Sea. In the Baltic we have always demanded absolute right of entry for British ships in unlimited numbers, both in peace and war.

It is worth enquiring whether in view of the Russian offer, of the new legal situation of Great Britain as a Member of

[1] Unimportant matters are omitted.
[2] L.N. Document C. 76, 1924, ix., p. 15.
[3] *E.g.*, *ibid.*, pp. 20-7, etc.

the League, and of the changed conditions of modern naval war, our traditional policy is not out of date. Of course, no Member of the League could accept a neutralization which forbade states to send their fleets to the Black Sea or Baltic in support of the Covenant of the League. But if this right were secured, would the traditional British policy still be sound?

The answer must depend upon the following questions.

First, will Great Britain ever in the future want to send ships to the Black Sea or the Baltic, except in support of joint action against an aggressor who has violated the Covenant or some treaty supplementary thereto? The answer would seem to be a decisive negative. What British interest could induce us, either *against* the Covenant or in pursuance of a bilateral war, to send our fleet into either of these seas? The case on this point will be still stronger if the Covenant is completed by new agreements finally outlawing all aggressive war.

Second, is it, in fact, probable, in the modern conditions of naval war, that we shall be able to send ships either into the Baltic or the Black Sea, except when we have the active support of at least a considerable number of riparian powers? During the late war the Russian Navy was for some years actively co-operating with Great Britain, yet Germany, defending the Kattegat and the Sound by floating mines, closed them so effectively that throughout the war no single British surface vessel reached the Baltic.[1] It must also be remembered that in the future any ship sent to the Baltic would have in its narrow seas to run the tremendous risks of large-scale air attack.

Third, all this being so, is it not, in fact, the true interest of Great Britain to clear the Baltic as far as possible of ships of war, and by agreeing to Russia's conditions, to reduce Russian naval strength as much as may be? What could Great Britain lose under the proposed arrangement? And might she not greatly gain?

The case seems strong enough, at least, to justify a thorough reconsideration with an open mind of our traditional policy

---

[1] It has been said that only two submarines got in, of which one was lost. But, so far as the author is aware, no official figures have been published.

about neutralization of the open sea. This reconsideration should certainly be given when there is a chance of a new naval arrangement, perhaps highly advantageous to the British fleet. Any neutralization that was accepted might, of course, be made conditional upon the acceptance by Russia of the general security system of the League of Nations, or at least of its obligations not to go to war. This is only likely to prove an obstacle to agreement until such time as Russia has made up her mind that a policy of disarmament and co-operation with other nations is in her own true interest.

CHAPTER XVI

THE TRAFFIC IN ARMS AND AMMUNITION AND THEIR MANUFACTURE BY PRIVATE ENTERPRISE

No general treaty of disarmament could be complete unless it dealt with the manufacture by private enterprise of arms and ammunition, and with the international traffic in them. That this is so is proved, if proof is needed, by the clauses on these subjects in the Treaties of Peace and in the Washington Convention. In particular, the provisions of the Washington Convention involved a great spontaneous sacrifice of government freedom—a sacrifice that would never have been made had the parties not thought it vital to their general success.

THE EVILS OF PRIVATE ENTERPRISE IN ARMS

Before the late war there was a considerable debate about the alleged evils of the private manufacture of, and the unchecked traffic in, arms. But since the Covenant was drafted, this debate, in principle at least, has ended. For Article 8 declares, in uncompromising terms, that " the Members of the League *agree* that the manufacture by private enterprise of munitions and implements of war *is open to grave objections.*" And it lays down that " the Council shall advise how the *evil effects* attendant upon such manufacture can be prevented."

On the trade in arms the Covenant is less explicit. By Article 23, paragraph (*d*), the Members of the League " entrust the League with the general supervision of the trade in arms and ammunition with the countries in which control of this traffic is necessary in the common interest." Here, again, is a duty laid upon the League with a clear instruction that *some* control is needed.

What are the " grave objections " to the manufacture of arms by private enterprise, as to the reality of which the Members of the League are all agreed ? The Temporary Mixed

Commission, charged by the Council with the study of the subject, has thus defined them:

" The objections that are raised to untrammelled private manufacture may be grouped under the following headings:[1]

" 1. That armament firms have been active in fomenting war scares and in persuading their own countries to adopt warlike policies and to increase their armaments.

" 2. That armament firms have attempted to bribe Government officials, both at home and abroad.

" 3. That armament firms have disseminated false reports concerning the military and naval programmes of various countries in order to stimulate armament expenditure.

" 4. That armament firms have sought to influence public opinion through the control of newspapers in their own and foreign countries.

" 5. That armament firms have organized international armament rings through which the armament race has been accentuated by playing off one country against another.

" 6. That armament firms have organized international armament trusts which have increased the price of armaments sold to Governments."

What are the evils of the international trade in arms? They are the same as the evils of private manufacture, for, of course, the trade is but another part of the activity of those who make the arms. But to those described above there may perhaps be added another evil due especially to the traders: the fact that throughout all the uncivilized, backward, or disorganized portions of the world vast quantities of arms and ammunition have been let loose. These arms make the task of government in such places more difficult than it should be, and much increase its cost in men and money; they sometimes even lead to general social chaos, of the kind into which the Chinese Tuchuns, with foreign arms, have sunk their nation.

[1] Report of the Temporary Mixed Commission, 1921, A. 81, 1921; C. 321, 1921, p. 11.

Few people to-day dispute the folly of permitting unchecked private enterprise in arms. Even before the war so orthodox a writer as the editor of the *Times Engineering Supplement*, commenting on " the present interchange of ideas and traffic in war material between nations " as " a remarkable product of modern commerce and diplomacy," added that although it was " regarded with complete equanimity, it involves what is perhaps the most momentous paradox of the age."[1]

A few illustrations showing various aspects of the " paradox " may be given. Before the war, a director of a great armament firm (Armstrong, Whitworth and Co.), in repudiating a suggestion that armament firms ever had resort to any of the methods set forth above, reassured his shareholders by telling them to look upon the firm as " equipping the police of the world. The ultimate appeal," he said, " for all order was force, and a great armament firm furnished the means for the suppression of disorder. That was really how they ought to be regarded."[2] At the very moment when that director used these words, his firm were making armaments for Turkey. Just twelve months later, the armaments provided by them and by another British firm, with which they were in close alliance, were inflicting upon the chosen flower of the Empire the hellish holocaust of Anzac.[3] One of the directors of the firm had been only a few years before, first, Director of Naval Intelligence in the British Admiralty, and later Secretary of the supreme military authority of the Empire, the Committee of Imperial Defence.[4] There is something peculiarly revolting to the public conscience in the thought that British capital, British brains, British enterprise, and the services of Englishmen who had gained unique knowledge and experience in the highest posts of public trust and honour, should have helped to organize and to equip the war machine which was to slaughter tens of thousands of Britain's sons.

The arms trade still goes on, and there have been few stranger examples of it than the trade of recent years with China. The

---

[1] *Times Engineering Supplement*, June 25, 1913.

[2] April 18, 1914, quoted by G. W. Ferris, *War Traders*, p. 101.

[3] Cf. facts cited by Dr. Hugh Dalton in the House of Commons, March 11, 1926.

[4] Mr. Philip Snowden in *Hansard*, March 18, 1914.

powers all protest that the Chinese civil war is not only disastrous to the Chinese people, but that it imperils most important foreign interests and even threatens to cause a great Asiatic war. Yet they have allowed their armament firms to pour into China ever since 1918 an unceasing stream of arms and ammunition which have been paid for by the compulsory growth and sale of opium—that is to say, at the price of the political and social debauchery of the Chinese. And the half-hearted efforts made in 1919, and again at Washington in 1921, to snuff the traffic out, only served to show that the Governments knew what was going on and that with that knowledge they did nothing to bring it to an end.[1]

And every year on all the distant frontiers of the Empire British officers and men are " sniped " by rifles produced for private profit by Western armament firms.

Proposals of the Temporary Mixed Commission

To meet the evils involved in these two problems of private manufacture and the trade in arms, the Temporary Mixed Commission made practical and elaborate proposals.

Their proposals on the arms traffic were ultimately embodied in an international convention agreed to at a League of Nations Conference held in Geneva in 1925. This Convention had a double purpose: first, publicity, by a system of Governmental licence for all international transactions in arms of every kind; second, the effective prohibition of the import of arms into certain backward portions of the world where it was believed that they would create social or political disturbance.[2]

For private manufacture a separate scheme was prepared by the British Government representative, Sir Hubert Llewellyn Smith, of the Board of Trade. His draft agreement laid down important rules. It provided that no company or private firm should engage in the production or sale of armament

---

[1] On April 8, 1919, the American Minister at Peking proposed that the powers should impose an embargo on the export of arms to China. This was formally agreed to, but never enforced. Similar proposals were put forward at the Washington Conference on January 31, 1922. and again abandoned without any serious effort to carry them through, Compare Buell, *The Washington Conference*, pp. 270-1.

[2] The text of the Convention is given in L. N. Document A. 16, 1925, ix.

without a Government licence; that no such licence should be granted if the applying company or anyone among its responsible management or owners had any controlling interest in any organ of the public press; that a licensed company should be obliged to inform the Government of all the foreign orders it accepts; that it should never, without Government consent, come under the control of any foreign interest; that it should issue no " bearer " shares which carry voting power; that every licencee should furnish to the Government every year a sworn declaration that he had fulfilled all the necessary conditions of the licence, false declarations to be punishable by the severest penalties.[1] This proposal was adopted by the Temporary Mixed Commission, but no steps have yet been taken to summon a Conference on the subject.

This fact, however, need not be much regretted. For the questions both of private manufacture and of the traffic in arms are wholly altered when they are made part, as it was intended by the authors of the Covenant that they should be part, of a general scheme for reduction and limitation of national armaments. When they are treated as separate isolated problems, when the purpose aimed at is the prevention of some special form of political corruption, the checking of unnecessary scares, the avoidance of artificial armament competition, the measures needed may differ widely from what is needed when they are dealt with as one part of a larger whole.

For this reason there is no need to discuss in detail the proposals of the Temporary Mixed Commission. We may pass on at once to what is needed in the general disarmament treaty—that is to say, a supplementary agreement for such measures of control upon the manufacture of and trade in arms as will secure the faithful observance of the armament limits that have been accepted.

THE PROVISIONS NEEDED IN A GENERAL TREATY

It is obvious that once armament limitations are agreed to, the whole problem will become very different from that of attempting to control the operations of private companies when their sales and markets are unrestricted in any way.

[1] For text of this proposal vide L. N. Document A. 31, C. 631, 1922, p. 23.

In view of this fundamental change, what measures are required ? The following suggestions are based on the discussions of the Temporary Mixed Commission and of the Arms Traffic Conference of 1925, but are adapted to meet the new situation which will be created by a disarmament treaty.

It will be observed that no attempt is made to distinguish between measures required for private manufacture and measures required for the traffic; on the contrary, the two are dealt with together. This is plainly right. At the end of its study of the two problems even the Temporary Mixed Commission, though it tried to deal with them separately, came to the firm conclusion that " the subject of private manufacture could not be divorced from the subject of traffic in arms."[1] It will be obvious in what follows that the measures required for controlling manufacture and those required for controlling the traffic must of necessity overlap.

(i.) As proposed by Sir Hubert Llewellyn Smith, no private company or other firm should be allowed to manufacture arms of any kind, either for sale at home or for export abroad, without a licence from the central Government or Governments in whose territory or territories its factories may be.

(ii.) The granting of such a licence should be made conditional upon fulfilment of the conditions proposed by Sir Hubert Llewellyn Smith (vide pp. 305-6 above). Faithful observance of these conditions should be attested every year by sworn declaration which should be subject to verification by Government or by international authority.

(iii.) The export of arms from one country to another should not be permitted by the Government of the country from which they are exported without a separate Government licence specially granted for each consignment.

(iv.) Such an *export* licence should only be furnished by the Government of the exporting country, in return for an *import* licence from the Government of the country to which the arms are destined to be sent.

(v.) All these three licences, to manufacture, to export, and to import, should be communicated immediately to the Secretary-General of the League, and should be published by him

[1] L.N. Document A. 31, C. 631, C.T.A. 173, p. 24, 1924.

in the official journal or some other organ of the League before the actual transfer of arms from one country to another is permitted to take place.

These last three provisions would be merely adaptations of principles already accepted in the Arms Traffic Convention of 1925. The same principles were also applied in a different form in Article 16 of the Washington Convention.[1]

(vi.) All licensed manufacturers, companies, or firms should be required to publish full accounts of their armament business, and to submit such accounts to public audit.

This measure was tentatively proposed by the Temporary Mixed Commission in its Report of 1921.[2]

(vii.) If it were proved by the public audit or by an international enquiry that the accounts of any licensed firm were not in order, the Government which had granted its licence to manufacture should be required to cancel it.

(viii.) All the signatory Governments should undertake not to allow upon their territory the production of any weapon or means of war which is forbidden by the disarmament treaty; and to oblige both their Government arsenals and private manufacturing firms within their jurisdiction to observe whatever limits of maximum size or calibre are laid down by the treaty for warships, artillery, or other implements of war.

This undertaking would, of course, be no more than a general adoption of the provisions of Article 15 of the Washington Naval Convention.[3]

(ix.) The signatory Governments should give an undertaking, similar to that of Article 18 of the Washington Convention, that they will sell no war material of any kind from the stocks of their national defence forces, nor so dispose of any such material that it may become the property of another state. In other words, they should agree never to allow arms or ammunition which they have prepared under the disarmament treaty for the use of their own troops to pass to other countries. There are several reasons why the general adoption of this

[1] Q.v., Appendix IV, p. 344, *infra.*
[2] L. N. Document A. 81, 1921; C. 321, 1921, p. 12.
[3] Q.v., Appendix IV, p. 343.

Washington provision is required. First, if a sudden large sale of Government stocks of arms were made by one country to another, it might completely upset the balance of the agreed disarmament ratio, and perhaps even render possible disloyal aggression by the purchasing state. Second, sales of second-hand material, being made, as almost certainly they would be, at prices well below the current market cost, might destroy the basis of the limitation of armament by budgetary appropriation, if that plan were to be adopted. Third, such sales might lead to undesirable relationships between Governments which it would be better to avoid.

The arguments for this Washington type of self-denying ordinance are perhaps stronger, as certainly they are more obvious, in respect of warships than in respect of other kinds of arms. But the three reasons just indicated lead to the conclusion that they really apply with almost equal force to armament of every kind.

(x.) Next, there is the question whether the principle of Article 17 of the Washington Convention should be generally applied; whether, that is to say, it should be laid down that no signatory power which is engaged in war shall use armaments prepared upon its territory for a foreign state.

At first sight it seems obviously desirable to secure its general application at least in respect of warships, and perhaps also in respect of armament of all kinds. But it must be remembered that if a general system of security is adopted which outlaws resort to war, except on behalf of the League of Nations and in joint defence against aggression, such an undertaking, if it did not lose its meaning altogether, would at least be much less obviously necessary than it was in the situation with which the authors of the Washington Convention had to deal.

(xi.) Finally, it must be asked whether the above provisions could be applied even if some arms-producing countries were to stand outside the disarmament treaty altogether, and were thus to keep their hands free of all restrictions upon their right to manufacture and trade in arms. This was, in fact, a capital difficulty in the preparation of the Arms Traffic Convention.[1]

Of course, the case is unlikely to arise if a general dis-

[1] Owing to the attitude of the U.S.A.

armament treaty is made, but even if it did, even if some one or two producing countries did stand aside, the resulting difficulty about trade and manufacture could still be overcome. The Temporary Mixed Commission once actually discussed a plan for the purpose, to wit, a mutual agreement among the signatory parties that they would boycott all arms manufactured in, or sold by, a non-signatory country, forbidding not only their purchase, but even their transport across their respective territories. Governments which are seriously resolved to disarm will not hesitate to agree upon such a measure of reprisal as this against a country which deliberately decides to stand aside. And if they did agree, it can hardly be doubted that, with the full publicity above proposed, their joint action would successfully protect them against the unfair competition of non-cooperating states.

THE LIMITATION OF POTENTIAL ARMAMENT PRODUCTION

Another question concerning the manufacture of armaments remains to be discussed: that of the limitation of the potential capacity of states to produce armament of different kinds after war has broken out. This is a matter to which the French Delegation to the Council Committee in December, 1925, attached a great importance, as is shown by the records of the debates. They urged that it was useless to limit armament in time of peace, if Governments were left free to maintain a great industrial machine for armament production, with which they could forthwith increase their strength whenever they might treacherously decide to go to war. They therefore demanded that measures should be taken to limit the capacity of states for armament production in time of war.

Can this be done? The answer depends on two further questions: First, is it desirable to limit and control industrial organizations, whether Government or private, which are capable of being converted to the production of arms and ammunition? Second, if it is desirable, is it practicable to do so?

As to the first of these questions, the answer, if it is considered from the point of view of disarmament alone, would no doubt be " Yes." The best is always best.

As to the second, the answer is less clear. The desired limitation could only be made by restricting the numbers of machines of certain types existing within the jurisdiction of different states. It would obviously be difficult to do anything of the sort, but before considering how the difficulties could be overcome, it may be well to narrow down the issue by determining what kinds of armament machinery it is necessary to discuss.

To begin with, plant for poison-gas production may be excluded. Nothing further could be done beyond the proposals discussed in Chapter XIV above.

Second, it is not practicable to limit the machinery used for making aircraft. There is no specialized machinery for military aircraft which is not equally required for commercial aircraft, and most of it, indeed, is required for commercial motor-cars as well. Nothing, therefore, can be done.

Third, there is no purpose in endeavouring to limit the machinery required for making warships. Warships take so long to build that production by an aggressor after war had been declared can safely be neglected.

There remain tanks, artillery, shells, machine-guns, and rifles, the machinery for making which it is desirable and which it may be possible to limit. They may be taken in turn.

1. *Tanks.*—The machinery required for the manufacture of a tank is, in part at least, specialized, and can be used for the production of no ordinary commercial article. The possession of more than a fixed amount of such specialized machinery might, therefore, be forbidden by international treaty, and the prohibition could, in all probability, be made effective.

2. *Artillery.*—Similarly, most of the machinery for the production of guns of all calibres is special, and serves no peaceful purpose. Again, therefore, it might be limited in amount, and observance of the limitation might be effectively controlled.

3. *Shells.*—The machinery required for making shells is almost entirely machinery used for peaceful products of commercial engineering. Thus the casting, turning, and filling of shells can all be carried out without special adaptation of factory plant. While, therefore, it may be possible by supervision to control the amount of a nation's shell production in

time of peace, it would not be possible to limit its capacity for such production after war had broken out, without limiting its capacity for ordinary commercial engineering—which obviously cannot be done.

4. *Machine-Guns and Rifles.*—The machinery required for making the barrels of machine-guns and rifles is specialized; both the machines which turn out the barrels and the gauges required for testing them are expensive, and serve no peaceful purpose. This machinery, therefore, could also be effectively limited in amount.

Thus the potential capacity of nations to produce tanks, artillery, machine-guns, and rifles during war could theoretically be limited by a disarmament treaty.

But another difficulty now arises. If armament machinery is to be limited in amount, how much should be allowed to any given state? Experts, no doubt, could decide roughly how much was needed to produce the annual quota of weapons which, under the disarmament treaty, any state may be allowed.[1] But that would not give the answer that is required; for the ratio in machinery could not vary directly with the general ratio of strength allowed to different states. Most countries do not produce themselves the armaments they use, nor is it desirable that they should do so. To oblige them to would merely be to broadcast throughout the world the specialized knowledge and technical organization which is needed for armament production—an obvious folly. But if this be so, then there must remain some measure of legitimate international trade in arms, even after the disarmament treaty has been made; and it cannot be known beforehand between what countries this traffic will take place, from what producer state purchasing Governments will desire to buy. Since this is so, it will plainly be difficult to find any rational basis for the ratio of the amount of armament machinery to be allowed to different producing states.

To meet this difficulty, at least in part, either of two things might be done.

First, an agreement might be made, by separate negotiation among the producing states, laying down the maximum amounts

---

[1] This in fact was done for ex-enemy states by Allied experts.

of armament machinery, whether in Government arsenals or private factories, which each of them would allow upon its territory. Either a fixed maximum of machinery might be adopted, equal in amount for all producing powers, or each of them might be allowed an amount proportionate to the output of its "heavy" engineering industry. This second plan, which would establish a special ratio among industrial states in their capacity for arms production, would have the advantage of corresponding roughly to the *status quo*, and might, on that account, seem reasonable to the Governments concerned.

Second, it might be agreed that instead of putting any artificial limit on armament machinery, the Governments should merely undertake not to subsidize, in time of peace, the maintenance of such machinery by private firms. Thus Government arsenals would be limited by the armament appropriation permitted in the annual budget,[1] and the producing power of private firms would not exceed that of the machinery which their owners, within the general limits of permitted armament, could put to profitable commercial use. This would be safe in practice, for without a subsidy no firm could possibly afford to tie up its capital without return, as it would do if it kept in idleness the expensive machinery required for making tanks and guns.

It is evident that these suggestions would all be complicated to work in practice, that their observance would be, in some ways, difficult to control, and that they might involve some interference with private enterprise. It is doubtful, therefore, whether there is any of them which the Governments will in fact be ready to accept.

Nor, happily, will it be of great importance if the Governments reject all action in the matter. There would be obvious advantage in forbidding subsidies to private firms, and that plan, perhaps, it would be worth while to press. But for the rest, the limitation of potential capacity to produce armament in time of war is in truth a question of secondary importance.

[1] Arrangements supplementary to those described in chap. ix. above would, of course, have to be made if the cost of arsenals were included in the armament appropriation. This could, no doubt, be done.

It is so for a simple reason, to wit, that for the production of tanks and guns, and so on, a long period is required, and therefore Period A is of much greater duration than in respect of other factors of military strength. Supplies of poison-gas and aircraft can be quickly multiplied; artillery and tanks cannot, even if the machinery for their production is in existence. For guns, the time before they could be brought into action in any numbers could hardly be less than six to nine months, however efficient were the preparatory arrangements that were made. For tanks, the period would be as long. Even for shells, to the production of which the peace-time machinery of engineering shops could be applied, the time required before they were delivered in the field would probably be at least about six months. At the time when the production of munitions in Great Britain was most efficient—in 1917 and 1918—nine months on the average elapsed before shells ordered by the War Office were ready for use in France. It is forgotten sometimes how long the processes of shell production—casting, machining, filling, testing, inserting fuses, general assembly, transport here and there—must inevitably take. The period could in special cases have been reduced, but only by delaying the delivery of other kinds of armament and supply. It is, in fact, a complete illusion to think that an engineering industry can be magically transformed into an immense munition plant, producing in a few days or weeks finished products ready for the field. This cannot happen even if the necessary specialized machinery exists; if it, too, has first to be produced, the inevitable delay becomes, of course, longer, but in any case it is a lengthy period of time.[1]

The above argument leads to the following conclusions:

First, there will be real value in limiting by the disarmament treaty not only weapons, but also ammunition, as proposed

[1] Cf. the following statement by Major Lefebure: "I admit that, for many types of heavy armament, an effectively long period would be required for expansion to much larger establishment, if the means of production were actually seriously reduced, in the first place. I have been analyzing evidence of such expansion in the recent war, and the figures are very surprising. For some types of armament, the figures afford a very poor case for the so-called normal convertible industries." (*Problems of Peace and War*, The Grotius Society, vol. vii, p. 158.)

in Chapter IX above, since additional supplies of ammunition will take so long to produce that an aggressor even with great industrial resources would take grave risks.

Second, if potential capacity for war production can be effectively restricted by any of the plans above proposed, it will reduce the supplies of tanks, artillery, rifles, and machine-guns available even to the most advanced industrial states for a prolonged period of time. This, however, will be of increasingly less importance if the present development of gas and aircraft goes on.

Third, even if no such restriction can be made, even if states must be left free to keep all the armament machinery they want, the result will not be fatal to a disarmament scheme. For if existing stocks of shells cannot be increased in less than six or nine months, and if the time for guns and tanks is longer still, there will be a protracted period during which joint action can be taken by states co-operating in support of the Covenant against an aggressor state, before that aggressor can exploit the advantage of its industrial resources upon the field of battle.

Fourth, the questions involved are so intricate, and raise such complicated problems of the organization and control of private and Government industry, that the whole matter should be referred for full investigation to the expert Economic Sub-Commission, which will assist the Preparatory Disarmament Committee of the League.

CHAPTER XVII

RIGHTS OF INVESTIGATION AND MUTUAL CONTROL

It has always been assumed in League discussions on disarmament that no scheme could inspire the general confidence that is required unless it provided specific guarantees that its undertakings would be faithfully observed. It has been also agreed that such guarantees must take the form of a mutual right of investigation and control.

It is true that there is no precise stipulation of the Covenant which provides for mutual control. The obligations of Article 8 are confined to a simple duty " to interchange full and frank information as to the scale of their armaments, their military and air programmes, and the condition of such of their industries as are adaptable to warlike purposes." But those who have responsibly discussed disarmament at Geneva have always urged that Governments cannot be expected to sacrifice their liberty of action, and to reduce their military preparations for national defence, unless they have some material assurance that their good faith will not be betrayed by the failure of other disloyal signatory states to observe the limits of armament they accept; and they have further urged that such a material assurance can only be found in some system of impartial investigation and control. For this reason the authors of the Draft Treaty of Mutual Assistance inserted as their Article 12 the following stipulation:

> " The High Contracting Parties undertake to furnish to the military or other delegates of the League such information with regard to their armaments as the Council may request."[1]

The authors of the Geneva Protocol—and they were the responsible Ministers of State of the most important powers

[1] *Report of the Third Committee to the Fourth Assembly, League of Nations Document A., III., 1923, iv, p. 9.*

in Europe—in their turn adopted the following provisions in their Articles 7 and 8:

> " If one of the signatory states is of opinion that another state is making preparations for war, it shall have the right to bring the matter to the notice of the Council."[1]

> " Should the Council be of opinion that the complaint requires investigation, it shall, if it deems it expedient, arrange for enquiries and investigations in one or more of the countries concerned. Such enquiries and investigations shall be carried out with the utmost possible despatch, and the signatory states undertake to afford every facility for carrying them out."[2]

These provisions of the Draft Treaty of Mutual Assistance and the Protocol had their roots in practical necessity. In any concrete discussion of disarmament, as the previous chapters of this book may have served to show, the question continually arises: How can the signatory states be sure that the limitations accepted will in practice be observed ? Thus, not only the history of previous debates, but also what lawyers call " the reason of the thing," make it seem most probable that no scheme of disarmament will succeed which is without provision for some form or other of mutual control. It is, therefore, the plain duty of the Preparatory Committee to discuss the matter and to make proposals, for without such proposals their general plan can be neither technically nor politically complete.

What proposals should they put forward ? The answer will be a matter of differing opinion, but before it is discussed some preliminary principles may be suggested, about which there will be no dispute.

First, the system to be established, like those proposed in the Draft Treaty of Mutual Assistance and the Protocol, must provide for mutual control through the organs of the League. A power of investigation conferred on individual states would be open to obvious and grave objection, and would lead to the

---

[1] *Geneva Protocol*, Article 8, para. 2.

[2] *Ibid.*, Article 7, para. 2.

sort of friction caused by the Allied Commission in Germany and elsewhere. Such an experience as that of these Commissions bears a warning for the future. Therefore, the right of investigation should be entrusted to the Council of the League, to whom a signatory Government must first address any complaints which it may have to make. The Council would thus be made responsible to all the signatories for carrying out the investigations that may be required.

Second, if a system of control is to be set up at all, it must be efficacious. This is essential in the interests of the states which, in reliance upon the protection it affords, will reduce their armaments; and it is no less essential in the interests of the League. A system which did not give real guarantees of faithful observance, a system under which a Government might, without detection, be guilty of large-scale violation of its disarmament obligations, would be no better than a trap for loyal states, and might involve the League itself, were its responsibility engaged, in grave disaster.

Third, the arrangements made must consist of two main parts. On the one hand, the right must be conferred on every signatory state to demand, if it desires to do so, investigation through the organs of the League into the armaments of any other signatory state; and the right must be conferred upon the Council of the League to organize and despatch Commissions of Enquiry whenever it may think that a case for such action has been made. On the other hand, duties must be imposed upon all the signatory states to receive such Commissions of Enquiry within their respective jurisdictions whenever the Council may judge it wise to send them, and to give to these Commissions all facilities of every kind for the fulfilment of their task.

Fourth, there should be set up some workable and standing machinery for the actual conduct of investigations if they should be needed. No doubt the work might be done in many cases by an *ad hoc* Commission created for each separate enquiry as it arose; but experience in the League has shown that there may be immense practical advantage in using regular and established machinery at international crises.

Fifth, if the above principles are accepted, investigation

alone will not end the responsibility of the Council towards the signatory powers. For it may decide, as the result of its investigations, that there has been, as alleged by the complaining state, excessive military preparation in violation of the disarmament undertakings. If so, it must obviously be empowered to do something to end an irregular and perhaps a dangerous situation. It would seem that for this purpose it should have rights similar, at least in principle, to those which would have been conferred upon it by Article 7 of the Geneva Protocol. These rights, indeed, appear to be the minimum of what the Council would require if it were called upon to deal with a definite violation of the disarmament treaty.[1]

Such being the main principles upon which a system of mutual control should be founded, what mechanism should the Preparatory Committee propose for the actual conduct of investigations that may be required ?

It has been widely assumed in past discussion of the matter that, when the moment came for general disarmament, the Members of the League would voluntarily accept for themselves the system of control prepared by the Council in 1924 for the supervision and control of Germany, Austria, Hungary, and Bulgaria.[2] For this reason it may be worth while to give a summarized account of this system. Its provisions are embodied in a Report drawn up by a mixed commission of jurists and representatives of the Permanent (Military) Advisory Commission, who worked on the basis of a scheme originally drawn up by the Permanent Advisory Commission

---

[1] Para. 4, Article 7, *Geneva Protocol :* " If the result of such enquiries and investigations is to establish an infraction of the provisions of the first paragraph of the present article " (*i.e.*, an undertaking not to exceed the level of armaments accepted) " it shall be the duty of the Council to summon the state or states guilty of the infraction to put an end thereto. Should the state or states in question fail to comply with such summons, the Council shall declare them to be guilty of a violation of the Covenant or of the present Protocol, and shall decide upon the measures to be taken with a view to end as soon as possible a situation of a nature to threaten the peace of the world."

[2] In pursuance of duties imposed on it by Article 213 of the Treaty of Versailles, Article 159 of the Treaty of St. Germain, Article 143 of the Treaty of Trianon, and Article 104 of the Treaty of Neuilly.

as a whole. This Report was adopted by the Council on March 14, 1925.[1]

The scheme contains, of course, two main parts. First, it confers the following rights upon Commissions of Enquiry appointed by the Council of the League:

(i.) Such a Commission may be sent at any time by the Council of the League into any of the four countries subject to control on the demand of any state Member of the League. Only one of its members may be a national of a state which is a neighbour to the country where the enquiry is to take place.

(ii.) Its members may take all such steps as they may deem necessary or expedient to satisfy themselves that in respect of—

> Recruitment,
> Organization,
> Numerical strength,
> Armament of the Army,
> Armament of the Navy,
> Armament of the Police Force or other similar organizations,
> Preparations for mobilizing military or naval personnel,
> Military training carried on by private institutions or associations,
> National legislation concerning armament of the country where investigation is in progress,

the provisions of the relevant Peace Treaty have been observed.

(iii.) A Commission may appoint sub-commissions or groups who may spend as long as they think necessary in inspecting any factory, depôt, or other place, or in carrying out any operations which in their opinion are required.

(iv.) For such purposes they must have absolute freedom of movement, and may enter and search any building, public or private.

[1] *League of Nations Document* C, 158, 1925, ix., C.P.C. 165.

(v.) A Commission shall be entitled to examine any books or documents relating to the transport of goods by whatever method.

(vi.) Local investigations shall be carried out by the groups of at least three members of the Commission of different nationalities.

Second, the scheme imposes the following duties upon the Government of the country subject to investigation:

(i.) On receipt of a notification from the Council that an investigation will be made, the Government must take all measures to ensure that the Commission of Investigation can accomplish its mission in complete freedom and without resistance, whether active or passive, from any authority or from the local population.

(ii.) It must designate a ministerial department with which the Council and the Commission can correspond and make practical arrangements for their work.

(iii.) This Ministry must supply to the Commission all the information or documents which it may request.

(iv.) All other Ministries must place at the disposal of the Commission all their archives and correspondence bearing on the subject-matter of the investigation, and in particular must furnish detailed lists showing the exact location and quantities of arms, munitions, and war material, as well as returns relative to the effective strength of units.

(v.) Qualified liaison officers are to be attached to the Commission of Investigation, and to its sub-committees during the whole duration of their mission. These officers must be furnished with formal written orders to comply with any request made in the course of its mission by the Commission of Investigation.

(vi.) They must also hold a written authority giving them full powers in relation to any military, naval, or civil authority, or any individual, to enforce the rights of the Commission of Investigation.

(vii.) Instructions shall be issued by the Government to all provincial and local authorities, military, naval, or civil, and to the private owners and managers of factories, enjoining them to comply at once with any request of the Commission and requiring police authorities to supply whatever assistance or protection may be needed.

(viii.) Copies of the orders and instructions mentioned in (v.), (vi.), and (vii.) must be sent to the Council of the League, together with a certificate to the effect that they are fully effective in the national law of the country concerned.

If this scheme is considered in relation to the discussion in previous chapters of the practical problems of control, it will be seen that as far as any paper scheme can do so, it adequately provides what is required.

But it will no doubt be thought by many that such a scheme will never, in fact, be generally accepted, because it would involve a sacrifice of military liberty to which no Government in present-day conditions can be expected to agree. It may be useful, therefore, without the formulation of any dogmatic conclusions, to state quite simply the arguments in favour of its general acceptance.

First, then, armament control is a matter in which differential treatment for the ex-enemy states would be particularly difficult to defend. Once the other Members of the League have accepted limitations on their national armaments, on what grounds can they reasonably refuse for themselves measures which, after prolonged consideration, the Council of the League has itself decreed to be necessary in respect of Germany and her late Allies? German opinion will probably regard their attitude on this point as the acid test of the sincerity of the other Governments in their professed intention to disarm. And, of course, unless the scheme were generally accepted it would be hard to maintain that Germany was being treated on " a footing of full equality " in the League.

Second, the general adoption of the scheme would go far towards inspiring real confidence in the signatory states that control over armament limitations would be effective. It is true that against some sorts of secret preparation—*e.g.*, gas and aircraft—even this scheme of investigation might possibly fail. But it must be remembered that it would supplement, and not replace, the secret services which most countries now maintain. The general staffs to-day are rarely in error about the preparations which their neighbours make. With their assistance a League Commission of Investigation could rarely fail to find out the truth. For these reasons it may be hoped that the general adoption of the Council's system would inspire the confidence that is required.

Third, to invert the argument, any plan that falls far short of this in the stringency of its provisions will in all probability *not* inspire the confidence that is required. It must be remembered that the Permanent Advisory Commission, in their first Report upon the question, virtually asserted that in their view this scheme was the minimum which would permit really effective investigation in Germany and the other states concerned. " The extent of the general discussion, which continued for some ten meetings, is," they said, " a testimony to the efforts made to arrive at proposals which should be reasonable and at the same time *calculated to render the enquiries really efficacious, failing which the Commission thinks that the Council's exercise of its rights would be illusory and even dangerous.*"[1]

Last, it may be asked if it is really necessary in the age in which we live to take account of the sacrifice of military liberty involved. It is not as if this scheme meant permanently resident foreign Commissions of Control; it means no more than an exceptional enquiry when *prima facie* evidence of dishonourable conduct has been shown. A country which observed its obligations could have nothing to fear, and would never have to submit to investigation. And are there not new overriding interests, which, for all Governments, now that a great new international policy is by their common consent to be adopted, should come before the old shibboleths of freedom and secrecy in military preparation—shibboleths which so far, be it noted, have failed to bring us security from war ? Nor can it be said that the generality of Governments will be unlikely to agree. France, the military leader of the world,

---

[1] *League of Nations Document* C. 503 (*a*), 1924, IX, p. 2.

whose general staff has always exercised great influence on her national policy, is not only ready now to accept investigation by the League into French armaments, but has pressed for a general system of League control ever since the Covenant was first discussed. Germany is already bound by the system above described; without a doubt the smaller states will follow the lead which the Great Powers give them. There can, in fact, be little question that if Great Britain were ready to consent, the general adoption of the scheme would be rapidly secured.

As to whether or not Great Britain *ought* to consent, no conclusion need be suggested. No doubt other alternative plans for mutual control could be devised. But the Council scheme for the ex-enemy countries is a useful and a thorough piece of work, and its general adoption would be the simplest way of avoiding difficulties that must otherwise inevitably arise.

CHAPTER XVIII

CONCLUSIONS

THERE are other parts of a disarmament treaty, not discussed in the preceding pages, which may give rise to technical difficulties of various kinds, and concerning which, therefore, it may be thought that proposals should have been put forward. The arrangements for the actual execution of reduction clauses; the conditions in which it shall be held that disarmament according to the treaty has or has not been carried out; the number of ratifications required to bring the treaty into force, and the question of what states must be among the ratifying powers; the revision of the original scales of armament adopted, and the mechanism for the consultation and agreement that will be needed; the problem of the increase of armament during an international dispute, and of the suspension of the disarmament clauses if war should for any reason actually break out—these are matters which collectively make up a not inconsiderable part of the technical difficulty of disarmament, upon which the general treaty must lay down clear rules, and for which, therefore, the Preparatory Committee and the Council, if their plans are to be complete, must make proposals.

But they are matters which, after all, are of secondary importance, and there can be little doubt that when the major problems have been successfully solved, whatever supplementary arrangements are necessary to bring the agreed scheme into force will be quite simply made. There is no purpose in complicating present issues by considering all the consequential questions which will arise when the main plan of action has been once agreed. "First things first."

That, indeed, might well be the motto which the Preparatory Committee should adopt. There will be much importance in the way in which they set about their work. If they try to make at their first meeting a rigid scheme, with all the scales and ratios included, they will almost surely fail.

325

Those who expect any such result from their first meeting do not know disarmament for the infinitely intricate affair it is. But if they start cautiously, conscientiously, it might also be said scientifically, with the study of the factors of military strength which they desire to limit; if, having settled on the factors, they next agree upon the methods by which each separate factor can be controlled; if, with that agreement, they draft a model skeleton treaty with " x," " y," " z," instead of figures; if after that—and only after that—they start discussion of the ratio, of the strength which different countries ought to be allowed; then by this gradual process of construction a disarmament treaty will slowly but certainly emerge.

It is a process which may strain the patience of the Preparatory Committee, and perhaps still more the patience of those who observe its labours from outside. Great patience will undoubtedly be needed.

But patience is justified, perhaps even compromise may be justified, by the hopes for which the present labours of the League give ground. It is these hopes, indeed, which make it right to explore every avenue and every plan by which a definite result, even a disappointing definite result, may be secured. In justice, in logic, in common sense, there is, once a policy of disarmament has been decided, only one plan which deserves consideration—the general adoption of the system imposed upon the ex-enemy states by the Treaties of Peace. But it is almost certain, however much the reasons may be deplored, that that is outside the realm of practical politics at the present time. Need we therefore despair ? Are the difficulties which inevitably result too serious to be overcome ? It has been the purpose of this book to show that they are not. And if they are once overcome, whether in the ways proposed above or by other simpler or more intricate devices, if a scheme is once agreed, if a comprehensive limitation of all kinds of armament is once set up, then further progress will be virtually assured. The first relief may not be very great; the prevention of great expansion in air forces, the curtailment of new construction in the fleet, these perhaps may be the first modest benefits we feel. But even if this were so, we could be confident that when the first revision period came we should be able to demand a great all-round percentage cut in the scales of armament first adopted, and to do so with the knowledge that the claim could hardly be opposed. For then there would be no problem of what factors should be limited, no dispute of method, no ratio to be made; all the Governments would know that by a simple automatic tested system of reduction they would be able, not only at no risk, but, on the contrary, with obvious advantage to their national safety, to cut down the burden of unproductive taxation which their peoples bear. That hope it is which justifies patience, compromise, and unremitting effort, and which will make the adoption of any definite comprehensive scheme, however small its first reductions, a great and a decisive victory for the League.

But if that be the starting point, what is the goal? When will disarmament be complete? When will victory be absolutely assured? Perhaps we may borrow our standards from the director of a great armament firm whose words were quoted above. Armaments, he said, were for the purpose of " equipping the police of the world. . . . The ultimate appeal for all order is force, and a great armament firm furnishes the means for the suppression of disorder."[1] The same conception appears in the Treaty of Versailles. There it is provided that the German army " shall be devoted exclusively to the maintenance of order within the territory and to the control of the frontiers."[2] When armament is recognized finally and universally as the means for the suppression of national and international disorder, when armies are devoted to the maintenance of order and the control of frontiers, then the work of disarmament will be done. But that means that disarmament will not be the labour of a day.

Frankly, what chance is there now of success? Surely a great chance, on one condition: that Great Britain should give the lead. America stands ready, ardent if doubting; Germany, eager for the equality which only our disarmament can bring; France, democratic France, ready to take a risk for reconciliation; Russia, using fair words, fairer than could have been expected; all the smaller powers enthusiastic for results for which they have been waiting long. The influence of the

[1] *Cf.* p. 304, *supra.*   [2] Article 160, Treaty of Versailles.

British Empire, in every question of international affairs, is almost infinitely great; in this grave matter, if it were wisely, firmly used, who doubts that it would be decisive?

How could the lead be given? The Washington Conference has taught us. The British experts should prepare draft plans to lay before the League, all their technical knowledge and skill and information should be placed at its disposal, and the British Government should make a generous offer of large reductions, especially of naval armaments on the lines proposed in Chapter XI above, provided always, of course, that other powers will also co-operate and help. If our Government did this, so great would be the psychological effect, that the Preparatory Committee, the Council, and at last the Conference itself, could hardly fail.

And why, once more, does disarmament matter? Above all other reasons, because it is a part, and an essential part, of the great complex of changes which at long last will rid the world of war. The pacific settlement of international disputes, the removal of the causes of international misunderstanding, the practice of open dealing among nations, the promotion of all forms of inter-governmental co-operation—to these it is a vital complement. In the last analysis, indeed, the struggle against the age-long misery of war can only be won in the hearts and minds of men. In that struggle victory will come slowly; it will come from constant and unwearying effort; it will come from steady and persistent progress, first on this part of the line and then on that. But when a general treaty of disarmament is signed, the central bastion of the enemy defences will be captured, and from that moment the forces of progress will march onward, irresistible and even, it may be, unresisted.

APPENDICES

APPENDIX I

Article 8 of the Covenant of the League of Nations

The Members of the League recognize that the maintenance of peace requires the reduction of national armaments to the lowest point consistent with national safety, and the enforcement by common action of international obligations.

The Council, taking account of the geographical situation and circumstances of each State, shall formulate plans for such reduction for the consideration and action of the several Governments.

Such plans shall be subject to reconsideration and revision at least every ten years.

After these plans shall have been adopted by the several Governments, the limits of armaments therein fixed shall not be exceeded without the concurrence of the Council.

The Members of the League agree that the manufacture by private enterprise of munitions and implements of war is open to grave objections. The Council shall advise how the evil effects attendant upon such manufacture can be prevented, due regard being had to the necessities of those Members of the League which are not able to manufacture the munitions and implements of war necessary for their safety.

The Members of the League undertake to interchange full and frank information as to the scale of their armaments, their military, naval, and air programmes, and the condition of such of their industries as are adaptable to warlike purposes.

APPENDIX II

QUESTIONNAIRE REFERRED BY THE COUNCIL OF THE LEAGUE
OF NATIONS TO ITS PREPARATORY COMMITTEE ON
DISARMAMENT

Question I.

WHAT is to be understood by the expression " armaments " ?

(a) Definition of the various factors—military, economic, geographical,
etc.—upon which the power of a country in time of war depends.

(b) Definition and special characteristics of the various factors which
constitute the armaments of a country in time of peace; the different
categories of armaments (military, naval and air), the methods of
recruiting, training, organizations capable of immediate military
employment, etc.

Question II.

(a) Is it practicable to limit the ultimate war strength of a country,
or must any measures of disarmament be confined to the peace
strength ?

(b) What is to be understood by the expression " reduction and
limitation of armaments " ?

The various forms which reduction of limitation may take in the
case of land, sea, and air forces: the relative advantages or disadvantages
of each of the different forms or methods: for example, the reduction
of the larger peace-time units or of their establishment and their equipment, or of any immediately mobilizable forces: the reduction of the
length of active service, the reduction of the quantity of military equipment, the reduction of expenditure on national defence, etc.

Question III.

By what standards is it possible to measure the armaments of one
country against the armaments of another—e.g., numbers, period of
service, equipment expenditure, etc. ?

Question IV.

Can there be said to be " offensive " and " defensive " armaments ?
Is there any method of ascertaining whether a certain force is organized
for purely defensive purposes (no matter what use may be made of it
in time of war), or whether, on the contrary, it is established for the
purposes in a spirit of aggression ?

Question V.

(*a*) On what principle will it be possible to draw up a scale of armaments permissible to the various countries, taking into account particularly:

Population;
Geographical situation;
Length and nature of maritime communications;
Density and character of the railways;
Vulnerability of the frontiers and of the important vital centres near the frontiers;
The time required, varying with different States, to transform peace armaments into war armaments;
The degree of security which, in the event of aggression, a State could receive under the provisions of the Covenant or of separate engagements contracted towards that State ?

(*b*) Can the reduction of armaments be promoted by examining possible means for ensuring that the mutual assistance, economic and military, contemplated in Article 16 of the Covenant, shall be brought quickly into operation as soon as an act of aggression has been committed ?

Question VI.

(*a*) Is there any device by which civil and military aircraft can be distinguished for purposes of disarmament ? If this is not practicable, how can the value of civil aircraft be computed in estimating the air strength of any country ?

(*b*) Is it possible or desirable to apply the conclusions arrived at in (*a*) above to parts of aircraft and aircraft engines ?

(*c*) Is it possible to attach military value to commercial fleets in estimating the naval armaments of a country ?

Question VII.

Admitting that disarmament depends on security, to what extent is regional disarmament possible in return for regional security ? Or is any scheme of disarmament impracticable unless it is general ? If regional disarmament is practicable, would it promote or lead up to general disarmament ?

* * * * *

The Preparatory Committee will begin its work on the basis of the above Questionnaire.

APPENDIX III

MILITARY CLAUSES OF THE TREATY OF PEACE WITH HUNGARY, 1920

IN order to render possible the initiation of a general limitation of the armaments of all nations, Hungary undertakes strictly to observe the military, naval, and air clauses which follow.

SECTION I.: MILITARY CLAUSES

CHAPTER I

GENERAL

ARTICLE 102.

Within three months of the coming into force of the present Treaty, the military forces of Hungary shall be demobilized to the extent prescribed hereafter.

ARTICLE 103.

Universal compulsory military service shall be abolished in Hungary. The Hungarian Army shall in future only be constituted and recruited by means of voluntary enlistment.

CHAPTER II

EFFECTIVES AND CADRES OF THE HUNGARIAN ARMY

ARTICLE 104.

The total number of military forces in the Hungarian Army shall not exceed 35,000 men, including officers and depot troops.

Subject to the following limitations, the formations composing the Hungarian Army shall be fixed in accordance with the wishes of Hungary:

(1) The effectives of units must be fixed between the maximum and minimum figures shown in Table IV annexed to this Section.

(2) The proportion of officers, including the personnel of staffs and special services, shall not exceed one-twentieth of the total effectives with the Colours, and that of non-commissioned officers shall not exceed one-fifteenth of the total effectives with the Colours.

(3) The number of machine guns, guns and howitzers shall not exceed per thousand men of the total effectives with the Colours those fixed in Table V annexed to this Section.

The Hungarian Army shall be devoted exclusively to the maintenance of order within the territory of Hungary, and to the control of her frontiers.

ARTICLE 105.

The maximum strength of the staffs and of all formations which Hungary may be permitted to raise are given in the Tables annexed to this Section; these figures need not be exactly followed, but must not be exceeded.

All other organizations for the command of troops or for preparation for war are forbidden.

ARTICLE 106.

All measures of mobilization, or appertaining to mobilization, are forbidden.

In no case must formations, administrative services or staffs include supplementary cadres.

The carrying out of any preparatory measures with a view to requisitioning animals or other means of military transport is forbidden.

ARTICLE 107.

The number of gendarmes, Customs officers, foresters, members of the local or municipal police or other like officials may not exceed the number of men employed in a similar capacity in 1913 within the boundaries of Hungary as fixed by the present Treaty. The Principal Allied and Associated Powers may, however, increase this number should the Commission of Control referred to in Article 137, after examination on the spot, consider it to be insufficient.

The number of these officials shall not be increased in the future except as may be necessary to maintain the same proportion between the number of officials and the total population in the localities or municipalities which employ them.

These officials, as well as officials employed in the railway service, must not be assembled for the purpose of taking part in any military exercises.

ARTICLE 108.

Every formation of troops not included in the Tables annexed to this Section is forbidden. Such other formations as may exist in excess of the 35,000 effectives authorized shall be suppressed within the period laid down by Article 102.

CHAPTER III
RECRUITING AND MILITARY TRAINING

ARTICLE 109.

All officers must be regulars (officers *de carrière*). Officers now serving who are retained in the Army must undertake the obligation to serve in it up to the age of 40 years at least. Officers now serving who do not join the new army will be released from all military obligations; they must not take part in any military exercises, whether theoretical or practical.

Officers newly appointed must undertake to serve on the active list for 20 consecutive years at least.

The number of officers discharged for any reason before the expiration of their term of service must not exceed in any year one-twentieth of the total of officers provided for in Article 104. If this proportion is unavoidably exceeded, the resulting shortage must not be made good by fresh appointments.

ARTICLE 110.

The period of enlistment for non-commissioned officers and privates must be for a total period of not less than 12 consecutive years, including at least 6 years with the Colours.

The proportion of men discharged before the expiration of the period of their enlistment for reasons of health or as a result of disciplinary measures or for any other reasons must not in any year exceed one-twentieth of the total strength fixed by Article 104. If this proportion is unavoidably exceeded, the resulting shortage must not be made good by fresh enlistments.

CHAPTER IV

SCHOOLS, EDUCATIONAL ESTABLISHMENTS, MILITARY CLUBS AND SOCIETIES

ARTICLE 111.

The number of students admitted to attend the courses in military schools shall be strictly in proportion to the vacancies to be filled in the cadres of officers. The students and the cadres shall be included in the effectives fixed by Article 104.

Consequently all military schools not required for this purpose shall be abolished.

ARTICLE 112.

Educational establishments, other than those referred to in Article 111, as well as all sporting and other clubs, must not occupy themselves with any military matters.

CHAPTER V

ARMAMENT, MUNITIONS, AND MATERIAL

ARTICLE 113.

On the expiration of three months from the coming into force of the present Treaty, the armament of the Hungarian Army shall not exceed the figures fixed per thousand men in Table V annexed to this Section.

Any excess in relation to effectives shall only be used for such replacements as may eventually be necessary.

ARTICLE 114.

The stock of munitions at the disposal of the Hungarian Army shall not exceed the amounts fixed in Table V. annexed to this Section.

Within three months from the coming into force of the present Treaty the Hungarian Government shall deposit any existing surplus of armament and munitions in such places as shall be notified to it by the Principal Allied and Associated Powers.

No other stock, depot or reserve of munitions shall be formed.

ARTICLE 115.

The manufacture of arms, munitions and war material shall only be carried on in one single factory, which shall be controlled by and belong to the State, and whose output shall be strictly limited to the manufacture of such arms, munitions and war material as is necessary for the military forces and armaments referred to in Articles 104, 107, 113, and 114. The Principal Allied and Associated Powers may, however, authorize such manufacture, for such a period as they may think fit, in one or more other factories to be approved by the Commission of Control referred to in Article 137.

The manufacture of sporting weapons is not forbidden, provided that sporting weapons manufactured in Hungary taking ball cartridge are not of the same calibre as that of military weapons used in any European army.

Within three months from the coming into force of the present Treaty, all other establishments for the manufacture, preparation, storage, or design of arms, munitions or any other war material shall be closed down or converted to purely commercial uses.

Within the same length of time, all arsenals shall also be closed down, except those to be used as depots for the authorized stocks of munitions, and their staffs discharged.

ARTICLE 116.

The plant of any establishments or arsenals in excess of the amount required for the manufacture authorized shall be rendered useless or converted to purely commercial purposes in accordance with the decisions of the military Inter-Allied Commission of Control referred to in Article 137.

ARTICLE 117.

Within three months from the coming into force of the present Treaty all arms, munitions and war material, including any kind of anti-aircraft material, of whatever origin, existing in Hungary in excess of the quantity authorized shall be handed over to the Principal Allied and Associated Powers.

Delivery shall take place at such points in Hungarian territory as may be appointed by the said Powers, who shall also decide on the disposal of such material.

22

ARTICLE 118.

The importation into Hungary of arms, munitions and war material of all kinds is strictly forbidden.

The manufacture for foreign countries and the exportation of arms, munitions and war material shall also be forbidden.

ARTICLE 119.

The use of flame throwers, asphyxiating, poisonous or other gases, and all similar liquids, materials or devices being prohibited, their manufacture and importation are strictly forbidden in Hungary.

Material specially intended for the manufacture, storage or use of the said products or devices is equally forbidden.

The manufacture and importation into Hungary of armoured cars, tanks or any similar machines suitable for use in war are equally forbidden.

TABLE I.—COMPOSITION AND MAXIMUM EFFECTIVES OF AN INFANTRY DIVISION.

Units.	Maximum Effectives of each Unit.	
	Officers.	Men.
Headquarters of an Infantry Division	25	70
Headquarters of Divisional Infantry	5	50
Headquarters of Divisional Artillery	4	30
3 Regiments of Infantry[1] (on the basis of 65 officers and 2,000 men per regiment)	195	6,000
1 Squadron	6	160
1 Battalion of Trench Artillery (3 Companies)	14	500
1 Battalion of Pioneers[2]	14	500
Regiment Field Artillery[3]	80	1,200
1 Battalion Cyclists (comprising 3 Companies)	18	450
1 Signal Detachment[4]	11	330
Divisional Medical Corps	28	550
Divisional parks and trains	14	940
Total for an Infantry Division	414	10,780

[1] Each Regiment comprises 3 Battalions of Infantry. Each Battalion comprises 3 Companies of Infantry and 1 Machine Gun Company.
[2] Each Battalion comprises 1 Headquarters, 2 Pioneer Companies, 1 Bridging Section, 1 Searchlight Section.
[3] Each Regiment comprises 1 Headquarters, 3 Groups of Field or Mountain Artillery, comprising 8 Batteries; each Battery comprising 4 guns or howitzers (field or mountain).
[4] This Detachment comprises 1 Telegraph and Telephone detachment, 1 Listening Section, 1 Carrier Pigeon Section.

TABLE II.—COMPOSITION AND MAXIMUM EFFECTIVES FOR A CAVALRY DIVISION.

Units.	Maximum Number Authorized.	Maximum Effectives of each Unit.	
		Officers.	Men.
Headquarters of a Cavalry Division ..	1	155	50
Regiment of Cavalry[1]	6	30	720
Group of Field Artillery (3 Batteries) ..	1	30	430
Group of motor machine guns and armoured cars[2]	1	4	80
Miscellaneous services	—	30	500
Total for a Cavalry Division ..	—	249	5,380

[1] Each Regiment comprises 4 Squadrons.

[2] Each group comprises 9 fighting cars, each carrying 1 gun, 1 machine gun, and 1 spare machine gun, 4 communication cars, 2 small lorries for stores, 7 lorries, including 1 repair lorry, 4 motor-cycles.

NOTE.—The large Cavalry Units may include a variable number of regiments and be divided into independent brigades within the limit of the effectives laid down above.

TABLE III.—COMPOSITION AND MAXIMUM EFFECTIVES FOR A MIXED BRIGADE.

Units.	Maximum Effectives of each Unit.	
	Officers.	Men.
Headquarters of a Brigade	10	50
2 Regiments of Infantry[1]	130	4,000
1 Cyclist Battalion (3 Companies)	18	450
1 Cavalry Squadron	5	100
1 Group Field or Mountain Artillery (3 Batteries)	20	400
1 Trench Mortar Company	5	150
Miscellaneous services	10	200
Total for Mixed Brigade	198	5,350

[1] Each Regiment comprises 3 Battalions of Infantry. Each Battalion comprises 3 Companies of Infantry and 1 Machine Gun Company.

TABLE IV.—MINIMUM EFFECTIVES OF UNITS WHATEVER ORGANIZATION IS ADOPTED IN THE ARMY.

(*Divisions, Mixed Brigades, etc.*)

Units.	Maximum Effectives (for Reference).		Minimum Effectives	
	Officers.	Men.	Officers.	Men.
Infantry Division	414	10,780	300	8,000
Cavalry Division	259	5,380	180	3,650
Mixed Brigade	198	5,350	140	4,250
Regiment of Infantry	65	2,000	52	1,600
Battalion of Infantry	16	650	12	500
Company of Infantry or Machine Guns	3	160	2	120
Cyclist Group	18	450	12	300
Regiment of Cavalry	30	720	20	450
Squadron of Cavalry	6	160	3	100
Regiment of Artillery	80	1,200	60	1,000
Battery of Field Artillery	4	150	2	120
Company of Trench Mortars	3	150	2	100
Battalion of Pioneers	14	500	8	300
Battery of Mountain Artillery	5	320	3	200

TABLE V.—MAXIMUM AUTHORIZED ARMAMENTS AND MUNITION SUPPLIES.

Material.	Quantity for 1,000 Men.	Amount of Munitions per Arm (Rifles, Guns, etc.).
Rifles or Carbines[1]	1,150	500 rounds.
Machine Guns, heavy or light	15	10,000 rounds.
Trench Mortars, light	} 2	{ 1,000 rounds.
Trench Mortars, medium		{ 500 rounds.
Guns or Howitzers (field or mountain)	3	1,000 rounds.

[1] Automatic rifles or carbines are counted as light machine guns.

N.B.—No heavy gun—*i.e.*, of a calibre greater than 105 mm.—is authorized.

APPENDIX IV

WASHINGTON NAVAL CONVENTION

CHAPTER I

GENERAL PROVISIONS RELATING TO THE LIMITATION OF NAVAL ARMAMENT

ARTICLE I.

THE Contracting Powers agree to limit their respective naval armament as provided in the present Treaty.

ARTICLE II.

The Contracting Powers may retain respectively the capital ships which are specified in Chapter II, Part 1. On the coming into force of the present Treaty, but subject to the following provisions of this Article, all other capital ships, built or building, of the United States, the British Empire and Japan shall be disposed of as prescribed in Chapter II, Part 2.

In addition to the capital ships specified in Chapter II, Part 1, the United States may complete and retain two ships of the " West Virginia " class now under construction. On the completion of these two ships the " North Dakota " and " Delaware " shall be disposed of as prescribed in Chapter II, Part 2.

The British Empire may, in accordance with the replacement table in Chapter II, Part 3, construct two new capital ships not exceeding 35,000 tons (35,560 metric tons) standard displacement each. On the completion of the said two ships the " Thunderer," " King George V," " Ajax " and " Centurion " shall be disposed of as prescribed in Chapter II, Part 2.

ARTICLE III.

Subject to the provisions of Article II, the Contracting Powers shall abandon their respective capital-ship building programmes, and no new capital ships shall be constructed or acquired by any of the Contracting Powers except replacement tonnage which may be constructed or acquired as specified in Chapter II, Part 3.

Ships which are replaced in accordance with Chapter II, Part 3, shall be disposed of as prescribed in Part 2 of that Chapter.

Article IV.

The total capital ship replacement tonnage of each of the Contracting Powers shall not exceed in standard displacement, for the United States, 525,000 tons (533,400 metric tons); for the British Empire, 525,000 tons (533,400 metric tons); for France, 175,000 tons (177,800 metric tons); for Italy, 175,000 tons (177,800 metric tons); for Japan, 315,000 tons (320,040 metric tons).

Article V.

No capital ship exceeding 35,000 tons (35,560 metric tons) standard displacement shall be acquired by, or constructed by, for, or within the jurisdiction of, any of the Contracting Powers.

Article VI.

No capital ship of any of the Contracting Powers shall carry a gun with a calibre in excess of 16 inches (406 millimetres).

Article VII.

The total tonnage for aircraft-carriers of each of the Contracting Powers shall not exceed in standard displacement, for the United States, 135,000 tons (137,160 metric tons); for the British Empire, 135,000 tons (137,160 metric tons); for France, 60,000 tons (60,960 metric tons); for Italy, 60,000 tons (60,960 metric tons); for Japan, 81,000 tons (82,296 metric tons).

Article VIII.

The replacement of aircraft-carriers shall be effected only as prescribed in Chapter II, Part 3, provided, however, that all aircraft-carrier tonnage in existence or building on the 12th November, 1921, shall be considered experimental, and may be replaced, within the total tonnage limit prescribed in Article VII, without regard to its age.

Article IX.

No aircraft-carrier exceeding 27,000 tons (27,432 metric tons) standard displacement shall be acquired by, or constructed by, for or within the jurisdiction of, any of the Contracting Powers.

However, any of the Contracting Powers may, provided that its total tonnage allowance of aircraft-carriers is not thereby exceeded, build not more than two aircraft-carriers, each of a tonnage of not more than 33,000 tons (33,528 metric tons) standard displacement, and in order to effect economy any of the Contracting Powers may use for this purpose any two of their ships, whether constructed or in course of construction, which would otherwise be scrapped under the provisions of Article II. The armament of any aircraft-carriers exceeding 27,000 tons (27,432 metric tons) standard displacement shall be in accordance with the requirements of Article X, except that the total number of guns to be carried in case any of such guns be of a calibre exceeding 6 inches (152 millimetres), except anti-aircraft guns and guns not exceeding 5 inches (127 millimetres), shall not exceed eight.

ARTICLE X.

No aircraft-carrier of any of the Contracting Powers shall carry a gun with a calibre in excess of 8 inches (203 millimetres). Without prejudice to the provisions of Article IX, if the armament carried includes guns exceeding 6 inches (152 millimetres) in calibre the total number of guns carried, except anti-aircraft guns and guns not exceeding 5 inches (127 millimetres), shall not exceed ten. If alternatively the armament contains no guns exceeding 6 inches (152 millimetres) in calibre, the number of guns is not limited. In either case the number of anti-aircraft guns and of guns not exceeding 5 inches (127 millimetres) is not limited.

ARTICLE XI.

No vessel of war exceeding 10,000 tons (10,160 metric tons) standard displacement, other than a capital ship or aircraft-carrier, shall be acquired by, or constructed by, for, or within the jurisdiction of, any of the Contracting Powers. Vessels not specifically built as fighting ships nor taken in time of peace under Government control for fighting purposes, which are employed on fleet duties or as troop transports or in some other way for the purpose of assisting in the prosecution of hostilities otherwise than as fighting ships, shall not be within the limitations of this Article.

ARTICLE XII.

No vessel of war of any of the Contracting Powers, hereafter laid down, other than a capital ship, shall carry a gun with a calibre in excess of 8 inches (203 millimetres).

ARTICLE XIII.

Except as provided in Article IX, no ship designated in the present Treaty to be scrapped may be reconverted into a vessel of war.

ARTICLE XIV.

No preparations shall be made in merchant ships in time of peace for the installation of warlike armaments for the purpose of converting such ships into vessels of war, other than the necessary stiffening of decks for the mounting of guns not exceeding 6-inch (152 millimetres) calibre.

ARTICLE XV.

No vessel of war constructed within the jurisdiction of any of the Contracting Powers for a non-Contracting Power shall exceed the limitations as to displacement and armament prescribed by the present Treaty for vessels of a similar type which may be constructed by or for any of the Contracting Powers; provided, however, that the displacement for aircraft-carriers constructed for a non-Contracting Power shall in no case exceed 27,000 tons (27,432 metric tons) standard displacement.

ARTICLE XVI.

If the construction of any vessel of war for a non-Contracting Power is undertaken within the jurisdiction of any of the Contracting Powers, such Power shall promptly inform the other Contracting Powers of the date of the signing of the contract and the date on which the keel of the ship is laid; and shall also communicate to them the particulars relating to the ship prescribed in Chapter II, Part 3, Section I (*b*), (4) and (5).

ARTICLE XVII.

In the event of a Contracting Power being engaged in war, such Power shall not use as a vessel of war any vessel of war which may be under construction within its jurisdiction for any other Power, or which may have been constructed within its jurisdiction for another Power and not delivered.

ARTICLE XVIII.

Each of the Contracting Powers undertakes not to dispose by gift, sale or any mode of transfer of any vessel of war in such a manner that such vessel may become a vessel of war in the Navy of any foreign Power.

ARTICLE XIX.

The United States, the British Empire and Japan agree that the *status quo* at the time of the signing of the present Treaty, with regard to fortifications and naval bases, shall be maintained in their respective territories and possessions specified hereunder:

1. The insular possessions which the United States now holds or may hereafter acquire in the Pacific Ocean, except (*a*) those adjacent to the coast of the United States, Alaska and the Panama Canal Zone, not including the Aleutian Islands, and (*b*) the Hawaiian Islands;

2. Hong-Kong and the insular possessions which the British Empire now holds or may hereafter acquire in the Pacific Ocean, east of the meridian of 110° east longitude, except (*a*) those adjacent to the coast of Canada, (*b*) the Commonwealth of Australia and its territories, and (*c*) New Zealand;

3. The following insular territories and possessions of Japan in the Pacific Ocean, to wit: the Kurile Islands, the Bonin Islands, Amami-Oshima, the Loochoo Islands, Formosa and the Pescadores, and any insular territories or possessions in the Pacific Ocean which Japan may hereafter acquire.

The maintenance of the *status quo* under the foregoing provisions implies that no new fortifications or naval bases shall be established in the territories and possessions specified; that no measures shall be taken to increase the existing naval facilities for the repair and maintenance of naval forces, and that no increase shall be made in the coast defences of the territories and possessions above specified. This restriction, however, does not preclude such repair and replacement of worn-out weapons and equipment as is customary in naval and military establishments in time of peace.

ARTICLE XX.

The rules for determining tonnage displacement prescribed in Chapter II, Part 4, shall apply to the ships of each of the Contracting Powers.

CHAPTER II

RULES RELATING TO THE EXECUTION OF THE TREATY—DEFINITION OF TERMS

PART I.—CAPITAL SHIPS WHICH MAY BE RETAINED BY THE CONTRACTING POWERS.

In accordance with Article II ships may be retained by each of the Contracting Powers as specified in this Part.

(Only the British Schedules are reproduced, as an illustration of them all.)

SHIPS WHICH MAY BE RETAINED BY THE BRITISH EMPIRE.

Name.	Tonnage.
Royal Sovereign	25,750
Royal Oak	25,750
Revenge	25,750
Resolution	25,750
Ramillies	25,750
Malaya	27,500
Valiant	27,500
Barham	27,500
Queen Elizabeth	27,500
Warspite	27,500
Benbow	25,000
Emperor of India	25,000
Iron Duke	25,000
Marlborough	25,000
Hood	41,200
Renown	26,500
Repulse	26,500
Tiger	28,500
Thunderer	22,500
King George V	23,000
Ajax	23,000
Centurion	23,000
Total tonnage	580,450

On the completion of the two new ships to be constructed and the scrapping of the "Thunderer," "King George V," "Ajax," and "Centurion," as provided in Article II, the total tonnage to be retained by the British Empire will be 558,950 tons.

PART 2.—RULES FOR SCRAPPING VESSELS OF WAR.

The following rules shall be observed for the scrapping of vessels of war which are to be disposed of in accordance with Articles II and III.

I. A vessel to be scrapped must be placed in such condition that it cannot be put to combatant use.

II. This result must be finally effected in any one of the following ways:

(*a.*) Permanent sinking of the vessel;

(*b.*) Breaking the vessel up. This shall always involve the destruction or removal of all machinery, boilers and armour, and all deck, side and bottom plating;

(*c.*) Converting the vessel to target use exclusively. In such case all the provisions of paragraph III of this Part, except sub-paragraph (6), in so far as may be necessary to enable the ship to be used as a mobile target, and except sub-paragraph (7), must be previously complied with. Not more than one capital ship may be retained for this purpose at one time by any of the Contracting Powers.

(*d.*) Of the capital ships which would otherwise be scrapped under the present Treaty in or after the year 1931, France and Italy may each retain two sea-going vessels for training purposes exclusively, that is, as gunnery or torpedo schools. The two vessels retained by France shall be of the "Jean Bart" class, and of those retained by Italy one shall be the "Dante Alighieri," the other of the "Giulio Cesare" class. On retaining these ships for the purpose above stated, France and Italy respectively undertake to remove and destroy their conning-towers, and not to use the said ships as vessels of war.

III.—(*a.*) Subject to the special exceptions contained in Article IX, when a vessel is due for scrapping, the first stage of scrapping, which consists in rendering a ship incapable of further warlike service, shall be immediately undertaken.

(*b.*) A vessel shall be considered incapable of further warlike service when there shall have been removed and landed, or else destroyed in the ship:

1. All guns and essential portions of guns, fire-control tops and revolving parts of all barbettes and turrets;
2. All machinery for working hydraulic or electric mountings;
3. All fire-control instruments and range-finders;
4. All ammunition, explosives and mines;
5. All torpedoes, war-heads and torpedo tubes;
6. All wireless telegraphy installations;
7. The conning-tower and all side armour, or alternatively all main propelling machinery; and
8. All landing and flying-off platforms and all other aviation accessories.

IV. The periods in which scrapping of vessels is to be effected are as follows:

(*a*.) In the case of vessels to be scrapped under the first paragraph of Article II, the work of rendering the vessels incapable of further warlike service, in accordance with paragraph III of this Part, shall be completed within six months from the coming into force of the present Treaty, and the scrapping shall be finally effected within eighteen months from such coming into force.

(*b*.) In the case of vessels to be scrapped under the second and third paragraphs of Article II, or under Article III, the work of rendering the vessel incapable of further warlike service in accordance with paragraph III of this Part shall be commenced not later than the date of completion of its successor, and shall be finished within six months from the date of such completion. The vessel shall be finally scrapped, in accordance with paragraph II of this Part, within eighteen months from the date of completion of its successor. If, however, the completion of the new vessel be delayed, then the work of rendering the old vessel incapable of further warlike service in accordance with paragraph III of this Part shall be commenced within four years from the laying of the keel of the new vessel, and shall be finished within six months from the date on which such work was commenced, and the old vessel shall be finally scrapped in accordance with paragraph II of this Part within eighteen months from the date when the work of rendering it incapable of further warlike service was commenced.

PART 3.—REPLACEMENT.

The replacement of capital ships and aircraft-carriers shall take place according to the rules in Section I and the tables in Section II of this Part.

Section I.—*Rules for Replacement.*

(*a*.) Capital ships and aircraft-carriers twenty years after the date of their completion may, except as otherwise provided in Article VIII and in the tables in Section II of this Part, be replaced by new construction, but within the limits prescribed in Article IV and Article VII. The keels of such new construction may, except as otherwise provided in Article VIII and in the tables in Section II of this Part, be laid down not earlier than seventeen years from the date of completion of the tonnage to be replaced, provided, however, that no capital ship tonnage, with the exception of the ships referred to in the third paragraph of Article II, and the replacement tonnage specifically mentioned in Section II of this Part, shall be laid down until ten years from the 12th November, 1921.

(*b.*) Each of the Contracting Powers shall communicate promptly to each of the other Contracting Powers the following information:

1. The names of the capital ships and aircraft-carriers to be replaced by new construction;
2. The date of Governmental authorization of replacement tonnage;
3. The date of laying the keels of replacement tonnage;
4. The standard displacement in tons and metric tons of each new ship to be laid down, and the principal dimensions, namely, length of waterline, extreme beam at or below waterline, mean draft at standard displacement;
5. The date of completion of each new ship and its standard displacement in tons and metric tons, and the principal dimensions, namely, length at waterline, extreme beam at or below waterline, mean draft at standard displacement, at time of completion.

(*c.*) In case of loss or accidental destruction of capital ships or aircraft-carriers, they may immediately be replaced by new construction subject to the tonnage limits prescribed in Articles IV and VII and in conformity with the other provisions of the present Treaty, the regular replacement programme being deemed to be advanced to that extent.

(*d.*) No retained capital ships or aircraft-carriers shall be reconstructed except for the purpose of providing means of defence against air and submarine attack, and subject to the following rules: The Contracting Powers may, for that purpose, equip existing tonnage with bulge or blister or anti-air attack deck protection, providing the increase of displacement thus effected does not exceed 3,000 tons (3,048 metric tons) displacement for each ship. No alterations in side armour, in calibre, number or general type of mounting of main armament shall be permitted except:

1. In the case of France and Italy, which countries within the limits allowed for bulge may increase their armour protection and the calibre of the guns now carried on their existing capital ships so as not to exceed 16 inches (406 millimetres) and
2. The British Empire shall be permitted to complete, in the case of the " Renown," the alterations to armour that have already been commenced but temporarily suspended.

Section II.—*Replacement and Scrapping of Capital Ships.*

BRITISH EMPIRE.

Year.	Ships Laid Down.	Ships Completed.	Ships Scrapped (*Age in Parentheses*).	Ships Retained. Summary.	
				Pre-Jutland.	Post-Jutland.
			Commonwealth (16), Agamemnon (13), Dreadnought (15), Bellerophon (12), St. Vincent (11), Inflexible (13), Superb (12), Neptune (10), Hercules (10), Indomitable (13), Temeraire (12), New Zealand (9), Lion (9), Princess Royal (9),Conqueror (9),Monarch (9),Orion (9), Australia (8), Agincourt (7), Erin (7), 4 building or projected[1]	21	1
1922	A, B[2]	..	.. ..	21	1
1923	..	..	.. ..	21	1
1924	..	..	.. ..	21	1
1925	..	A, B	King George V (13), Ajax (12), Centurion (12), Thunderer (13)	17	3
1926	..	..	.. ..	17	3
1927	..	..	.. ..	17	3
1928	..	..	.. ..	17	3
1929	..	..	.. ..	17	3
1930	..	..	.. ..	17	3
1931	C, D	..	.. ..	17	3
1932	E, F	..	.. ..	17	3
1933	G	..	.. ..	17	3
1934	H, I	C, D	Iron Duke (20),Marlborough (20),Emperor of India (20), Benbow (20)	13	5
1935	J	E, F	Tiger (21), Queen Elizabeth (20), Warspite (20), Barham (20)	9	7
1936	K, L	G	Malaya (20), Royal Sovereign (20)	7	8
1937	M	H, I	Revenge (21), Resolution (21)	5	10
1938	N, O	J	Royal Oak (22)	4	11
1939	P, Q	K, L	Valiant (23), Repulse (23)..	2	13
1940	..	M	Renown (24)	1	14
1941	..	N, O	Ramilies (24), Hood (21) ..	0	15
1942	..	P, Q	A (17), B (17)	0	15

[1] The British Empire may retain the " Colossus " and " Collingwood " for non-combatant purposes after complying with the provisions of Part 2, III (*b*).

[2] Two 35,000-ton ships, standard displacement.

NOTE.—A, B, C, D, etc., represent individual capital ships of 35,000 tons standard displacement laid down and completed in the years specified.

Note Applicable to all the Tables in Section II.

The order above prescribed in which ships are to be scrapped is in accordance with their age. It is understood that when replacement begins according to the above tables the order of scrapping in the case of the ships of each of the Contracting Powers may be varied at its option; provided, however, that such Power shall scrap in each year the number of ships above stated.

PART 4.—DEFINITIONS.

For the purposes of the present Treaty, the following expressions are to be understood in the sense defined in this Part.

Capital Ship.

A capital ship, in the case of ships hereafter built, is defined as a vessel of war, not an aircraft-carrier, whose displacement exceeds 10,000 tons (10,160 metric tons) standard displacement, or which carries a gun with a calibre exceeding 8 inches (203 millimetres).

Aircraft-Carrier.

An aircraft-carrier is defined as a vessel of war with a displacement in excess of 10,000 tons (10,160 metric tons) standard displacement designed for the specific and exclusive purpose of carrying aircraft. It must be so constructed that aircraft can be launched therefrom and landed thereon, and not designed and constructed for carrying a more powerful armament than that allowed to it under Article IX or Article X as the case may be.

Standard Displacement.

The standard displacement of a ship is the displacement of the ship complete, fully manned, engined, and equipped ready for sea, including all armament and ammunition, equipment, outfit, provisions and fresh water for crew, miscellaneous stores and implements of every description that are intended to be carried in war, but without fuel or reserve feed water on board.

The word " ton " in the present Treaty, except in the expression " metric tons," shall be understood to mean the ton of 2,240 pounds (1,016 kilog.).

Vessels now completed shall retain their present ratings of displacement tonnage in accordance with their national system of measurement. However, a Power expressing displacement in metric tons shall be considered for the application of the present Treaty as owning only the equivalent displacement in tons of 2,240 pounds.

A vessel completed hereafter shall be rated at its displacement tonnage when in the standard condition defined herein.

Chapter III

MISCELLANEOUS PROVISIONS

Article XXI.

If during the term of the present Treaty the requirements of the national security of any Contracting Power in respect of naval defence are, in the opinion of that Power, materially affected by any change of circumstances, the Contracting Powers will, at the request of such Power, meet in conference with a view to the reconsideration of the provisions of the Treaty and its amendment by mutual agreement.

In view of possible technical and scientific developments, the United States, after consultation with the other Contracting Powers, shall arrange for a conference of all the Contracting Powers which shall convene as soon as possible after the expiration of eight years from the coming into force of the present Treaty to consider what changes, if any, in the Treaty may be necessary to meet such developments.

Article XXII.

Whenever any Contracting Power shall become engaged in a war which in its opinion affects the naval defence of its national security, such Power may after notice to the other Contracting Powers suspend for the period of hostilities its obligations under the present Treaty other than those under Articles XIII and XVII, provided that such Power shall notify the other Contracting Powers that the emergency is of such a character as to require such suspension.

The remaining Contracting Powers shall in such case consult together with a view to agreement as to what temporary modifications, if any, should be made in the Treaty as between themselves. Should such consultation not produce agreement, duly made in accordance with the constitutional methods of the respective Powers, any one of said Contracting Powers may, by giving notice to the other Contracting Powers, suspend for the period of hostilities its obligations under the present Treaty, other than those under Articles XIII and XVII.

On the cessation of hostilities the Contracting Powers will meet in conference to consider what modifications, if any, should be made in the provisions of the present Treaty.

Article XXIII.

The present Treaty shall remain in force until the 31st December, 1936, and in case none of the Contracting Powers shall have given notice two years before that date of its intention to terminate the Treaty, it shall continue in force until the expiration of two years from the date on which notice of termination shall be given by one of the Contracting Powers, whereupon the Treaty shall terminate as regards all the Contracting Powers. Such notice shall be communicated in writing to the Government of the United States, which shall immediately transmit a certified copy of the notification to the other Powers and inform them of the date on which it was received. The notice shall be deemed to have been given and shall take effect on that date. In the event of notice of termination being given by the Government of the United States, such notice shall be given to the diplomatic representatives at Washington of the other Contracting Powers, and the notice shall be deemed to have been given and shall take effect on the date of the communication made to the said diplomatic representatives.

Within one year of the date on which a notice of termination by any Power has taken effect, all the Contracting Powers shall meet in conference.

ARTICLE XXIV.

The present Treaty shall be ratified by the Contracting Powers in accordance with their respective constitutional methods and shall take effect on the date of the deposit of all the ratifications, which shall take place at Washington as soon as possible. The Government of the United States will transmit to the other Contracting Powers a certified copy of the *procès-verbal* of the deposit of ratifications.

The present Treaty, of which the French and English texts are both authentic, shall remain deposited in the archives of the Government of the United States, and duly certified copies thereof shall be transmitted by that Government to the other Contracting Powers.

In faith whereof the above-named Plenipotentiaries have signed the present Treaty.

Done at the City of Washington the 6th day of February, 1922.